City Bound

CITY BOUND

Urban Life and Political Attitudes among Chicano Youth

Martín Sánchez Jankowski

UNIVERSITY OF NEW MEXICO PRESS
Albuquerque

Library of Congress Cataloging-in-Publication
Data

Jankowski, Martín Sánchez, 1945–
  City bound.

  Bibliography: p.
  Includes index.
  1. Mexican American youth—Political
activity.   2. Mexican American youth—
Attitudes.   3. Mexican American youth—
Southwest, New—Political activity.
4. Mexican American youth—Southwest,
New—Attitudes.   5. Southwest, New—
Politics and government.
  I. Title
E184.M5J36   1968   979   85–24502
ISBN 0-8263-0847-3
ISBN 0-8263-0848-1 (pbk.)

To my parents—
Leo and Anna Jankowski

Contents

Figures

Tables

Preface

THIS BOOK has its origins in a graduate course I took in the mid-1970s. While reading for that course on ethnicity in America, I became intrigued with the experiences of the countless people who made their way from distant lands to the various ports of entry of the United States. Their separation from loved ones, of breaking away from everything familiar with no guarantees that the pain and suffering endured would lead to a more comfortable future, and then the adjustment to a new environment—these were events that I knew could tell us much about change and survival.

Most of the ethnic groups I was reading about found themselves in cities. Thus one aspect of the experience that I found particularly fascinating was the process by which members of these different groups went about reconciling the values, norms, and customs of the old country of origin with those found in American cities. With so many ethnic groups inhabiting various parts of each major urban American area, I came to realize that, just as Robert Park had suggested, cities were an ideal laboratory for social analysis. As I kept reading, I continued to think how exciting it must have been to be a field researcher while these immigrants were undergoing social assimilation and urbanization. Then it occurred to me that I ought not to feel that history had passed me by, that America still had ethnic groups immigrating to cities and that these groups were involved in the same process that the older European groups had been involved in. One such ethnic group that was going through the urbanization and assimilation process was the Chicano (Mexican-American). Here was an opportunity to study a group involved in the urbanization and cultural adaptation process some fifty years after most European ethnic groups had gone through it. Thus, I came to believe that it was important to begin to examine the various aspects of the process as they relate to Chicanos. In the study that follows I pursue an inquiry into one such aspect: how urban life and the process of cultural adaptation affects the attitudes of Chicanos towards politics.

As I mentioned, this project began while I was a graduate student, and I should like to thank three men who encouraged and supported my interest in this subject. They are Wayne A. Cornelius, Lloyd Etheredge, and Ithiel de Sola Pool. Sadly, Ithiel de Sola Pool died before the book came out. Given the fact that he continually supported the project, I should have liked to have been able to hand him a copy, but that is not to be. Yet, because he was a teacher who made a difference, his imprint is on this book.

I am also indebted to Joel Krieger, George Breslauer, Peter Lupsha, and Andrés Jímenez, who gave of their time to comment on portions of earlier drafts.

In addition, I am particularly indebted to three of my colleagues at Berkeley. Claude Fischer and Jack Citrin read the entire manuscript and provided extensive comments that helped me clarify many of my ideas. Michael Rogin deserves special mention because he not only read the entire manuscript, he read it more than once. His comments helped me in rethinking many of my ideas and in redrafting portions of the manuscript.

Two other people deserve my thanks: Cheryl Publicover read the manuscript and pointed out where it needed clarification; and Michele Dillon painstakingly proofread the text during the final stages.

Last, and most important, my primary debt is to those young men and women who consented to participate in this study. They not only gave of their time in 1976–77, but they also consented to be re-interviewed in 1982.

A project as large as this one could not have been completed without financial assistance. In this regard, I am grateful to the Weatherhead Foundation for a generous grant that enabled me to complete two-thirds of the project. I should especially like to thank Dr. Richard P. Weatherhead, President, and Professor Richard Eells, Trustee, for their personal support of me and the project. In addition, I should like to thank the Ford Foundation for its financial assistance that enabled me to finish the final phase of the study.

Appropriately, I shall point out that none of the people or agencies I have mentioned ought to be held responsible for any of the interpretations and/or deficiencies that may exist in the book. For that, one must look to me alone.

Now for two personal notes. This book is dedicated to my parents, Leo and Anna Jankowski, two people who have been a guiding force in my life. They have always shown me what the word *courage* means, and for that I shall always be grateful. They have also been my first critics, yet most importantly they have continually demonstrated love and understanding, which has sustained me on some very long roads—for that, no words can express my feelings.

My wife, Carmen, came into my life at the tail end of this project. While she has had little to do with its completion, she has a great deal to do with making it meaningful.

Berkeley, California
1985

1

Introduction

THE STATUE OF LIBERTY looks out over the ocean toward distant lands and proclaims, "Give me your tired, your poor, your huddled masses yearning to breathe free, the wretched refuse of your teeming shore." Throughout American history the world has complied. This has resulted in a country composed of diverse ethnic groups, many of which have faced the problems of socioeconomic and political integration into a new national community. The experiences of these groups in assimilating into the main sociocultural fabric of American society have been the focus of much research, and the data which have emerged from these studies have provided a greater understanding of the process of integration and the consequent changes in the socioeconomic and political status of these groups.[1]

Until very recently most of these studies focused on European ethnics. While the Statue of Liberty faces east and most of America's immigrants came from the east (primarily Europe and Russia), a great many have come from other regions of the world. Some of these ethnic groups even inhabited areas of America before these areas were incorporated into the present-day United States. Unfortunately, there have been fewer studies of these non-European groups, and so less is known about their process of assimilation.[2]

One such ethnic group is the Mexican Americans (Chicanos/Hispanics),[3] and the present work treats the experiences of this group. Although the subject of ethnic assimilation includes cultural, economic, and political assimilation, this work is concerned primarily with political assimilation, specifically the political socialization of Chicano youth.[4] While concentrating on political socialization, the volume considers economic and cultural assimilation as well, be-

1

cause political socialization does not occur in isolation from cultural values and norms. Many studies have documented the influence of cultural orientation on the process of political socialization.[5]

There are many reasons why a study of the political attitudes of Chicano youth is important. Chicanos constitute a large ethnic group in America, numbering, according to the 1980 census, eight million people. In addition, they are the fastest growing ethnic group in the country. If the present trend continues, it is estimated that by the year 2000 Chicanos will replace blacks as the nation's largest non-white minority.[6] Because the Chicano population is concentrated primarily in the southwestern part of the United States, they have potentially significant political power in that area. Indeed, as the general population in the Southwest continues to increase, the importance of the Chicano in national politics (particularly in presidential elections) likewise will increase. Hence, the study of political attitudes of young Chicanos becomes a salient issue.

In addition to the fact that Chicanos are a growing political force in American politics, the study of this group poses interesting questions concerning political integration.[7] Here is an ethnic group that has been associated with the United States for more than a hundred years and that, for most of this time, has been effectively disenfranchised from the American political system. In Texas and many of the other Southern states, the poll tax and literacy tests were used to exclude Chicanos from political participation.[8] In addition, because Spanish was the dominant language among Chicanos, many found it difficult to understand the candidates and/or to read the ballots. Further, in many areas of the Southwest, physical intimidation was used to inhibit Chicano political participation. Finally, the combination of racial discrimination in the socioeconomic sphere and the political alienation mentioned above caused a great majority of the Chicano population to feel that politics were meaningful only to Anglos. As a result, they withdrew psychologically from the political process, thereby reducing the Chicano electorate to a marginal element in the American political arena.

With the recent success of organizations such as the Southwest Voter Registration and Education Project in registering previously unregistered Chicano voters, political analysts must take Chicano voters into account. They must ask whether Chicanos, as a result of being a culturally distinct minority unintegrated into the mainstream of American political life, will behave differently from other

Americans. Chicanos, for the most part, have continued to maintain the Spanish language, which distinguishes them from the English-speaking majority. Being non-white (a mixture of Indian and Spanish), they are racially different from the American majority. They have suffered historically from racial discrimination.[9] One questions whether the Chicano experience can be equated with the experience of black Americans. But if the Chicano experience differs from that of whites, the history of the Chicanos in the U.S. is not the same history as that of black Americans. They did not experience the institution of slavery as did blacks; on the other hand, they were conquered by the United States and their own land was taken.

The fact that Chicanos are members of a group whose land was appropriated is not in any way intended to convey that the Chicano experience is comparable to the experience of Native Americans or to that of the French ethnic group in Quebec, Canada. To make the argument that these experiences are completely comparable would diminish the importance of emigration from Mexico and, in a sense, misrepresent the Chicanos' historical experience. In fact, emigration from Mexico has continued since 1848, with the largest exodus taking place after 1910, when the ravages of the Revolution in Mexico forced many Mexicans to relocate in the United States. Although the number of emigrants from Mexico has varied since 1848, there has been a relatively constant flow in both directions (Mexico to the United States, and back to Mexico).[10]

With this stated, the reader must be cautioned to keep one fact in mind about the Mexican experience. Many Mexicans who now live in New Mexico and south Texas can trace their family origins to those geographic areas that were taken from Mexico by the United States. On one hand, this has produced a rationale for identifying strongly with the United States: Mexicans were residents of a part of the United States prior to the incorporation of that land into this country, and therefore Mexicans should be accepted (and not discriminated against) as Americans. On the other hand, because the Mexicans were a conquered group and Mexico borders the United States, Mexicans, unlike blacks, have their country of origin as a close symbol of counter-identification. How these factors affect Chicano political thought and behavior needs to be studied.

This work focuses on the formation of political attitudes and the nature of political socialization among Chicano youth (adolescents). Despite the importance of this group, little is known about them.

Most political socialization studies have focused on whites and blacks.[11] Studies comparing black Americans with whites report that blacks participate in elections at a higher level than do whites of comparable socioeconomic backgrounds. An important study by Verba and Nie explains this occurrence in terms of "black consciousness," that is the awareness among blacks of a common history, both as an American ethnic group and as a deprived racial group.[12] Subsequent studies have stressed the importance of "black consciousness" in black political participation.[13] These findings about black Americans have been reinforced by the few studies that have been done on the political socialization of Chicano children. These studies have found that ethnic identification played a critical role in the Chicanos' formation of political attitudes and behavior.[14]

The Chicano experience shares something with both that of the black and that of the European ethnics who migrated during the nineteenth and early part of the twentieth century.[15] For example, the racism experienced by the black has also been experienced in some form and degree by Chicanos.[16] In addition, the problems faced by European ethnics of reconciling old cultural values, norms, and language to an entirely new set also is faced by Chicanos. Thus while the Chicano experience has not been unique, this study of Chicano political socialization considers issues peculiar to their social position in society.

As with studies of all ethnic groups, this work considers those general questions associated with an ethnic group's level of assimilation into the dominant social fabric of a given society. Thus, in an effort to understand the formation of political attitudes and behaviors, the study has devoted significant attention to the topic of Chicano assimilation into the mainstream of American culture. How Americanized have Chicanos become?

Chicanos:
Bound for the City

Like most other ethnic groups that have immigrated to the United States, Chicanos today find themselves living in urban centers. Until the 1960s, Chicanos lived primarily in rural areas or were members of small or medium-sized communities. During the 1960s and 1970s Chicanos became more urban; they moved in large numbers to the major metropolitan areas of the Southwest and Midwest. They also were experiencing an immense increase in population that was due in part to better living and health conditions, which reduced infant and maternal mortality rates. In addition, the influx of undocumented workers from Mexico increased and those workers began to shift from rural agricultural employment to urban, service-oriented jobs. The result was a Chicano population that was more than 87 percent urban in 1980, living in large metropolitan areas.[17] Any analysis of Chicano assimilation and political socialization must consider the effects of living in a new urban environment.

Traditionally, the principal lines of analysis in political socialization research have focused on the effects of family, school, peer groups, and the mass media as socializing agents in the development of political attitudes.[18] The approach of this work differs from this traditional method of inquiry, in that it concentrates on four explanatory variables that influence the political attitudes of Chicano youth. They are: social class standing; urbanism (i.e., population density of a person's neighborhood, ethnic heterogeneity of the neighborhood, and the length of time the person has lived in the city); the degree to which the individual has remained tied to his/her ethnic culture; and the socioeconomic and political character of the city of residence. There are two reasons for this emphasis. First, it provides a broader understanding of the factors that influence political attitudes. Although the family, the school, the peer group, and the mass media are important agents in the socialization of any group of individuals, as the evidence clearly indicates, these agents influence individuals as part of the larger social context. These agents are themselves influenced by the social, economic, political, and physical environments in which they operate. For example, a family may in fact influence a child in a particular political direction, but the family itself is influenced by such factors as its socioeconomic standing, the neighborhood in which it resides, and the overall socioeconomic and political character of the city of residence.

The second reason for focusing on these variables, two of which concern urban culture, is that the vast majority of Chicanos now live in cities. Documentation of the effects the urban experience is having on them tests and extends the work of three prominent schools of urban sociological thought as they relate to ethnic assimilation and to the general impact of urban living on ethnic group attitudes and behavior.

FIGURE 1.1
The Louis Wirth Model of Urbanism's Impact on the
Retention of Ethnic Cultures

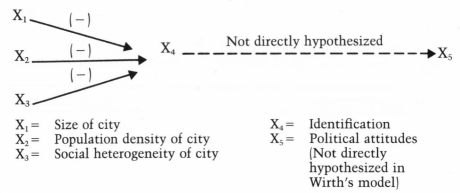

$X_1 =$ Size of city	$X_4 =$ Identification
$X_2 =$ Population density of city	$X_5 =$ Political attitudes
$X_3 =$ Social heterogeneity of city	(Not directly hypothesized in Wirth's model)

NOTE: $(-)$ means this factor has undermined traditional culture.

Chicanos, Ethnicity, and the City

There are three major theories concerning the effects of urbanism on ethnic group assimilation. The first is that of members of the Chicago school of urban sociology, most notably Wirth and Park.[19] They theorized that the spatial organizations of cities provide a unique set of social relationships that influence people's attitudes and behavior. The city changes the attitudes of ethnics about maintaining their particular folk culture, according to members of the Chicago school, by assimilating them into the values and norms of the community as a whole. Thus it has been argued that, generally by the second generation and certainly by the third, most of those ethnic individuals who lived in the city would be assimilated into the dominant Anglo-American culture.[20] If the concern for the development of political attitudes were to be coordinated with Wirth's theory as it relates to urbanism and ethnic assimilation, the resulting conceptual model would look something like Figure 1.1.[21]

The other school of thought concerning ethnic assimilation comprises the work of those whom Smith, in *The City and Social Theory,* has called the "neighborhood solidarity" theorists, of whom Gans, Suttles and Jacobs are the most notable.[22] These theorists (particularly Gans) have argued that urbanism, or the urban environment, has no effect on an individual ethnic's assimilation into the main-

FIGURE 1.2
The "Neighborhood Solidarity" Model

$$X_1 \xrightarrow{\text{Unrelated}} X_2 \xrightarrow{(+)} X_3 \xrightarrow{(+)} X_4 \xrightarrow{\text{Not directly hypothesized}} X_5$$

$X_1 =$ Urban variables (size, population density, heterogeneity)
$X_2 =$ Socioeconomic status of the individual or group
$X_3 =$ Ethnic composition of the neighborhood
$X_4 =$ Degree of identification and use of traditional cultural institutions
$X_5 =$ Political attitudes (not included in model)

NOTE: (+) means this factor has reinforced traditional culture.

stream of Anglo-American culture. Whether ethnics assimilate or not has more to do with the socioeconomic conditions in which they find themselves than with anything else. Those who maintain ethnic ties are in the lower class, living in lower-class neighborhoods; members of the middle class will assimilate or already have assimilated. Again, if the propositions of the neighborhood solidarity theorists were to be diagrammed conceptually in their most basic form, the diagram would look something like Figure 1.2.[23]

In this model, living in the city has no effect; the only thing that affects cultural retention is the social class status of the individual as well as the social class/ethnic character of the neighborhood in which he/she lives. If an individual is economically mobile, becomes middle class, and moves to a middle-class neighborhood, he/she will leave the old traditional values behind and become assimilated into Anglo-American society. In this conceptual framework, urban contextual variables have no effect at all.

Both the conceptual framework of the Chicago school and that of the "neighborhood solidarity" theorists guided the field of urban sociological inquiry[24] until a number of Marxist urban sociologists introduced some important analytical critiques and suggestions.[25] The most fundamental critique was directed at the theoretical positions of both the Chicago school and the "neighborhood solidarity" theorists, which the Marxists argued, failed to take into account that city life was dominated by class antagonisms and that these antagonisms were the result of the general capitalist organization of the whole society.[26] As Smith stated:

My critique is grounded in the assumption that the overall
class structure and political economy of a society, rather than
its degree of urbanization, largely determines the patterned
opportunities and constraints that affect both the persistence
and change of people's everyday lives.[27]

Urban political scientists, such as Katznelson, in *City Trenches:
Urban Politics and the Patterning of Class in the United States*,[28]
likewise have argued, from a Marxist perspective, that the social
and political patterns of interaction in cities can be understood best
by understanding the larger contextual organization of the economy.
The organization of the national economy, Katznelson has argued,
explains a great deal about behavioral patterns at the local and even
the neighborhood level:

It is, in brief, crucial to avoid the temptation to study
moments of crisis in isolation from the wider society and its
history. In this book, it was only after I had accounted for the
origins of the basic elements of the political culture of the
American working class that I could make sense of the urban
movements of the 1960s, the crisis of which they were a part,
and its resolution. The social and political life of northern
Manhattan could not be understood either in its own terms,
or by an exclusively structural-institutional account of older
American cities in advanced capitalism. The relationship of
Washington Heights-Inwood [the area Katznelson studied] to
the wider society made its boundaries permeable; more
important, the distinctive character of class formation in the
United States provided widely shared rules for urban
politics.[29]

There are two parts to the Marxist model that should be emphasized. The first has to do with the premise that the overall structure
of the economy is related to the economic organization of cities.
The second part has to do with the causal links between the general
economic structure of the country and the socioeconomic and political structures found at the city level. The Marxist approach adds
an important dimension to the analysis of human interaction as it
takes place in the urban environment because it points out that the
economic conditions of a particular society influence the cultural
and political norms of its inhabitants. In this model, those ethnics
who migrate to urban areas can expect to encounter economic con-

FIGURE 1.3
Marxist Model of the Effect of Urbanism on People's
Attitudes toward Traditional Culture and Politics

Not directly hypothesized

$$X_1 \longrightarrow X_2 \longrightarrow X_3 \longrightarrow X_4 \text{-------------------} X_5$$

$X_1 =$ Overall economic structure
$X_2 =$ The urban structure (local economic organization and spatial arrangement to accommodate economy)
$X_3 =$ Work/social relations
$X_4 =$ Cultural orientation
$X_5 =$ Political orientation (not hypothesized)

ditions that will require most of them to make cultural adjustments. These new conditions to which migrants must learn to adapt, the Marxists have argued, are dictated by the general economic organization of the society. Thus, in the case of the United States, capitalism requires a rational work schedule. Since Anglo-American culture has dominated the society, the work schedule will follow the cultural norms of the dominant culture (language, for example), and the eventual consequence will be that the cultural norms of all ethnic groups involved in this national capitalist enterprise will approximate those of the dominant culture. Interestingly, the Marxist model, which has the dynamics of capitalism assimilating divergent peoples into a unified whole, is similar to the Wirth model, while the fact that the Marxist model can predict interethnic conflict based on class standing also makes it similar to the model of the "neighborhood solidarity" theorists.

In the analysis that follows, each of these theories is tested as to its efficacy in explaining the urban experience of the Chicano youth involved in the study on which this work is based and how that experience influenced their political socialization. The study examined the ways in which the urban ecological conditions of population density and neighborhood ethnic heterogeneity, along with the length of time a particular person had lived in the city, affected cultural retention and attitudes toward politics. These variables incorporate many (although by no means all) of Wirth's concerns regarding urbanism's impact on the individual. The study also examined the socioeconomic standing of each individual, and how his/her socioeconomic position affected cultural retention and political attitudes. In examining SES (socioeconomic status) the hypotheses of

FIGURE 1.4
Path Model Representing Urban Contextual Variables,
Socioeconomic Variables, and Political Variables*

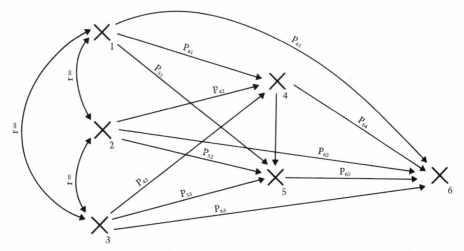

* =   All coefficients are significant at the .05 level or beyond on
      a two-tailed "t" test
$X_1 =$ Length of residence in the city
$X_2 =$ Population density in neighborhood
$X_3 =$ Ethnic homogeneity in respondent's neighborhood
$X_4 =$ Socioeconomic status
$X_5 =$ Traditional cultural values (retention of)
$X_6 =$ Dependent political variable

the "neighborhood solidarity theorists" and, to some extent, of the
Marxists were tested. In addition, the comparison of cities permitted
more direct testing of the Marxist model.

To separate the effects of all these variables, a Path Analytic Model
(see Figure 1.4)[30] was employed, as described in Chapter III. In this
model (X_1) is the urban variable "length of time the respondent has
lived in the city," operationalized as the number of years the respondent has lived in his/her specific city; (X_2) is the "population
density of the respondent's neighborhood," measured as the number
of residents in a four-block square around the respondent's house;[31]
(X_3) is the "ethnic heterogeneity of the respondent's neighborhood,"
operationalized as the percentage of Chicanos (as a ratio of the number of ethnic groups) in the respondent's neighborhood; (X_4) is the

"socioeconomic status of the respondent," operationalized as the socioeconomic status (measured using the method employed by Duncan and Featherman and Hauser,[32] of the respondent's family; (X_5) is the degree to which the respondent has retained Chicano culture, operationalized as an index variable of the extent to which the respondent has retained the use of four cultural institutions;[33] and (X_6) is the dependent variable, or the respondent's attitude toward various political concepts and institutions.

In utilizing this model it is not suggested that the arrows imply causal relationships, even though path models usually imply causality. Rather, the path model is used to gain a better understanding of the interrelationships that exist between these variables as they affect political attitudes. Through the use of this model, many of the hypotheses of the Chicago school and the "neighborhood solidarity" theorists may be explored. The researcher's own theory is that neither of the processes hypothesized by these two conceptual schools of thought is universal when it comes to ethnic socioeconomic and political socialization. The determination of which one has the greatest impact depends on other characteristics, such as the socioeconomic organization and political culture of the society. Although this theory seems to coincide with the Marxist theory of urbanism, the study departs from that theory, not because of rejection of the premise that there are causal relationships between the national economic structure and political/social attitudes, but because the study extends the Marxist argument and focuses on a different locus of organization—the city. *It is my contention that the economic, social, and political organization of the city, not the country as a whole, is the variable which has the most impact on members of a particular ethnic group's (Chicanos, in this case) retention of traditional culture and their socialization toward politics, precisely because this variable sets the parameters for what constitutes acceptable and unacceptable behavior.* In comparing three cities with distinct social and economic environments, this work shows how such factors as social class, urban ecological conditions, and cultural retention interrelate with these distinct environments to affect the political attitudes of the Chicano youth studied.

A Tale of Three Cities: Caste, Class, and Mass

The three cities investigated in this study are San Antonio, Texas; Albuquerque, New Mexico; and Los Angeles, California. These cities are all large metropolitan areas, they have large numbers of Chicanos living in them, and they have been magnet cities for Chicano migration. Since each of these cities is large, a key element in both Wirth's and the Chicago school's schema for defining urbanism, it is logical to assume that the social forces within each of these urban environments would produce similar attitudes and behaviors among the Chicanos residing there. However, this is not the case. The cities of Albuquerque and Los Angeles have patterned similarities in the ways in which the city's environment affects the attitudes and behaviors of the Chicano youth who live there, but for different reasons. The environment of San Antonio has produced a different attitudinal response among the Chicanos who live there. How could this occur? These cities are all large, densely populated, and heterogeneous, but more factors than size, population density, and heterogeneity affect an ethnic group's attitudes and behaviors. This study has found that these attitudes are influenced by: (1) the economic organization of the city and its concomitant social structure; (2) the city's ethnic composition; (3) the history of ethnic relations; (4) the openness of the political system; and (5) the codes (legal system) by which the population is controlled. In sum, it is the interaction of these conditions that forms a city's *modus vivendi*, and this *modus vivendi* is what ultimately has the most impact on the formation and maintenance of people's attitudes.

Each of the three cities investigated in this study has a different character with regard to social relations between ethnic groups. In San Antonio social relations are permeated by the legacy of a "caste-like" social structure that dominated the entire south Texas region for most of the twentieth century.[34] In other words, Chicano/Anglo social relations in San Antonio society are influenced more by inherited ethnic origin than by other criteria such as level of socioeconomic attainment. Thus, in spite of economic success, a Chicano usually is not socially equal to an Anglo who holds an equivalent economic position. This type of social relationship tends to strengthen social/ethnic segregation and to encourage the maintenance of two strongly ethnic-conscious communities. It also limits social relations between Anglos and Chicanos to the workplace and reinforces dominant/subservient patterns of ethnic interaction.[35]

One factor that has contributed to the persistence of "caste-type" elements in the social relations of San Antonio has been the fact that San Antonio does not have the ethnic diversity of cities like Los Angeles and Albuquerque.[36] Ethnically, Chicanos comprise about

58 percent of the city's population, Anglos about 34 percent, and blacks about 8 percent.[37] Migration into San Antonio from eastern cities has not been significant, and the result has been the maintenance of two dominant ethnic groups with a long history of ethnic antagonism. This antagonism began before Texas succeeded in gaining independence from Mexico and has continued to the present. Ironically, the Alamo, a "national shrine" in Texas, is in San Antonio and is a constant reminder to both Anglo-Texans and Chicano-Texans of past conflict and present animosity.[38]

In addition to San Antonio's ethnic composition and history of ethnic antagonism, the city's economic structure is a contributing factor in maintaining the "caste-like" character of its social relations. The local economy is dominated by tourism and by government employment on the five military bases located within the city limits.[39] These structural foundations of San Antonio's economy have remained fairly constant—the economy has not been diversifying and expanding, and the city has not experienced an influx of large numbers of new workers (either manual or professional) from the East or Midwest. The result of this economic situation is the maintenance of a rather closed economic system that limits the opportunities of its Chicano citizens, the overwhelming majority of whom occupy a lower socioeconomic status, to pursue many avenues of economic mobility.[40]

The political structure of San Antonio was closed to Chicanos until very recently.[41] At the time of the initial phase of this study, 1977, there was only one Chicano on the city council, a remarkable statistic given the fact that the city was over 50 percent Chicano. In 1984 there were four Chicanos on the city council and a Chicano mayor; however, this does not signal a changing of the guard in terms of political power. The Anglo-American community controls much of the economic activity in San Antonio, primarily through the power of the banks, and as a result it controls a great deal of local government activity.[42] Therefore, even with the addition of more Chicanos to the city council, the political system is perceived by Chicanos to operate in its traditional manner, i.e., Chicano participation is perceived to be restricted to support for a Chicano politician who acts as an ambassador from the *barrio* (Chicano districts) to the outside world. At the same time, this politician's power to aid Chicanos also is perceived to be confined by the power of the Anglo-American in the everyday business of the local economy. This is not the public perception in Los Angeles or Albuquerque, where diversified and expanding economies have given the impression of dispersed economic and political power.

The legal system in San Antonio reflects a hard line "law and order" approach, and the police department has been stricter and more physical in the Chicano community than it has been in the Anglo-American. Given the history of Texas police relations with Chicanos, particularly that of the Texas Rangers, the police and the courts in San Antonio have an image among Chicanos consistent with their past role as agents and institutions operating to maintain the status quo and, in the process, to control the Chicano community.[43]

In sum, San Antonio, the tenth largest city in the United States, qualifies as a "city" according to the criteria put forth by Wirth and the Chicago school; however, the urbanism of San Antonio nurtures attitudes and behaviors quite different from those found in Los Angeles and Albuquerque.

Albuquerque, the second city in our study, can best be described as a "class-oriented" city because its social relations, as they pertain to Chicanos, are dominated by issues related to social class standing. It is smaller than our other two cities. In fact, it has less than half their population, but it is one of the fastest growing cities in the nation.[44] As a fast-growing city, it has both properties associated with its past and a set of new properties associated with the new form it is assuming.

At one time Albuquerque shared many of San Antonio's attributes. It was a service-oriented town, with the primary economic activities associated with government, principally the military.[45] The population was composed mainly of two ethnic groups: Hispanos (Chicanos) and Anglos, although there were a small number of American Indians and blacks.[46] Ethnic antagonisms between Chicanos and Anglos did exist in Albuquerque, but they never reached the degree of severity experienced in Texas, for some crucial historial reasons. One of these historical factors is the existence of a well-developed upper and middle class among the Chicanos before the United States conquered New Mexico in 1848.[47] Those social classes, for the most part, maintained themselves after annexation, creating the impression that Chicanos could become middle class and thereby reducing the resentment associated with feelings of victimization in a "caste-like" system such as San Antonio's. This impression of access to social mobility has continued to the present. The fact that Albuquerque, like Los Angeles, has experienced economic growth promotes optimistic feelings of social mobility. Also, Albuquerque's economy, although to a lesser extent than that of Los Angeles, is more evenly dispersed among the service, manufacturing, commercial, and government.[48] This has produced more fluidity in the labor market and more optimism with regard to the existence of options. Thus, at the societal level in Albuquerque, a person who is identified as ethnically "Mexican" (not a positive connotation in New Mexico) can, with economic mobility, become identified as "Spanish," which carries with it the connotation of being racially Caucasian (instead of *mestizo*, which the label "Mexican" carries) and socially on a par with the Anglo middle and upper classes.

Formal politics in Albuquerque has the appearance of being open to all who want to enter the political arena, regardless of ethnic origin. This is so despite the fact that social class background is perceived to be an important factor in participation in the various levels of government. The appearance that the system is open to Chicanos and that there is a far greater range of possibilities for personal involvement for the middle class has been reinforced by the fact that Chicanos have participated in the upper levels of government in Albuquerque (and in New Mexico as a whole) since the region became part of the United States, but most of those who have been involved at these levels have been middle- and upper-class Chicanos.[49]

The legal institutions in Albuquerque periodically have been accused of being discriminatory in their dealings with Chicanos. However, over time they have gained the reputation, whether justified or not, of being relatively fair to all citizens and effective in protecting the public.

Thus, for Albuquerque, a moderately but steadily expanding economy, combined with the increasingly diverse ethnic population resulting from immigration from the East has produced the perception that there are opportunities for all citizens, regardless of ethnicity, to pursue their ambitions. The Albuquerque economy has been able to integrate a significant number of its immigrants, but at various rates of speed. These different rates of economic integration have resulted in enormous social class differences, particularly between the Chicano population, with few professional or technical skills, and the immigrants from the East, who are generally young and professional. However, because Albuquerque's economy eventually has been able to integrate people into its various labor markets, its citizens, including Chicanos, believe that eventually hard-working individuals will become economically mobile. As a result, the Chicanos in this study were found to react to urban life, as predicted by the theories of Wirth and the Chicago school, with social class standing regulating the rate of individual reaction.

Los Angeles is the third city in the study, and, like San Antonio and Albuquerque, it has its own distinctive character. Los Angeles can best be described as a "mass city," in that the social relations that exist in Los Angeles are best characterized as those existing in a mass society. Los Angeles is geographically so expansive that it gives the appearance of having no boundaries. This appearance is aided by the fact that the surrounding region is all urban, so that people never really know when they have entered Los Angeles or left it. Most people agree that the mere distance involved in getting from one part of the city to another through the maze of freeways is quite overwhelming at times. It has the psychological effect of creating an image that the city has no end.

In addition to its size, Los Angeles has an extremely heterogeneous population. There exist in Los Angeles, perhaps more than in any city in the world, a variety of life styles, all influencing one another. This diversity, which makes it difficult to agree on a governing norm, also adds to the mass character of the city. As in New York, there are a multitude of ethnic groups, each with a sizable constituency. For example, there are a million Chicanos in Los Angeles County, yet Chicanos make up only 10 percent of the population. Although each group may have a large proportion of its members living in one particular area of the city, one can find representatives of each of the groups throughout the city, and in many cases in sizable numbers.[50]

The history of ethnic relations in Los Angeles is complex. There has been competition among all ethnic groups in the marketplace, and antagonisms have existed, but ethnic antagonisms and social isolation have not occurred with the intensity or breadth with which they have been manifested in other cities in the country—San Antonio or Boston, for example.[51] There is a history of acceptance and a perception among Los Angeles' citizens that there is more tolerance in the Los Angeles community. Of course, some of the ethnic antagonisms have been eased by the fact that Los Angeles' local economy has experienced steady growth. Its economy is diversified, blending manufacturing, commercial, and service sectors into one of the strongest urban economic systems in the United States.[52] This has produced a diverse labor market, with more fluidity and a perception among its citizens that there is a wide range of options for employment. The heterogeneity in the labor market, as opposed to a stratified labor market with few options, like San Antonio's, makes a difference in the impact that the city has on individuals. There is also a sense of openness to the political system. This does not mean that Chicanos have had equal representation in city government; in fact, there has only been one Chicano on the city council in its history. However, those politicians who have recently been elected, including Mayor Bradley, himself a black, have been able to portray the political system as being open to those who want to participate. Also, the legal system of Los Angeles, while perhaps not one of the most sensitive in the country, still is administered, particularly by the police, in a way that makes all sectors of the city complain relatively equally about law enforcement.[53]

Last but not least, the avant-garde style of the media in Los Angeles has worked to connect various cultures to one another. There are anchor men and women on the local television stations representing various ethnic groups, but, perhaps more importantly, one can find Asian, Latin, black and white ethnic bands all playing creative pop music on the radio. This has minimized the effect of ethnocentrism among young people by giving the impression that there has been an interpenetration by all ethnic groups of one another's cultures. In essence, the media have been powerful in facilitating the assimilation of a multitude of ethnic groups in Los Angeles.[54]

In addition to the assimilative aspects of Los Angeles' society, the city's mass culture gives an interesting aspect to the effects of city life on ethnic attitudes toward culture and politics. The mass culture of Los Angeles is able, just as Wirth and the Chicago school hypothesized about cities, to assimilate diverse ethnic groups into the city's general cultural norm. Yet city life in Los Angeles also creates an underclass among many of the ethnic groups which the culture is in the process of assimilating. This underclass is composed of people from a variety of ethnic groups, although this work deals only with the Chicano underclass. Members of the Chicano underclass are second to fourth generation Americans and have lived in the city for quite some time. Their grandparents and perhaps even their parents maintained the traditional culture, but the younger generation no longer practices and/or knows this culture.

For the Chicanos who have achieved mobility, thus becoming middle class, the problems associated with cultural change have been relatively minimal; however, for those who have remained in the lower socioeconomic strata, the problems associated with cultural change have been immense. These people have given up the traditional cultural practices associated with their group of origin, just as the dominant society has expected them to do, but they have not experienced the prosperity enjoyed by members of other groups upon following this sociocultural prescription of socioeconomic mobility. Thus, although they have adopted the dominant culture, they live in poor areas composed mostly of people from their own ethnic group; they are culturally separated from those in their group who have maintained Chicano/Mexican culture—in essence, they are not fully part of either culture, Anglo or Chicano. They are, as Park and Wirth have pointed out, culturally marginal people—that is to say, members neither of one culture nor of the other.[55] This economically poor and culturally schizophrenic underclass, if not created, then greatly accelerated by Los Angeles' mass culture, exhibits attitudes and behaviors more extreme than those of other subgroups studied in this work.

To summarize, all of the conditions described in Los Angeles have acted to create a more integrated social structure, but the consequence has been that there are few social attachments to objects and/or people and places. The vast majority of middle-range relationships that one would find in other social settings (in fact, in other cities) are not extensive in Los Angeles. Those primary groups with which people could and would identify, such as ethnic organizations, do exist in Los Angeles, and they are not weak *per se;* however, as Kornhauser has stated with regard to mass societies in general, they are isolated from the larger society.[56] In this case, they are isolated from the larger Los Angeles society; although people feel somewhat attached to these groups, their identification is not sufficient (because these organizations or groups are so small compared to the larger society), nor do they provide for large-scale mobilization and participation in the larger society. There is the feeling that one can participate in the economic and political system, but there is also a sense that the size of Los Angeles inhibits any control that an individual may have over his/her life. The consequence is that people cease to care about many of the issues concerning the economy and polity, even though they continue to participate in both. The final consequence is that Los Angeles is culturally integrating. It produces attitudes among the Chicano youth who live there that are characteristic of those predicted by Wirth and the

Chicago school. At the same time (and contrary to the Wirth model), it also has a disorganizing effect which distinguishes it from San Antonio and Albuquerque.

An Overview of What Follows

The present work, dealing with the political socialization of Chicano youth, begins by analyzing the cultural context in which this socialization occurs. Chapter 2 is concerned with questions of ethnic assimilation and acculturation and how this process has been affected by living in each of the three cities studied. Questions related to the various schools of urban sociology are considered. The data presented in that chapter serve to provide a better understanding of Chicano ethnicity and establish a foundation for understanding the impact that ethnicity has on the acquisition of political attitudes. Chapter 3 begins to analyze the political attitudes of Chicano youth through the use of the path model, addressing their identification with the American political-economic system, and attempting to determine who identifies with the system and what factors influence that identification. In addition, the chapter discusses which members of the sample developed a sense of political disenchantment by embracing a radical ideology that challenges the existing political-economic arrangements in the United States, and attempts to explain the foundation for that diffuse sense of estrangement.

Following this analysis of how Chicanos view their political world, Chapter 4 investigates the manner in which they translate this political world view into involvement in the American political system. The chapter focuses on conventional forms of involvement, such as the youths' conception of voting and their political partisanship. Questions posed are: What do they think of voting? Do they expect to vote? Do they think it is important? What do they think will be the result of their voting? With which political party, if any, do they identify? How are their thoughts on these issues influenced by their city life?

Chapter 5 continues the investigation of political involvement, but switches the focus to unconventional modes of political participation. Rather surprisingly, a large number of young people were found to support these modes of participation. The chapter analyzes the attitudinal support for political protest and violence and examines the factors in the new urban environments that influence individuals' attitudes in supporting or rejecting these forms of participation.

Finally, Chapter 6 turns to the new immigrants to the Chicano community—the Mexican nationals, most of whom are in the United States without the benefit of legal papers. The number of illegal Mexican immigrants has been steadily increasing, and their impact on the Chicano community is not known. For example, does their presence in the community strengthen Chicano association with traditional culture, thereby affecting Chicano assimilation/acculturation? Does it affect the political attitudes of Chicanos? If so how? The history of other ethnic groups has demonstrated that succeeding waves of immigrants of the same group have had some impact on that group's political power vis-a-vis other groups in the political system. This was particularly true for the Irish, the Jews, and the Italians. In all of these cases the first generation of immigrants was found to be wealthier than those who arrived later, to discriminate against later arrivals, to be more politically conservative than the latter, and at the same time to be more politically powerful. In addition, precisely because they did arrive first and were more wealthy and established, they were the leaders of the community. Despite their disdain for the lower class members of their own group who had only recently arrived, the established leaders were forced to appeal to the new arrivals because these persons provided the political power base for the community. Keeping in mind the experience of these other ethnic groups, the situation of young Mexican nationals who have recently arrived in the United States is compared with that of Chicano youths who have lived in the U.S. for a considerable time.

Research Design

The initial study described in this work focuses on young adult Chicanos seventeen to nineteen years of age. The sample included 1,040 young people, all of whom were in their senior year of high school. This age group was chosen because it provided the most potential for identifying changes occurring in the Chicano community, since any changes occurring in attitudes toward culture and politics would be as detectable among this group as among older adults. In addition, the subjects would soon be graduating from high school and assuming various adult positions in American society. Thus this group provided an excellent opportunity for identifying trends within the Chicano community.

The data for the study were acquired in three ways. First, a lengthy questionnaire was administered to everyone who participated in the study. The questionnaire asked for background information and included various questions aimed at determining attitudes toward Chicano culture and politics. Several methodological techniques were used in the questionnaire, including Likert-scale and Semantic Differential-type questions.

In the second part of the study, 200 of the 1,040 people who completed the questionnaire were selected for in-depth interviews. These persons were selected randomly from each of the three cities, and an interview of about ninety minutes' duration was conducted with each. Each of the 200 interviews was then transcribed. The data provided by the interviews filled in some informational gaps in the responses to questionnaires. The interviews also helped to validate the information obtained from the questionnaires.

In the third part of the study, the researcher became a participant-observer in each of the three cities studied, which helped to clarify many of the ambiguities remaining after the questionnaire and interview data had been analyzed. It also pointed out a number of the subtle idiosyncracies that helped to explain the local environments in which the Chicanos in this study lived.

This initial study (survey questionnaire, in-depth interviews, and participant observation) was begun in September of 1977 and finished in December, 1978. In 1981–1982 the researcher received a grant from the Ford Foundation to do a follow-up study of those who participated in 1977–1978. Three hundred (100 in each city) of the original 1,040 people interviewed in 1977–1978 were randomly selected and asked if they would consent to being interviewed again. Nearly all of those selected agreed to be re-interviewed; however, in place of those who declined to participate or whom the researcher was unable to locate (because they had moved to an undisclosed address, or were deceased), other individuals were selected until the desired total of 300 was obtained. The follow-up study focused on what had happened to these young people in the four years since the original study was conducted. Particular attention was given to whether their attitudes toward Chicano culture and politics had changed. The data that were obtained from the follow-up study were then compared to the original 1977–1978 data. Surprisingly, few attitudinal changes had occurred in the four years since the original study had been completed. Where changes occurred, both the original findings and the new findings have been reported.

As the reader proceeds, it will become evident that almost no differences are reported which relate to gender. This is not to be considered an oversight on the part of the research design or analysis. At every juncture, the survey and interview data were checked against the researcher's participation-observation field notes to determine whether there were differences between the sexes in attitudes toward the various subjects examined. Few were found, and most of these were too slight to report as true differences; however, the few significant gender differences in attitudes have been reported.

Finally, a word on the identification of the people being quoted here. To protect confidentiality (which was agreed upon before administering the questionnaire and undertaking the interview), all names have been changed. Thus, although the respondents' genders, their places of residence, and the occupations of their parents are accurate, the name assigned to each of them is fictitious.

2

Chicano Ethnicity
and City Life

THIS CHAPTER addresses the ethnic acculturation of Chicanos. The issue of cultural retention/deterioration has important implications for ethnic group integration into a particular society. In turn, ethnic integration has been an important issue in political science, because it has been shown that those individuals (or groups) who have been integrated into the larger society have higher levels of trust in government, higher degrees of loyalty to the system, and a higher sense of political efficacy; and are more likely to participate in politics, particularly in political activities that are not conflict-oriented.[1] Thus, an analysis of Chicano assimilation can provide a foundation for understanding the development of political attitudes among Chicanos.

Like most of the ethnic groups that immigrated to America, Chicanos now live in cities. Thus, the process of Chicano ethnic acculturation is occurring with an urban context. From the work of the Chicago school of urban sociology, most notably that of Wirth and Park, it might be expected that the longer a Chicano has lived in a city, the less he/she will be involved with Chicano traditional culture and the more assimilated into the dominant Anglo-American society. According to Wirth and Park, this general process of assimilation occurs because the complex social structure of cities has an enormous influence on traditional views of the world. Hence the social adjustments required by living in a large, densely populated and heterogeneous area hastens the loosening of ties to traditional culture and encourages the acceptance of the cultural norms of the larger community. Urban living, they argued, not only breaks down various sub-cultural associations, but also integrates these individuals who make up these associations into the broader American society.[2]

A competing theory regarding the city's impact on ethnic assimilation has been advanced by Gans, among others. Gans observed that members of ethnic groups in urban environments continue to maintain the values associated with their country of origin. He argued that maintenance of ties to traditional cultural institutions or particular ethnic groups has more to do with social class standing than with urbanization *per se.*[3]

Although these two theoretical approaches may seem incompatible, they are not necessarily mutually exclusive. Whether a particular ethnic group responds in the manner theorized by Wirth and the Chicago school or in that posited by Gans depends on the social context of the particular city in which its members live. The study described in this work involved three cities with different social orientations (caste, class, mass), and this chapter will discuss ways in which these different social contexts affect the preservation/deterioration of traditional Chicano culture. Four cultural institutions that are considered to be of fundamental importance to Chicano culture will be analyzed: the nuclear family, the extended family, the Spanish language, and the Catholic Church. The study findings indicated that, in the cases of Albuquerque and Los Angeles, the argument of Wirth and the Chicago School is applicable. Although the data were not broken down into urban and rural, it is apparent that the longer a Chicano lives in each of these cities, the more assimilated he/she becomes, and that this is accelerated by socioeconomic mobility. In the case of San Antonio, it was also found that living in the city has no effect on the retention of Chicano culture; regardless of the time that the subjects have been living in San Antonio, they have retained their culture. In essence, the Chicanos in San Antonio remain separate and socially unintegrated into Anglo society.

Before proceeding with the analysis of the impact of city living on Chicano attitudes toward traditional cultural institutions, it is important to clarify two definitions: (1) the meaning of the term "traditional cultural institution," and (2) how culture is operationalized.

First, the use of the term "traditional cultural institution" does not imply that these cultural institutions are archaic or obsolete. No value judgment is attached to the concept. The term "traditional cultural institution" is used here to designate a cultural institution that has been retained by an ethnic gorup (in this case, Chicanos) over a long period of time. For example, the Spanish language has gone through changes that doubtless have altered some of its character; nevertheless, the language has been maintained, and it is referred to here as a "traditional cultural institution."

Second, the culture of a particular ethnic group is composed of a variety of phenomena. There are artifacts, festivals, institutions, values, attitudes, norms, etc. Even if the exclusive concern of this work were to analyze the impact of urbanism on cultural attachment, it would be most difficult, and perhaps impossible, to analyze exhaustively every aspect of a group's culture. For this reason, the work focuses on what have been some core institutional elements of Chicano culture: the nuclear and extended family, the Spanish language, and religion. There is no contention that these are the only elements or even the most important elements of Chicano culture, although it may be argued that they have played a fundamental role in the culture of most groups. It is important to note that other cultural variables were included in the questionnaire administered to the subjects of the study, but the unavoidable constraints imposed by the study's focus on political attitudes and behavior precluded the inclusion of the data on those additional aspects of culture.[4] It can, however, be reported, before turning to the findings for the cultural variables selected for discussion, that the same patterns found with regard to these variables existed for the other cultural variables as well.

The Nuclear Family

The institution which has been recognized by many sociologists as one of the most, if not *the* most, crucial in maintaining culture is the family structure. Its position is pivotal because of its primary role as a socializing agent in the personal growth of every individual. It is the family which has been given the primary responsibility of transmitting to the next generation those values that are considered worth preserving. It is not surprising that urban sociologists have looked to the family as a source for identifying changes in human populations and investigating whether living in an urban, as compared to a rural, environment creates major changes in the family structure, the way members of the family look at the world, or what family relations teach children.[5]

Wirth and Park would have argued that increased urbanization alters the structure and behavior of the traditional ethnic family, and that the "new" urban social structure will, after experiencing a period of disorganization, take on the family norms of the larger urban community.[6]

The sociological and anthropological characterization of the traditional Chicano nuclear family is that of a patriarchal structure, in which the father monopolizes both power and prestige while the mother and children assume secondary and/or subservient roles, and in which it is emphasized that primary obligations and loyalties are to the family and not to the individual.[7] This depiction of the traditional Chicano family is, in fact, remarkably similar to that of traditional family structures of other ethnic groups, and thus social scientists have assumed that there was nothing unique about the Chicano family experience. The Chicano family would undergo the same changes that families of other ethnic groups had undergone, and the catalyst for this change would be the assimilation process, stimulated by the association with an industrialized urban society.[8]

This depiction of the Chicano family and the accompanying assumptions concerning its transformation have been criticized heavily for their conceptual and empirical shortcomings. These criticisms have been summarized efficiently by Baca Zinn, who stated:

(1) Families [Chicano] are described in reference to a monolithic (traditional) family type, i.e., "traditional" family versus "modern" when there may in fact be a great deal of variation in the patterns of the Chicano family.

(2) "Family structure is reduced to cultural value orientations, i.e., the notion that Chicano family structure is determined by traditional cultural values alone" and any linkages between family structure and the larger society are omitted when they clearly have some impact.

(3) The Chicano traditional family structure will disappear with increasing modernization and acculturation, i.e., acculturation has been the major framework of explaining changes in family patterns when conditions such as common occupational positions, residential concentration and dependence on common institutions and services may act to reinforce the kinship structure.[9]

Wirth and Park perhaps are vulnerable to two of Baca Zinn's criticisms: they have assumed, first, that there is a monolithic family structure that is considered traditional, and second, that there is a linear process of change whereby the traditional family structure evolves into something new which represents the pervasive norm of the city. Although the study described here focused on the impact of the city on the Chicano, the data set consisted of Chicanos 17 to 19 years of age, none of whom were married, and thus did not allow for an analysis of either the family structure or inter-family relations. Yet data on the family and attitudes toward the family available from the questionnaire and from in-depth interviews provide some information concerning city experience and the family. Three significant variables, to be discussed below, are (1) the size of the respondents' families, (2) the number of respondents having mothers who work outside the home, and (3) the youths' attitudes toward women working outside the home. While these data are somewhat tentative, when they are considered together with the attitudes toward other cultural institutions presented in this chapter, they do provide supportive evidence as to how city life affects Chicano attitudes toward culture.

The Chicano population has been one of the fastest growing in the United States, and if this trend continues, Chicanos will overtake black Americans as the United States' largest ethnic group. When figures from the 1960, 1970 and 1980 censuses are compared, they show that the average size of the Chicano family has been decreasing, a trend consistent with that found in the rest of the nation. With regard to the size of the families of the subjects of this study, in San Antonio the average number of family members was 4.11, with a mean number of 4.25 for lower-class families and 3.97 for middle-class families. In Albuquerque, the mean family size was 3.99, with lower-class families having a mean of 4.23 and middle-class families a mean of 3.75. In Los Angeles, the mean family size was 4.00, with a mean of 4.21 for lower-class families and 3.89 for the middle class. These results are consistent with what often has been noted as a characteristic of socioeconomic standing—that middle-class couples have smaller families. Yet the differences reported above are not of a magnitude that would suggest that social class, as it applies to the families in this sample, is the most important factor influencing family size.

The variable that does have a significant impact on the size of the families of the Chicanos in this study is the length of time that the respondent has spent in the city, although this is not true in the case of San Antonio. The mean size of families from Los Angeles who had lived in that city less than ten years was 5.08, whereas for Chicano families who had lived in Los Angeles for more than 10 years, the mean was 2.92. In Albuquerque the same trend exists: for families who had lived in Albuquerque for less than ten years the mean size was 4.51, while residence for over ten years yielded a mean of 3.37. For San Antonio, the size of the family varied little with length of residence—those who had lived in the city for less than ten years had a mean family size of 4.16, while those who had lived there longer than ten years had an average of 4.06 members.

Interestingly, when the youth who had been in the city for under ten years were asked how many children their parents had had after the family arrived in the city, the mean number for Los Angeles was 0.17, while it was 1.13 for Albuquerque and 2.42 for San Antonio. This would appear to indicate that most of the families from Los Angeles and Albuquerque were relatively large upon arrival, and that the typical couple proceeded to have only one more child after arriving in the city.

Three reasons were given by the youth of Albuquerque and Los Angeles for their parents' decisions to limit the size of their families. The first was that the high cost of housing, food, and clothing in these cities had forced their parents to reduce the number of children they would otherwise have wanted just to make ends meet. The second was that these high costs reinforced, in those parents who were preoccupied with economic mobility, the tendency to eliminate any factors that would consume family resources and thus jeopardize that mobility. The third was that parents were influenced by the prevailing social norms to have fewer children because the majority of the other families in their neighborhoods had fewer children and they did not want to be looked upon as socially deviant.

Information from the in-depth interviews provides perceptions of the Chicano youths from Los Angeles and Albuquerque understanding as to why their parents only had one more child. Seventy-nine percent (170) of the youth in Los Angeles and Albuquerque who had lived in the city for under ten years and were from lower socioeconomic backgrounds said that their parents' decision on family size was influenced by the hardships that the new economic conditions had placed on the family's financial resources. Finding adequate housing had been a problem, and the prices for other necessities such as food and clothing, as well as for amenities such as entertainment, were generally much higher in their new cities than they had been in the places from which they had migrated. While it may not seem that economic hardship in and of itself would have been likely to produce a conscious effort to limit the number of children in the family, one must remember that most of these families had come to the city with the desire to be economically mobile. Hence the combination of this desire and the stark economic realities of the cities influenced them to have fewer children. In addition to these factors, according to the youth in this study, another factor influenced their families to have fewer children, and that was the prevailing norm of smaller families in these cities, as indicated above. The youth reported that most of the people they lived around had the same number of children that their parents had, and that they felt that this had had an impact on their parents. Two illustrative comments follow:

Armando, 18-year-old son of a warehouse worker in Albuquerque:

My parents were concerned with not having a real big family because it was expensive to live and there was no way to save [money] if they did . . . and then none of my parents' friends had big families, and none of the neighbors did either, and I think that influenced them, too.

Teresa, 17-year-old daughter of a worker in a plastics factory in Los Angeles:

I know that my parents were concerned with making ends meet and so they did not think they could afford a big family. Plus none of the people they knew, the people we lived around or their friends, had large families, so I don't think they wanted to be different from the rest.

For San Antonio, the data on number of children in the family indicate that this number is not affected by the length of time the family has been in the city. In addition, only 11 percent (16) of the youth in San Antonio whose families had lived in the city ten years or less said that economic conditions were harder for them there than they had been in their former homes. The prevailing attitude was that conditions were about the same, or if not the same, then at least manageable.

Miguel, 18-year-old son of a bartender:

I don't think economic hardship influenced my father because it really is not a lot different from the Valley where we lived before. If it did, it didn't do a whole lot because my mother had three kids since we moved here six years ago.

Norma, 18-year-old daughter of an office building window washer:

Well, my mother has had two kids since we moved here five years ago, so I don't think being in San Antonio changed their minds about having more kids. I never heard my parents mention that they thought it was too expensive to have more children, and nobody else I know seems to think about that; I mean my friends' mothers have all had more children since I have known them.

How do the youth from these cities view the family? In each city, the overwhelming majority of the youth wanted to be married some day, but there are some interesting differences within and between cities on some issues related to the family. When asked who should be the head of the household, the youth from Los Angeles and Albuquerque who had been in the city for five years or longer said that no one person should be the head of a family, but that it should be a fifty-fifty partnership. In contrast, the Chicanos who had been in the city for less than five years thought that the husband should be the head of the house. Interestingly, there was no difference between sexes on this issue. For the youth in San Antonio, length of residence in the city made no difference—both males and females thought that the man should be the head of the house.

When asked whether extramarital sex was permissible, 61 percent (fifty-two) of the youth in Los Angeles and 58 percent (thirty-four) of the youth from Albuquerque who had lived in the city for five years or less thought that extramarital sex was appropriate, but only for men. Women who had lived in the city for under five years did not believe that extramarital sex was appropriate for either gender. Those youth who did think it was permissible were almost exclusively male. In San Antonio there was no difference related to length of time in the city; 36 percent of the entire sub-sample (sixty-four men and fifty-five women) felt that extramarital sex was permissible, although nearly all of them (95 percent) restricted it to men.

These findings demonstrate that the youth in Los Angeles and Albuquerque who were recent migrants had arrived with traditional attitudes about male/female roles in the family, but that these attitudes were subject to change with longer residence in those cities.

The comments of two youths who had lived in the city for more than five years provide an illustration:

Mario, 18-year-old son of a shoe salesman in Los Angeles:

I don't think that a marriage will work if people [partners] cheat. I used to think so, though. I mean I used to think it was okay for dudes [men] to do it, 'cause that is the way everyone thought from the town [in rural California] that my family came from. But that's not the way things happen here and have the marriage work, 'cause if you do that [cheat], you are looking at divorce.

Carlos, 18-year-old son of a construction worker in Albuquerque:

I wanted to have a lot of women even after marriage. I believed it was the thing a man had to do, but after I lived here for a little while [his family was from rural southern New Mexico] I learned that it don't work that way here. The women here don't take that stuff; they'll leave you. Besides, I don't think it's right, now.

This change in attitude toward extramarital sex roles was stimulated by the fact that social conditions in Los Angeles and Albuquerque are different from those in the youths' communities of origin, which were primarily rural.[10] These are larger metropolitan communities with norms that incorporate a variety of values other than those associated with traditional Chicano male/female roles. The result is that the youth living in these cities understand that attitudinal changes are required for both men and women after arriving in the city if they are going to interact without conflict.

This transition does not occur in San Antonio, where the social norms, despite the size of the city, seem similar to those of the small communities from which the recent migrants have come. The economy in San Antonio is based on services to government and tourism, and is dominated by lower-wage jobs, most of which are occupied by Chicanos. The fact that the perceived cost of living in San Antonio is not radically different from that in the rural communities from which the Chicano youth came explains their failure to report that economic difficulty was a primary factor in determining the number of children that they would want in their family.[11] Forty-seven percent (156) said that they would like three children, 26 percent (eighty-six) said that they would like four children, and 23 percent (seventy-eight) indicated that they would like no more than two children. In addition, only 35 percent (116) said that they would want the wife/mother of the family to work. In the interviews there is little mention of economics as a determinant of attitudes with regard to desired family size or as to whether the women of the family should work. The concern for most of these youth was whether their prospective mates shared their attitudes on these issues. Two representative comments follow.

Ramon, 18-year-old son of a bricklayer:

I would like at least three kids. . . . What it will depend on is whether my wife wants to have them, 'cause she'll be doing most of the work, so I don't think I can make the whole decision. . . . I don't want my wife to work 'cause I think it's important that she stays home and takes care of the kids.

Lisa, 18-year-old daughter of a refrigerator repairman:

I don't know how many children I would like to have; that will depend on what my husband thinks, too. I think I would like about two or three. . . . I think I would work for a little while after I was married, but then I would probably quit once I had children. I think once you have children you [a wife] should definitely not work, but that depends on my husband's ideas, too.

These responses may be compared with those for Los Angeles and Albuquerque. Sixty-three percent (fifty-four) of the youth from Los Angeles and 68 percent (forty) of those from Albuquerque who had lived in the city less than five years said that they preferred to have two, or a maximum of three, children.[12] However, among those youth who had lived in the city for more than five years, 71 percent (fifty-two) from Los Angeles and 69 percent (forty-one) from Albuquerque said that they wanted to have a maximum of two children, and preferably only one.[13] This difference—of one child—between the youth living in Los Angeles and Albuquerque and those living in San Antonio is attributable to perceived economic difficulties in having more children. The youth who had lived in Los Angeles and Albuquerque for more than five years were influenced by the fact that it is expensive to raise children in both Los Angeles and Albuquerque, and their concern was that the size of their families not be so large as to detract from the quality of their lives by consuming most of the family's revenues. The comments of these two youths are representative:

Leticia, 17-year-old daughter of a postal worker in Los Angeles:

I want to have one child and maybe two, depending on how much money my husband and I make. . . . I really don't want to have two children if it means I can't do things or buy things. I know that might sound kind of bad, but it's expensive to raise children in L.A.

Raymundo, 18-year-old son of an electrician in Albuquerque:

Hey, I only want one kid 'cause it's too expensive to have a lot, and I want to be able to do things myself, and if you have kids you can't afford to do a lot of other things. When my family lived in Mora [small northern New Mexico town] it was a lot cheaper than Albuquerque. I guess I might have wanted more kids there, but in Albuquerque there is just no way I'm going to have more than one. That's it.

These attitudes are quite different from those of the youth from San Antonio. For the San Antonio youth, the most important factor in determining family size was the wishes of the other partner, while for the youth of Albuquerque and Los Angeles it was the potential of having an economically restricted life that determined their attitudes on family size.

To highlight further the differences between San Antonio on the one hand and Los Angeles and Albuquerque on the other, the youths' attitudes concerning whether the wife in a family should work may be examined. Sixty-nine percent (227) of the youth from Los Angeles and 64 percent (200) of those from Albuquerque thought that the wife should work both before and after having children. Their rationale was that the family would need the added income, especially if there had been an addition. Interestingly, there was no difference between the two cities, nor were there gender differences, with regard to the necessity of having the wife work. The following two comments are characteristic of the general comments on this issue.

Maria-Elena, 18-year-old daughter of an auto mechanic from Albuquerque:

I would want to work, and I don't think I would marry someone who didn't want me to. I know I would want to work after I had a child because I know I would probably have to, to keep the income we had about the same.

James, 17-year-old son of an architect in Los Angeles:

I would like, or I should say, we [he and his wife] would need to have my wife work to have any kind of reasonable income. . . . Yes, I would want my wife to work after she had a baby because we would need her income more than ever then.

Again, it was the youth's perception of their economic realities in Albuquerque and Los Angeles that influenced their attitudes about the family—this time with regard to the issue of the wife's working.

The data confirm the Chicago school's hypothesis regarding the impact of length of residence in the city on attitudes toward the family for both Los Angeles and Albuquerque. Of course, these are rough measures, and the fact that length of residence had an effect only in Los Angeles and Albuquerque, the two cities in the study with socioeconomic relations more closely resembling the type described by Wirth and the Chicago school, confirms a portion of Baca Zinn's hypothesis concerning the linkages between family structure and the larger society; that is, that socioeconomic conditions do matter.

Primary Group Relations:
The Extended Family

Having examined the attitudes of the youth toward the nuclear family, the study turned to a traditional institution in Chicano culture—the extended family system, or *compadrazgo*. Essentially the *compadrazgo* system is based on the tradition of godparents within the Roman Catholic Church. Every child is assigned godparents who assume the responsibility, in the event of the death of the natural parents, of providing for the religious instruction of the child. Furthermore, in the case of the death of both parents, the *comadre/compadre* usually assumes the responsibility of raising the godchild.

Yet the *compadrazgo* system is more than a religious pact; it is also a system which encourages close relationships, thereby extending social networks. These networks can provide resources in times of need. Information, temporary shelter, financial loans, labor, and material support are all included within the *compadrazgo* system. Chicanos are not the only ethnic group to have an extended family system—many other groups who came to the U.S. have had these systems and have used them as support systems in their new homeland.[14] It is the resource aspect of extended family systems like *compadrazgo* which has been of particular interest to urban sociologists, primarily because they have seen it as a functional institution for integrating groups into the urban community with a minimum of psychological and physical trauma.[15]

Urban sociologists like Wirth and Park have felt that the extended family is useful for the first generation, but that it eventually withers away as tasks performed by the extended family are assumed by societal and political institutions available to migrants in their new urban environments. Other urban sociologists, like the neighborhood solidarity theorists, believe that the primary group affiliations of kinship remain because they are both functional and the result of an unequal opportunity structure within the larger society.[16] Thus the Chicano *compadrazgo* system is interesting because it is precisely the type of cultural institution whose ability to remain viable would be debated by urban sociologists.

In San Antonio the *compadrazgo* system is still maintained, and there are few signs that any withering away is occurring. Ninety-five percent (322) of the Chicanos from San Antonio reported that they had *comadres* and *compadres*. In addition, 98 percent (315) of these youth knew who their *comadres* and *compadres* were, and 81 percent (255) said they were in contact with them more than five times a month. Table 2.1 presents the scores obtained from the semantic differential tests. Semantic differential scores in general, and these scores in particular, indicate whether a person values a particular concept—in this case his/her extended family. Thus the semantic differential test scores in Table 2.1 indicate that the Chicanos from San Antonio value *compadrazgo* as an important social institution, and that neither the length of time they have lived in the city nor their socioeconomic background has significant impact on how much they value the system. In addition, the interview data indicated that among the Chicanos from San Antonio, *compadrazgo* as an extended kinship network represents a system that provides for expanded social companionship. There is the feeling among the San Antonio Chicanos that *compadrazgo* is a means for parents to

Table 2.1

Semantic Differential Mean Scores for Compadrazgo by City of Residence, SES, and Length of Residence in the City[a]

	Length of Residence in the City						
	0–4 Years		5–9 Years		Over 10 Years		All	
San Antonio	1.97	(43)	2.10	(89)	2.21	(199)	2.09	(329)
Lower SES[b]	1.89	(32)	1.94	(52)	2.07	(114)	1.96	(197)
Middle SES	2.05	(11)	2.27	(37)	2.35	(85)	2.22	(132)
Albuquerque	2.01	(59)	2.87	(92)	3.65	(159)	2.84	(305)
Lower SES	1.80	(43)	2.34	(54)	2.88	(73)	2.34	(171)
Middle SES	2.23	(16)	3.40	(38)	4.42	(86)	3.35	(137)
Los Angeles	1.76	(85)	3.11	(92)	4.58	(151)	2.98	(315)
Lower SES	1.51	(57)	1.83	(56)	3.73	(74)	2.02	(180)
Middle SES	2.01	(28)	4.39	(36)	5.43	(77)	3.94	(135)

[a]Scores should be interpreted as positive when they are from 1–3.50; neutral when they are from 3.51–4.50; and negative when they are 4.51–7.00. Positive means that the respondent assumed a positive attitude toward *compadrazgo*, a neutral score indicates that the respondent did not care one way or the other, and a negative score indicates that the respondent assumed a negative attitude.

[b]Socioeconomic status was determined by an index developed by Duncan, "A Socioeconomic Index for All Occupations." In *Occupations and Social Status*, edited by Reiss (New York: Free Press, 1961), pp. 109–33, and elaborated on by Featherman and Hauser, "On the Measurement of Occupations in Social Survey," *Sociological Methods and Research 2* (Nov. 1973); however, the dichotomous variables Lower SES and Middle SES were derived from the SES assigned using the following formula: Youth whose parents were unemployed or working at blue-collar occupations, manual, semi-skilled jobs with incomes below $12,000 ($10,000 in San Antonio), and educational levels of high school or lower, were classified as Lower SES. Those whose parents were working at white-collar occupations (clerks, businessmen, professionals, etc.), or as highly trained technical workers, with incomes above $12,000 ($10,000 in San Antonio), and educational levels of high school and above, were classified as Middle SES.

become closer to people whom they already know as friends. It is a social mechanism that provides adults with a support group for interaction and entertainment. For example:

Jacinto, 17-year-old son of a small grocery store owner:

I see my *comadre/compadre* much of the time because they are good friends of my parents. My parents and them do things on the weekends and other times so they are around a lot.

Monica, 18-year-old daughter of a school bus driver:

My *comadre/compadre* are friends of my parents, so one or
the other goes out with my father or mother a lot of the time.
They are good friends to each of my parents which is good for
me too because I get to see them and I like them.

For these respondents, the *compadrazgo* system represented an increase in parental figures, not because they saw their *comadre* and
compadre as parents *per se*, but rather because it gave them the
feeling that there were friends nearby who would and could aid them.
They also believed that the help of these friends, in terms of advice
and psychological comfort, could be secured even if it were requested
by them and not by their parents.

Adelita, 18-year-old daughter of a bricklayer:

I like my *comadre* and *compadre*. They are friends of mine,
sort of like additional parents, because any time I want to
talk to them about some problem or something that is going
bad, they will listen.

Alberto, 17-year-old son of a city health inspector:

When I need to talk to somebody about something I don't feel
good about, you know, something I don't like or something
that was done to me, I can always go to my *compadre* or
comadre and they'll listen. So I can get support from them
and my parents.

In sum, the definition of *compadrazgo* given by the Chicanos of San
Antonio was that of an institution that provided the kind of social
ties associated with intimate friendships—that is to say, a relationship with people who are enjoyable to be around socially and who,
at the same time, may be counted on to be helpful in times of
personal/familial need.

In Albuquerque, the *compadrazgo* system is not as extensively
used as it is in San Antonio. Eighty-two percent (255) of the Chicanos
from Albuquerque said that they were aware that they had *comadres*
and *compadres*, with 87 percent (222) of this number reporting that
they knew who their *comadres/compadres* were. Forty-nine percent
(158) said that they had contact with their *comadre/compadre* more
than four times a month. There is a significant difference between

this figure and the percentage of Chicanos from San Antonio who said that they had contact more than four times a month.

When the effect of living in the city on the *compadrazgo* system is considered, much may be learned. The longer a Chicano family had lived in Albuquerque, the less contact they had with their *comadres/compadres* and the less importance they placed on the system. While this occurred regardless of class background, social class standing was not a passive factor in the process, but, rather, provided an accelerator effect. The decline in *compadrazgo* participation and the level of importance assigned to it thus is affected by the length of time an individual has lived in the city, with Chicanos of upper socioeconomic status being inclined to have both lower rates of participation and lower opinions of the system's value.

This phenomenon occurs for a variety of reasons. First, 60 percent of the recent migrants to Albuquerque were from northern New Mexico, where Chicanos/Hispanos historically have been the dominant ethnic/cultural group since permanent settlement began in the seventeenth century. *Compadrazgo* as a religious and social network system has been an integral part of the northern New Mexico communities for centuries. Most of these communities are small and isolated in rural and/or mountainous areas. Because these communities have been isolated, individuals have had to depend on local community support, and this support has come from extending familial networks through *compadrazgo*. The result has been the preservation of strong *compadrazgo* networks in this area. When people from northern New Mexico migrated to Albuquerque they felt attached to the *compadrazgo* system; it was, in fact, still valued. The belief that *compadrazgo* was still available, although not in the immediate area, aided these Chicano families in adjusting to an alien environment.

It is important to note that most of the recent migrants to Albuquerque who served as respondents in this study arrived without the benefit of a member of the extended family already living in the city. The data indicate that this situation occurred because these youth and their families were part of the first significant wave of immigration from the north, and so the extended family system was not yet extensively established for them in Albuquerque. This is quite different from the situation described in the literature on migrants and extended family systems, as well as from the situation in Los Angeles. The fact of not having a *compadrazgo* system already established in Albuquerque provided, for this generational segment of northern New Mexico migrants, the conditions that would make the system vulnerable to other social forces in the city. Once in the city, having left the *compadrazgo* system physically behind, Chicanos found that new social relationships, or friendship networks, developed, replacing one or more of the functional elements of the *compadrazgo* system. This gradual process is reflected in the value placed on *compadrazgo* by the Chicanos in Albuquerque, as seen in Table 2.1. The longer these Chicanos stayed in the city, the less they felt that the system was important.

The city's ability to diversify social relationships is also affected by housing arrangements. The availability of moderate income housing in Albuquerque makes living in ethnically heterogeneous neighborhoods more likely than in other cities because red lining, or racial/ethnic discrimination, in securing housing in mixed neighborhoods is not as pervasive as it is in other cities.[17] Thus, for many of the migrants who themselves were from communities that were predominantly Chicano/Hispano, exposure to an ethnically and culturally heterogeneous social environment has had the effect of diversifying cultural practices.[18] It is, therefore, understandable that the Chicanos in Albuquerque who were from ethnically heterogeneous neighborhoods had less knowledge of *compadrazgo*, used it less, and valued it less.

Marco, 18-year-old son of a lumber salesman:

We did not get to see our *compadre* or *comadre* that much because we lived in a neighborhood that was mixed between Anglo and Chicano, and most of my parents' friends were Anglos. So I just know I have a *comadre/compadre* and know they live on the other side of town, but I don't know more than that.

Bianca, 17-year-old daughter of a printer:

My parents moved to this neighborhood that had a lot of Anglos living in it and we did not get to see our *comadre* or *compadre* that much because many of my parents' friends were our Anglo neighbors instead of my *comadre/compadre* like before. . . . Also, when my parents had a new baby after we lived here, they asked one of their Anglo friends to be godparents. I mean, my brother doesn't really have a *comadre/compadre* because Anglos don't really have that, they have just godparents.

As has been mentioned, socioeconomic status is not a neutral agent in lessening the use and importance of *compadrazgo* in Albuquerque. As the socioeconomic status of Chicano families increases, the influence of the *compadrazgo* system in their lives decreases. New social and economic conditions for individuals have the effect of changing established cultural patterns. Thus the middle-class Chicanos reported that they did not view *compadrazgo* as a system that provided for personal needs; most of these needs were met by other people and other institutions. For them, *compadrazgo* was a part of Chicano culture to be remembered, but not something that was an integral part of their individual cultural orientation. Finally, socioeconomic status does not affect attitudes and behaviors related to *compadrazgo* in isolation from the local economic environment. Albuquerque's economy is growing, and most of the Chicanos there reported that their families' economic position had improved the longer they had lived in the city. Accompanying improved economic conditions for the family was a general move to secure structurally and "socially" better housing. In 88 percent (178) of the instances, this meant the family's moving to an ethnically/culturally/socially heterogeneous neighborhood, which in turn had an effect on attitudes and practices concerning *compadrazgo*.

The evidence presented for Albuquerque does not indicate that *compadrazgo* is dead. It does indicate, however, that the *compadrazgo* system is undergoing change, that much of this change is in the direction of the system's becoming increasingly less prevalent, and that living in the urban environment of Albuquerque, with its increasing social, economic, and cultural heterogeneity, is an important factor in its declining status.

In examining the *compadrazgo* system in Los Angeles, it is apparent that the Chicanos there were inclined to use *compadrazgo* the least, and, as compared to those in San Antonio and Albuquerque, knew the least about who their *comadres/compadres* were and valued the system the least. It is also in Los Angeles that the most powerful impact of the city is evident. As in Albuquerque, the Chicanos whose families had been in the city for less than five years were the ones who were the most involved in and supportive of *compadrazgo*. Eighty-three percent (fifty) of these Chicanos were members of families who had come either from Mexico or from rural sections of the Southwest, areas where the *compadrazgo* system was well entrenched. These recent immigrants therefore arrived in Los Angeles with a positive value orientation toward *compadrazgo*.

Upon their arrival in the city, their existing orientation toward *compadrazgo* was reinforced by the conditions they encountered, at least for a short time. First, *compadrazgo* acted as a psychological support system for 73 percent (sixty-two) of those Chicanos who had immigrated within the past five years. When their families arrived, members of the extended family were already living in the greater Los Angeles area. This was an important factor, although not the single most important, in the families' choosing Los Angeles over another city.[19] When they got to the city, the extended family aided in the adjustment process. There was the basic psychological support of knowing that there was someone in an alien city who could be called upon to help. In addition, 88 percent (fifty-three) of the Chicanos reported that they received informational assistance with regard to possible employment and housing opportunities. Finally, there was the availability of material support for the family if aid became necessary. Eighty-five percent (fifty-one) of the Los Angeles Chicanos mentioned such forms of support as the lending of money in time of need, the giving of help in the form of labor when needed, and the providing of security for the children in case of the death of their parents as reasons why their families found the *compadrazgo* system important.

Juanita, 18-year-old daughter of a painter:

When we moved to L.A. we got help from mine and my brothers' *comadre* and *compadre* [two sets]. They put us up until we found a place to live, helped us find a place to live, and helped us move. They also helped my father find a job.

Pedro, 17-year-old son of a gardener:

My family got quite a bit of help from our *compadre* who lived in the area. That is why my father picked L.A. over Chicago. . . . We stayed with them [*comadres/compadres*], and they helped my father find a job, and they helped us move, things like that.

However, the longer a Chicano family had lived in the city, the less the *compadrazgo* system was a part of their life, and the less important they thought it was. What factors influenced the process by which *compadrazgo* became less important the longer one had lived in Los Angeles? First, the size of the city does make a difference. Fifty-two percent (130) of the Chicanos who said they had *comadres/*

compadres said that they were fond of them, but that they rarely saw them in the course of a year. Their reason for not having more contact was that their *comadres/compadres* lived too far away from them and their families. Thus, not only were they not able to see them, but their parents had the same problem.[20] Although their *comadres/compadres* did live in the city of Los Angeles, or in the immediate metropolitan area, the city was so large geographically that they did not have the transportation to visit and/or could not motivate themselves psychologically to drive the long distance required. The result was that contact had been reduced to a level where the extended family existed in name only.

Belinda, 17-year-old daughter of a furniture worker:

We never visit our *comadre/compadre* very much 'cause they live on the other side of town [Santa Monica] and it's too far. My father doesn't feel like driving that far. So I don't know them very well.

Bert, 18-year-old son of a car salesman:

I don't see my *comadre/compadre* that often because they live in another part of the city [Inglewood] and it just seems it's such a long way to drive to visit. So I don't do it very often. I think they feel the same way . . . because we never see each other, we really aren't close.

Interestingly, size of city is a factor, as Wirth suggested, although he referred primarily to population size as opposed to geographic size. Perhaps this is one of the important differences between the Northeastern and Southwestern cities and the ways in which they affect the individuals who live in them. Southwestern cities are much more spread out horizontally, and thus population density is considerably less than that found in the vertical Northeastern cities. On the other hand, the Northeastern cities do not have the same physical distances to cope with as cities in the Southwest. It seems appropriate for future research, given the conditions that exist in the Southwestern cities, for urban sociologists to consider the physical dimension of the size variable when analyzing the effects of the city on individual attitudes, norms, and behaviors.

The city's ethnic heterogeneity was also a factor in lessening the importance of *compadrazgo* among the Chicanos of Los Angeles. The longer these Chicanos stayed in the city, the more they came into social contact with other people, some of whom were not of the same ethnic group. Friendships were established, and many of these substituted for the friendships that had, or would have, been assumed by the persons within the *compadrazgo* system. The fact that some of these friendships involved people from other ethnic groups reduced the importance of *compadrazgo*, with its internal dynamics and requirements centered on Chicano idiosyncracies. The importance of ethnic heterogeneity was felt most by those who lived in heterogeneous neighborhoods.

Jerry, 17-year-old son of an auto mechanic:

Some of my friends are not Chicano, and so I spend some time at their homes or just with them. I don't have as much time to spend with my *comadre/compadre* as I used to. I guess it's not as important to me as it used to be.

Arlene, 18-year-old daughter of a school teacher:

I used to see my *comadre* and *compadre* more, but I don't have as much time now because I have a lot of friends and they take time. And my friends are different. I have a lot of friends that are not Chicano, so my *comadre/compadre* are not as much a part of my life as they were before.

Heterogeneity within the urban work force also constituted a contributing factor. Many of the parents of the Los Angeles Chicanos worked in occupations where there were workers from other ethnic groups. Friendships were established at the work place, and many of these friendships not only filled one of the functional aspects of *compadrazgo*, as a friendship/social relationship, but led to asking people from other backgrounds to be *comadres/compadres.* However, when this was done, many of the functions traditionally assumed under *compadrazgo* were no longer assumed by the person(s) of a different ethnic origin. For the most part, these new participants assumed the role of godparents, which is only one aspect of the system, and a minor one at that.

Julie, 17-year-old daughter of a city government employee:

I can't say I see my *comadre* and *compadre* that often. They used to come over a lot, but my parents have a lot of other friends. My father has a lot of his friends from work over, so they [the parents] don't see them [the *comadre/compadre*] as much.

Benjamin, 18-year-old son of an auto worker:

I don't see my *comadre/compadre* because I really don't have time. I mean my father picked two people to be *comadre/ compadre*, but they were people he worked with and they weren't Chicano so they don't exactly act like the *comadre* and *compadre* my older sister has.

The impact of the urban economic system in Los Angeles on *compadrazgo* can be seen in conjunction with the influence of social class background. In general, the longer the Chicanos from Los Angeles had lived in the city, the more socioeconomically mobile they had become, although there was, to be sure, a considerable disparity in the degree and speed with which this had occurred. As socioeconomic mobility increases, there is less need to call on the *compadrazgo* system for assistance. Financial assistance, as well as informational˙ and housing assistance, becomes less needed. Social networks which have expanded because of divergent occupations, neighborhoods, and social settings also provide support systems that either parallel or replace that of the extended family. In either case, the consequence is a reduction in the extent to which *compadrazgo* is an integral part of these Chicanos' lives. Thus, 50 percent (sixty-nine) of the Chicanos from middle-class families do not know the names of their *comadre/compadres*, and of those who do know, only 32 percent (twenty-two) have any type of contact with them more than twice a year. In addition, for Los Angeles Chicanos, increasing time spent in the city, along with middle-class status, combine to produce lower opinions of *compadrazgo*, and these evaluations of the system by the middle class are lower than those given by the middle class of Albuquerque. In Los Angeles the middle-class youth not only evaluated *compadrazgo* as unimportant (see Table 2.1), but thought, as indicated in the in-depth interviews, that the system was detrimental to Chicanos as they became more socioeconomically mobile. Therefore, they felt that *compadrazgo*, along with other traditional cultural institutions, should be abandoned by Chicanos.[21] Two examples of this opinion are as follows:

Beverly, 17-year-old daughter of an architect:

I do not think that things like *compadrazgo* or other cultural things that Chicanos have held on to ought to continue. They just keep Chicanos thinking of themselves as separate [from the dominant community] and not of being a part of America.

Robert, 17-year-old son of a bank manager:

I think maybe I have a *comadre/compadre,* but I am not sure I have seen them. I really do not think that things like that [*compadrazgo*] are important and I don't think they should continue for Chicanos. I think Chicanos have to give up all that stuff [traditional culture] if they are going to make it in this country.

The lower-class Chicanos of Los Angeles were also found to be less involved in the *compadrazgo* system the longer they lived in the city. For example, 57 percent (thirty) of the Chicanos who were from lower socioeconomic backgrounds and who had been in Los Angeles for five to nine years visited their *comadre/compadre* more than twice a year, compared to 45 percent (thirty-three) who had been in the city for more than ten years. Like their middle-class counterparts, the Chicanos from lower socioeconomic backgrounds are also affected by the fact that the urban environment provides for many of the functions traditionally assumed by *compadrazgo.* Some of the material support, especially with regard to health and nutrition, is provided by the various government social agencies. Furthermore, as additional time is spent in the city, members of families of lower socioeconomic status, like their middle-class counterparts, receive additional information as to how to secure the type of assistance that is desired at a given time. Once that information has been obtained and the appropriate social agency contacted, the need for assistance from the extended family is reduced. Accompanying this reduction in assistance needed is a reduction in social contact among members of the extended family, which serves to undermine *compadrazgo.*

Despite the fact that *compadrazgo* had become less of a factor in their lives the longer they had resided in Los Angeles, lower-class youth still evaluated the system as being important, although here again the degree of importance assigned to it declines as length of residence increases. The length of time spent in the city also affects what the Chicanos from lower socioeconomic backgrounds mean when they say that they value *compadrazgo.* Those who have been in the city for less than ten years and have remained in a lower socioeconomic status want to preserve some parts of the system because they are marginally involved in it and find it beneficial. However, the vast majority of those who have been in the city for ten years or more would like to re-establish the system in their lives. This group of people is particularly interesting because they and/or their families came to Los Angeles with the hope of attaining middle-class status or higher. They have been in the city for more than ten years (in the case of some families, for two generations) and have remained in a lower socioeconomic status. Some have even slipped in socioeconomic status, having been forced to rely on public assistance. At some time during their residence in the city the *compadrazgo* system ceased to be a part of their lives, along with other traditional cultural institutions. This is a process that usually accompanies social mobility, but in these cases social mobility was not attained, thus lending additional evidence that the impact of Los Angeles' environment is quite powerful in eroding attachment to traditional cultural institutions independent of social class background.[22] For this group of lower-class Chicanos, *compadrazgo* was seen as something that could aid them in their everyday struggle to make life less frustrating and alienating. To illustrate:

Juan, a 19-year-old son of a mother who is the head of household and a maid:

I think a *comadre/compadre* would be important to have. I don't have any that I know . . . and I would really like to, because if my mom or our family needed some help we could call somebody we could count on like the *comadre/compadre.* I mean, right now we can't count on anybody, and sometimes I know my mom gets worried when she thinks of it—I know I do sometimes.

David, 18-year-old son of a widower who is a night watchman:

I really don't have anybody I can really talk to or count on. I mean I have friends, but they have their own things they have to do . . . I mean, they have their own responsibility. If I had a *comadre/compadre,* it would be somebody I could count on . . . yeah, somebody to help or talk to . . . you know, somebody to give a little security.

From the interview data the profiles of members of this group of lower-class Chicanos are very similar. Their families had come to Los Angeles from Mexico or other parts of the Southwest, primarily from rural areas, and they and their families had lived in Los Angeles for a considerable length of time, some for as many as two genera-tions. Very little socioeconomic mobility had been attained since they had arrived, and, as was mentioned earlier, some families had actually declined in socioeconomic status. Throughout the inter-views this group, more than any other, exhibited strong feelings of alienation, mentioning very little with which they could positively identify. These Chicanos from Los Angeles also exhibited high levels of frustration and aggression. In some ways their attitudes resembled the profile of Park's "marginal man" in that they were caught be-tween two worlds, having retained few of the cultural norms of the old country (in this case, Mexico), yet not having been integrated into the Anglo society.[23] It is important to call attention to this group now because they will, throughout the description of the study, and particularly in the political sections, present a consistent pattern of alienation, frustration, and favorable attitudes toward aggression.

Language: ¿Habla Español?

Language is probably the cultural variable that comes to mind first when people talk about ethnic groups. This is because, for every ethnic group, language encompasses not only a particular set of norms and characteristics, but also a world view. Language is the medium by which members of the group transmit information, and because of this it is a factor in defining group identity. Thus the importance of language is self-evident—it occupies a strategic cul-tural position in any ethnic group's continued existence as a distinct entity. It is probably for this reason that most ethnic groups who immigrated to the United States initially attempted to maintain their native languages. However, after residing in the United States for some period of time, members of these groups had to decide whether to continue to maintain the language of their homeland or willingly to give up their ancestral language in order to integrate themselves more fully into the fabric of American society.

Chicanos continually have had to confront the question of lan-guage loyalty and socioeconomic integration. The sociologist Glazer has remarked that of all the ethnic groups that are a part of United States society, the Mexican-American, or Chicano, has held most tenaciously to his/her native language.[24] Urban sociologists like Wirth would undoubtedly have replied that this has occurred because Chicanos until very recently have lived in small rural communities, communities with social structures that protect traditional culture and values; and that an examination of those Chicanos who lived in large urban areas would indicate that these persons have begun to assimilate. In point of fact, the visitor to many urban areas in the United States will encounter Hispanic peoples who are speaking half Spanish and half English, or, in many cases, primarily English with some Spanish. Are they exhibiting traits of individuals who are moving toward complete assimilation but are not yet quite there? Is this a system of social assimilation? Is this the stage theorized by Wirth as "personal disorganization," or by Park as that of "marginal man"? Or, conversely, does Glazer's finding continue to be true—do Chicanos, regardless of whether they live in an urban area, continue to maintain and perhaps even strengthen their loyalty to and usage of Spanish? These questions will be pursued further in this section.

Finally, the question of language loyalty, usage, and competence that is examined in this section is not one of interest to sociologists alone, but one that has been of interest to political scientists as well. Language is extremely important in determining a person's perceptions of politics because language involves symbols and the meanings assigned to symbols. Since politics involves communicating through the manipulation of symbols, political scientists are extremely interested in determining the effects of particular forms of language usage on political thought and behavior. Deutsch has pointed out that language is one of the major building blocks of nationalities because it gives people their strongest source of group identity. For Chicanos, the use of Spanish or English is important because it has the potential to affect their perceptions of American political life from the point of view of an ethnic minority, i.e., their role in politics and their allegiance to America. It is possible that language usage among Chicanos has important implications regarding political integration and involvement. Thus, an understanding of the status of language among the Chicanos in this study will provide a further foundation for understanding their political attitudes.

The empirical findings concerning language maintenance in the three cities in this study demonstrate the influence of language on cultural assimilation and politicization. In the case of San Antonio, 47 percent of the respondents (159) were completely fluent in Spanish in all situations.[25] Another 25 percent (eighty-five) said that they could speak and understand Spanish well, but had some difficulty when the subject matter was academic in nature. In everyday conversation, they were completely fluent. Thus, 72 percent (244) of these youth were fluent in Spanish. In looking at the language environment within the home, it appears that Spanish is the primary medium of communication. Forty-six percent (157) of the respondents' families communicate only in Spanish at home, and 23 percent (seventy-eight) speak half Spanish and half English. Only 12 percent (forty-one) said that no Spanish was spoken in the home. Clearly, the home language environment in San Antonio is, to varying degrees, oriented toward Spanish. Given that the home is one of the primary socializing institutions in American society, this is an important finding because it provides a better understanding of the conditions under which political attitudes are formulated.

What effect does living in an urban environment have? It appears that whether a person is fluent in Spanish has little to do with the urban characteristics of his/her neighborhood. There is no likelihood that a person living in a densely populated area will speak more or less Spanish than a person living in a less densely populated area. While one might expect that the degree of ethnic heterogeneity of a neighborhood would have some impact on language use because of the opportunity for contact with other ethnic groups, no effect of this nature was found. However, it is apparent that neighborhood heterogeneity does have an impact on the Chicano youth who live in Los Angeles and Albuquerque. Housing patterns partially explain differences among the cities. There are few truly integrated neighborhoods in San Antonio. Where there are integrated neighborhoods, this integration has occurred as a result of the real estate and banking establishment deciding to open up an area that previously had been inhabited entirely by whites. Thus the heterogeneous neighborhoods are only temporarily heterogeneous. The Anglo families usually do not intend to stay, so contact between them and their Chicano neighbors is minimal and any effect that social contact might have had on language is neutralized. This process of neighborhood change actually reinforces language maintenance because it strengthens ethnic perceptions of "in group"/"out group," thereby reinforcing "in group" solidarity.

The reason that language use in San Antonio is not affected by urbanism or socioeconomic status lies, in part, in the fact that San Antonio is a city quite different from other cities in the Southwest or in the United States. San Antonio does not have the ethnic heterogeneity of other cities. Practically speaking, the city is culturally divided into two communities: one Anglo-American, the other Mexican/Chicano. What this means in terms of language usage is that there is not a variety of linguistic groups that are somehow forced, through social contact, to communicate in a language neutral to each of them, such as English.[26] The fact that Chicanos comprise over 50 percent of the population of San Antonio is significant. The size of this population, when combined with the lack of ethnic heterogeneity of the city and a history of Spanish usage, has the effect of reinforcing each community's language orientation.[27]

Furthermore, in looking at the way in which these young Chicanos from San Antonio evaluated the Spanish language, it becomes apparent, through examining the data from the semantic differential scores, that it is a highly valued cultural trait, one that is viewed as not only subjectively important, but functionally useful as well. This latter perception differs from the perceptions of Spanish in the other two cities. Here, 84 percent (285) of the young Chicanos in the study saw the Spanish language as functionally useful on two counts. First, 46 percent (156) said that they saw Spanish as being an important tool for communicating with parents, relatives, and friends. Eighty-four percent (131) of the group said that they chose Spanish as their primary medium for expressing emotional sentiments, such as friendship, love, and anger, rather than using English for the same purpose. They preferred Spanish because they felt that the language was better able to communicate the sentiments they were trying to convey.

Luis, 18-year-old son of a bartender:

I prefer Spanish because it lets me express myself better. I mean, Spanish has the words that let me say what I mean better than English.

Dina, 17-year-old daughter of a professional cook:

I use Spanish with close friends and relatives because I can say things that I feel better than I could with English words.

The youth also said that Spanish was necessary because the other people they were communicating with thought in Spanish, and one had to be sensitive to their desires as well.

Don, 18-year-old son of a bakery worker:

I think speaking Spanish is important because most of the
people you come into contact with do, and you have to be
able to speak to them in the language they feel comfortable
in.

Nancy, 18-year-old daughter of a medical technician:

Speaking Spanish is necessary and important because you
have to be able to speak to these people who feel the most
comfortable in Spanish and there are a lot of people who feel
that way here.

Second, among 78 percent (223) of these young Chicanos, Spanish
was considered important because it is functional in everyday life
in San Antonio. They believed that a significant part of the everyday
business of San Antonio was conducted in Spanish, and that this
made the ability to speak Spanish valuable.

George, 18-year-old son of a butcher:

You need to know Spanish because a lot of business you have
to do during the day is in Spanish.

Tina, 17-year-old daughter of a lawyer:

Spanish is important because during the day Spanish is
spoken at work or whatever business you have to do. So you
need to be able to speak it.

Gans, along with other urban sociologists who have been referred
to as the "neighborhood solidarity theorists," has long argued that
subcultural traits are dependent on the inability of people to be
economically mobile, and that as long as a group is stuck in the
lower strata of the social structure it will continue to exhibit sub-
cultural norms. In other words, the large number of San Antonio
Chicanos who are proficient in Spanish is the result of their being
in a subculture that has found it difficult to become socioeconomically mobile. However, the data on language presented throughout this chapter do not support the contention of the "solidarity
theorists." Within the San Antonio sample, there were people representing a wide variety of socioeconomic backgrounds, as the city
has a growing Chicano middle class. Thus, although Chicanos in

San Antonio are predominantly lower-class, they are not exclusively so. When the socioeconomic standing of the Chicanos from San Antonio was analyzed to see if it had any direct impact on language usage or attitudes toward it, virtually none was found. The amount of Spanish spoken in the home, the level of proficiency, and the value placed on the language were essentially the same, regardless of socioeconomic status. Thus the data do not substantiate the contention of the "solidarity theorists" pertaining to social class and cultural maintenance, at least in terms of language maintenance in San Antonio.[28]

Wirth believed that the longer one was associated with a large urban area, the more one would be inclined to disassociate oneself from the traditions of the past. In the case of language, then, associations for a long period of time among large numbers of divergent ethnic groups within a heterogeneous urban area would influence all these ethnic groups toward more extensive use of English, which would in turn cause the abandonment of the native language and the acceptance of English as the language most commonly spoken. As seen in San Antonio, the length of time that the Chicanos in this study had lived in the city had no effect on their proficiency in Spanish. Thus the data for San Antonio confirm neither the theories of Wirth nor those of Gans on the issue of language loyalty and retention.

For those Chicanos who live in Albuquerque, proficiency in Spanish is on the decline. Only 34 percent (106) of the respondents were fluent in Spanish, and 37 percent (116) could not speak any Spanish at all. As one might expect, the amount of Spanish spoken in the home is directly related to the level of proficiency exhibited. In addition, the data indicate that only 34 percent (106) of the families sampled speak Spanish half of the time or more.[29] Thus, contrary to the findings for San Antonio, the "Spanish-dominant" language environment is shrinking in Albuquerque.

The case of Albuquerque is interesting in that maintenance of Spanish is affected by an individual's socioeconomic status. Those Albuquerqueans in the sample who are from middle-class families have not maintained fluency in Spanish, while individuals from lower-class families have. City life has an effect on maintenance of Spanish, but only in conjunction with social class standing. For example, the data indicate that those individuals who have recently migrated to Albuquerque from either northern New Mexico or Mexico are usually poor and from rural communities. They have come to Albuquerque to find work and to improve their lives; they are, in a sense, classic immigrants to the city. This group is Spanish-dominant, and thus use Spanish as their primary means of communication. The longer members of this group remain in the city, the less they maintain Spanish and the more they turn to English. It would appear from this trend that city life in Albuquerque has an effect on language maintenance; however, this is not an entirely accurate characterization. For those Chicanos who have lived in the city for more than five years and who have become middle-class, English is their primary language. When asked why they chose to speak English over Spanish, they responded that English was the primary language for doing business in middle-class occupations in Albuquerque, and that since most of their day involved speaking in English, there was little time to speak Spanish. Even at home, 94 percent (146) of the middle-class Chicanos in this study said that they spoke English because after using it all day for business it was easier to express themselves in English than to switch back to Spanish.

John, 17-year-old son of a stockbroker:

My parents speak Spanish at home, but I talk to them in English because after using English all day it is difficult to switch in the evening. I find it hard to express myself in Spanish because I don't use it during the day.

Thus in Albuquerque the neighborhood solidarity theory prevails: socioeconomic mobility produces a relinquishing of the group's traditional language and an acceptance of the dominant language.

The effects of the interrelationship between social class and city life are also evident if one looks at the impact of living in an ethnically heterogeneous neighborhood. The ethnic heterogeneity of an individual's neighborhood does have an effect on language maintenance in Albuquerque, but its effect works in conjunction with either the socioeconomic standing of the individual or his/her desire to be economically mobile. Those Chicanos who are middle-class and live in mixed neighborhoods are English-dominant.[30] Eighty-nine percent (ninety-three) of these Chicanos said that they spoke English because most of their friends were a mixture of Anglo and Chicano, and that even if they themselves could speak Spanish, nearly all of their friends could not.

Angelina, 18-year-old daughter of a professional photographer:

> I really have no opportunity to speak Spanish. My parents do
> not speak Spanish to us kids, and all my friends don't speak
> it at all, so I really have no one to make Spanish important.

Of course, it is important to point out that 87 percent (eighty-one)
of these middle-class Chicanos had only middle-class Chicano friends,
all of whom spoke only a small amount of Spanish, and this acted
to reinforce their usage of English.

Those Chicanos who were from lower socioeconomic backgrounds and living in ethnically heterogeneous neighborhoods were
also English-dominant. Fifty-one percent (twenty-three) of these Chicanos could understand Spanish, and 45 percent (twenty) could speak
some, but 84 percent (thirty-eight) said that they had lost their ca-
pacity to speak Spanish "comfortably." They said that since their
parents had been able to buy a new house outside the *barrio*, or
Chicano neighborhood, they were living much more comfortably.
They also expressed the desire to become economically mobile
themselves, and stated that in order for them to do so they would
have to be English-dominant. Spanish was simply not functional for
them.

Gregory, 18-year-old son of a lawyer:

> Spanish is not important, English is because if you want to
> make it in the world you have to be good in English, not
> Spanish. I want to make it [economically], and Albuquerque is
> a place you can, so I will devote my time totally to English.

Thus, this is a group of Chicanos who, having moved from poor to
upper-lower-class status, and having also moved physically from the
barrio to an ethnically heterogeneous neighborhood, want to use
this initial mobility as a springboard to middle-class status. This
group also has determined that use of English, at the expense of
Spanish, is necessary in order to do this.

What is interesting about the data on Albuquerque is the importance of social class standing in maintaining Spanish. Those Chicanos in the study who were middle-class had given up Spanish as
a part of their lives. Spanish was not practical for them to use in
their everyday lives. All of the occupations they were interested in
pursuing in the future required English and, because they were pri-

marily interested in socioeconomic mobility, Spanish had to assume secondary importance. In addition, because their friends were ethnically mixed, they said that few opportunities existed socially to make Spanish useful. This did not mean, however, that they thought that Spanish was totally unimportant. Ninety-four percent (140) of the middle-class youth said that they thought Spanish was important, but primarily for reasons of cultural identity. They wanted to have their language preserved, but they did not see it as something that they would have to preserve themselves. It was assumed that Spanish would always be spoken in the greater Albuquerque community, an assumption based on the perception that *barrios* still existed and that predominantly Spanish was spoken in these areas. Since those areas are overwhelmingly inhabited by Chicanos of lower socioeconomic status, this belief was based on the premise that lower-class Chicanos would be responsible for maintaining the Spanish language.

Camila, 17-year-old daughter of a clothing store owner:

I think Spanish is important for the Chicano community. It will always be spoken in the *barrios* and I think that's good. Most middle-class Chicanos like myself don't speak it, but the other Chicanos do, and I think it would be a loss for the entire Chicano community if some day Spanish was never spoken.

Chris, 18-year-old son of a real estate broker:

I don't speak Spanish, but I would never want it to die out because Chicanos would cease to be Chicanos. I really don't think I'll have to worry about that because it is still strong among the people who live in the *barrios*, they have gone through hard times, but they have kept the language and they will continue.

The Albuquerque Chicanos from lower-class backgrounds were more apt to be more fluent in Spanish than the middle class and to use it in some aspects of their daily lives. However, the use of Spanish among this group was confined to social relationships, away from their roles as students or workers. Spanish usage took place primarily in the home among relatives and occasionally around friends. Seventy-two percent (117) of the lower-class respondents also said that they thought they would use Spanish less in the future because there would be less opportunity to use it in the types of jobs they wanted to obtain. The jobs they mentioned most were of a professional or highly skilled nature, and they believed that there would not be enough people who could speak Spanish on their jobs, because these jobs would be held by an ethnically mixed workforce, or by Chicanos who would have difficulty carrying on a sustained conversation in Spanish.

Enrique, 17-year-old son of a construction worker:

My Spanish will go down if I were to get the job I would like to get, 'cause that kind of job [professional] usually only has people who speak only English, and almost all of those type of people couldn't speak Spanish if they wanted to; and that includes the Chicanos on the job, too.

However, at present these lower-class Chicanos do not have the jobs they desire, and they continue to find the *barrio* environment in which they live conducive to maintaining Spanish.

Mary, 17-year-old daughter of a plastics worker:

Even though I don't speak Spanish most of the day, I speak Spanish a lot when I get home, or I should say when I get to the neighborhood, because a lot of people speak it here [my *barrio*]. I mean, I have a lot of opportunity to speak it in my neighborhood.

Juan, 17-year-old son of a garbage collector:

Well, when you are at school you don't have time to speak Spanish and you don't have the opportunity either, but when I get to the *barrio* where I live I have a lot of places and people to talk to. After all, that's what most of the people speak down here. So I really don't have to worry about losing my ability to speak.

Interestingly, these data seem consistent with the assertions of the "neighborhood solidarity theorists." It will be remembered that these theorists hold that social class background is a function of the overall economic structure and that only changes in an individual's socioeconomic position will have an effect on his/her cultural orientations. Since they contend that cultural orientations are rooted in the social interaction of those primary groups with which an individual is consistently associated (for example, the Chicano lower class of Albuquerque) cultural retention will tend to be quite stable regardless of whether a person lives in an urban, suburban, or rural environment. Yet in Albuquerque the social class differences that do exist should not mandate the conclusion that social class influences attitudes apart from any influence from the larger urban environment of which it is a part. The urban community as a whole has had an important influence on how the Chicanos in this study view language. For example, the youth in Albuquerque believed that they could become economically mobile. In other words, they believed that the Albuquerque economy could provide them with the opportunity to improve their lives. They also believed that in order for this to occur they would need to be English-dominant and that Spanish was something that would have to assume secondary importance—reserved, as it were, for the purpose of cultural identity. While the middle class was more vocal in expressing this belief, the Chicanos from lower-class backgrounds also adhered to it; however, the latter group chose to speak Spanish at home and among close friends not simply because it was expected of them culturally, but, more importantly, because their economic position had not changed sufficiently for their cultural expectations to change to acceptance of English as the sole means of communication.

What is important to understand here is that the respondents are saying that the society of Albuquerque gives a mixed message to its members concerning language usage. The general society not only recognizes that Spanish has had a long history in New Mexico and that there are significant numbers of people who speak Spanish, but has engaged in activities, such as the provision of translators and the sponsoring of Spanish language/cultural events, that encourage some type of maintenance. This has been done to preserve New Mexico's unique Spanish and Indian identity, one in which Anglo New Mexicans take pride as well. This situation is nearly identical to that found in Quebec, Canada, where English-speaking Canadians are extremely proud of the fact that Canada has a French culture because it adds to the overall Canadian identity. This does not mean that the English speakers in Canada would like to learn to speak French; in point of fact, most resist this.[31] (Similarly, in the case of New Mexico, most members of the Anglo-American community have not learned Spanish.) However, Anglophone Canadians are fond of the fact that there is a French Canadian society. In fact, a great deal of the resistance to Quebec's separatism among English-speaking Canadians has focused on the loss that it would present to Canada in terms of cultural identity.

Yet despite the fact that the Anglo society in Albuquerque is proud of the community's Hispanic/Indian origins, it does nothing in its everyday economic activity to indicate that socioeconomic mobility can occur without English being the dominant means of communication. This leads to the universal conclusion that to have a chance of achieving the "better life," one will have to conduct most of one's daily activities in English.[32] This was also true in the case of Quebec until the coming to power of the French separatist party, the Parti Québécois, which proceeded to pass legislation requiring all official business in the province to be conducted in French, including public education.

In sum, the evidence on language maintenance among Chicanos in Albuquerque does not suggest that the city's environment is unimportant in explaining attitudes toward language simply because social class standing, rather than size, density, or heterogeneity, is the primary explanatory variable. Rather, socioeconomic and political structures exist within the physical configuration called a city, and these structures vary in the types of conditions that they provide for ethnic groups to maintain their languages. As the evidence suggests, Albuquerque provides a different cultural environment from that of San Antonio, which encourages language maintenance.

The case of the Chicanos who live in Los Angeles constitutes another unique case study of the effects of city life on language maintenance. Although nearly 36 percent (120) of the sample were found to be fluent in Spanish, 69 percent (199) either did not know any Spanish or knew very little. The most telling aspect of language maintenance among the Chicanos in Los Angeles is that Spanish proficiency and usage in the home continue to decline the longer one lives in the city. What is more, this decline in maintenance occurs regardless of social class status. The evidence would suggest that simply living in Los Angeles is sufficient to cause an erosion in the use and proficiency of Spanish; thus, there is no "neighborhood solidarity effect" found in Los Angeles. In effect, this supports Wirth's proposition that urbanism facilitates the assimilation process. Those who have travelled to Los Angeles are no doubt surprised by these findings, having heard Spanish spoken throughout the city. Yet there are explanations as to why the general traveler's observations of the amount of Spanish spoken in Los Angeles and the data from this study are not incompatible. First, the Chicano population in Los Angeles is quite large, and has continued to grow each year. Part of this growth is attributable to natural population increase; however, one of the most significant factors has been immigration either from other parts of the Southwest, predominantly rural areas, or from Mexico. The Chicanos who come to Los Angeles usually arrive from areas that are Spanish-dominant; i.e., areas where Spanish is spoken both fluently and readily. Thus the recent Chicano migrants to Los Angeles usually arrive with a high propensity to speak Spanish. Once these people have arrived in the city, two factors interrelate to produce a gradual shift from Spanish to English dominance. The first has to do with the reasons why the individual or his/her family moved to Los Angeles. Ninety-four percent (186) of the Chicanos in the study who had moved to Los Angeles said that their family had moved to the city in order to improve their economic conditions. In 87 percent (169) of these cases the respondents reported that their parents thought that Los Angeles was the only place where they would have a chance to improve their socioeconomic status. Eighty-one percent (158) said that their parents believed, given their perception of the city's growth, that if they could not make it in Los Angeles it was not likely that they would be able to make it in another city. In a sense, Los Angeles was perceived as the last chance to experience middle-class comfort.

Geraldo, 18-year-old son of a worker in a furniture factory:

My parents came to Los Angeles [from rural south Texas] because they decided to try to have a better life, you know, to become middle class. And they thought that Los Angeles was the best place to do that. I remember them talking and they said that if they could not do it in LA, it just could not be done. They thought, I should say they still think, that if you work hard, LA is the place you can make it.

Margie, 17-year-old daughter of a textile worker:

My parents work very hard and try to save their money. They want to be middle class like other people do. They still think that LA is the only place for Chicanos to have a chance to do that. We lived in other cities [El Paso, Tucson, Bakersfield] before we moved here, but my parents thought LA had the best opportunities. I know they think, or my dad does, 'cause he says it all the time, if you can't make it in LA, you won't be able to make it anywhere else.

With these perceptions and with these motives for moving to the city, these families were prepared to make the necessary accommodations in order to become economically mobile. They were prepared to be functionally fluent in English because they understood that English was the language used for economic activity in Los Angeles. In addition, the mothers of many of these families, who traditionally had been charged with cultural/language socialization, had begun to work outside the home to help with the family income.

> Lupe, 17-year-old daughter of a hotel clerk and a house cleaner:
>
> Before my mother went to work the house was totally in Spanish, but after she went to work where she had to speak English, she had to practice her English, and she did that at home. Then we started to use English a lot more.

Thus, for many of these families, English was now being spoken during most of the work day by most of the members. It should be noted that there were some families in the study (ninety-eight, or thirty percent) where the mother did not work outside the home and where Spanish was spoken much of the time. In these homes the youth still reported that over a period of time less Spanish was used. They attributed the decline in Spanish usage primarily to the fact that they, as members of the family, were responsible for introducing more English into the home. They went on to say that they thought they used English around the house because they spoke it while at school, and because most of their friends spoke English. Thus, in homes where the mothers do not work and are Spanish dominant, there is still a general shift from Spanish to English; however, this shift is a slower one.

The second factor which causes a change in Spanish maintenance in Los Angeles has to do directly with urbanism. The heterogeneity of Los Angeles is an important factor, and takes on a number of different forms. First, Los Angeles is ethnically heterogeneous, with a large number of diverse ethnic groups, each with a language of its own. Sometimes these ethnic groups live relatively close to one another within the same neighborhood, and at other times they live in entirely different sections of the city. Because of the spatial pattern of the city, there are times when individuals are forced to come into contact with individuals of another ethnic group.[33] This happens most often in the work place, but it happens in other commercial and social situations as well. Given this forced contact between divergent linguistic groups, English is agreed upon socially as the language for mutual communication. In this way, English becomes an incrementally larger part of an individual's everyday life, and 61 percent of the Chicanos in this study reported that they used English more as the result of meeting other people who also were from a non-English-speaking culture.[34]

Daniel, 17-year-old son of a city recreation worker:

Well, I felt most comfortable in Spanish until we moved to an area where there were a lot of Asians. It was there that I used English a lot more because I had to talk to them [Asians], and I couldn't speak their language, and they couldn't speak Spanish, so we spoke in English.

Christina, 18-year-old daughter of a hospital worker:

I speak Spanish fluently, but I use English more because a lot of the people who I talk to speak English. Most of them speak another language, but we talk English because it is one we all agree on. It's real strange, isn't it?

The mass media of Los Angeles also have an enormous impact on language maintenance in the city. Only New York can compare with Los Angeles with regard to the variety of media systems in operation, and these systems have an enormous impact on the language one uses. Although newspapers, radio, television, and records utilizing a variety of languages, including Spanish, do exist in Los Angeles, the vast majority of media utilize English. In addition, most of the new media trends, such as video discs, use English first. Young people are especially vulnerable to influences in music and to television, and thus they listen to English over a significant amount of time. Thus, not only do the youth in this study use English in school, but they hear English a great deal when they listen to music, watch television, or go to the movies. Seventy-six percent (249) of the Chicanos from Los Angeles said that they listened primarily to English media. Eighty-four percent (209) said that this was because most of the new records and movies were in English. Finally, 77 percent (192) said that they discussed the new, avant-garde music in English because it was easier to do so.

This does not mean that these youth did not listen to Spanish media. Fifty-eight percent (145) said that they listened to Spanish programs on the radio and television, and 67 percent (97) of this group said that they found these programs enjoyable. However, 81 percent (202) said that, while it was important to have Spanish programs available, they preferred the programs in English because the new, avant-garde musical programs, on both radio and television, were being produced in English. Again, the fact that this group is an adolescent one is important because adolescents are highly receptive to new ideas and new technologies, and thus the advances in English language programming are particularly seductive. Media do affect language usage and, ultimately, language maintenance.

Ricardo, 17-year-old son of a professional cook:

The Spanish-speaking stations are good, but I listen to mostly the English ones because that is where the new music comes out of. . . . I think my friends and I speak more English because we talk most of the time about music.

What is particularly important about these findings concerning language preference and its relationship to media technology is that, whatever the influence on the shift in language orientation, the fact remains that the socialization process will result in these youth acquiring beliefs and behavior patterns that are likely to endure well into adulthood and may remain with them permanently.

Language and Cultural Nationalism

Thus far discussion has focused on the factors in the city, both social and ecological, that have enhanced Spanish language maintenance or have contributed to a decline in Spanish usage. Yet this discussion would not be complete without commenting on another factor which relates to the question of language, and this is the cultural/political nationalism that exists among some of the youth in this study. In all three cities, 19 percent (eighty-nine) of those who were Spanish-dominant said that they continued to speak Spanish in preference to English because for them it was a way to resist the Anglo (European) seizure and domination of the Southwest. These attitudes seem to originate in the home, and they are related to socioeconomic standing (84 percent, or seventy-five, of the youth expressing these attitudes are from lower SES homes). Of the eighty-nine youth who said that they maintained Spanish because of nationalistic attitudes, 91 percent (eighty-one) said that they developed their ideas about language and nationalism as a result of being told stories when they were younger about the Anglo seizure of power and the Chicano resistance.[35] These stories all include the belief that the Southwest was Mexican territory, that Chicanos were the rightful heirs, and that the subordinate position in which Chicanos find themselves today is directly related to Anglo expropriation of this land. Thus the young people reasoned that, while the Anglo may have taken their land, he was not going to take their language away from them.

Alberto, 18-year-old son of a machine shop worker in San Antonio:

I won't speak English when there is a choice. I always speak Spanish because my feeling is the Anglo may have taken the land away from us, but he won't take the language away, at least not from me.

Jovita, 17-year-old daughter of a meat packer in Albuquerque:

My father used to tell me about how the Anglo came into our land, took the land away from us and then tried to take our culture, too. My feeling is that I don't have any power to get the land back, at least not now—maybe that will change—but I do have the power to keep my language, and I will!

There are, however, some variations in the findings among cities. Forty-two percent (thirty-seven) of those who said that their language maintenance was due to cultural nationalism were from Los Angeles, 38 percent (thirty-four) were from Albuquerque, and 20 percent (eighteen) were from San Antonio. The explanation for this difference among cities has to do with the fact that cultural nationalism has been stronger in California and New Mexico than in Texas. This is because in California nationalism grew out of Chicanos' reaction to not having experienced economic mobility while having given up much of their culture, which they were told was inferior to that of the Anglos. In New Mexico nationalism has been in existence for decades, particularly in the Chicano-dominated northern part of the state, from which nearly all of the 38 percent of the respondents who said that they maintained language for nationalist reasons had come. This nationalism has grown out of an extreme pride in what Hispanic New Mexicans consider to be their unique culture, combined with the ethnic antagonisms they have had with Anglo Americans in the area. As for the fact that comparatively fewer of the San Antonio respondents remained loyal to their primary language as a result of nationalism, this may be attributed to the amount and severity of the intimidation that the Anglo community exerts on the Chicano community if it hears of anything resembling Chicano nationalism. This has resulted, over many years, in lower levels of nationalism among the Texas Chicanos.

Because the historical experience of the Chicanos is clearly different from that of the white Europeans who immigrated to the United States by choice, it has important implications for understanding the differences in attitudes concerning loyalty to one's mother tongue.[36] In this sense, all of these Chicano groups share a common historical relationship to American society, one that closely resembles that of the French to Canadian society.[37] Just as questions of language maintenance and nationalism are important in Canada, they are equally important for Chicanos in the United States. Hence the issues related to language loyalty and nationalism among the Chicanos in this study are completely interrelated and mutually reinforcing. It is therefore important to point out that this segment of our sample, expressing a cultural/political nationalism, will reappear at various stages in the analysis of political attitudes.

The Catholic Church

Religion has been responsible for giving individuals a view of the world, a set of moral and ethical values, and, in some cases, group and personal identity, particularly when it has been associated with a specific ethnic group.[38] Thus, when organized, religion has provided institutions for the development of its own dogma and has constituted a source of influence on parishoner thought and behavior.

Urban sociologists have often argued that religiosity has declined among urban residents despite the fact that urban areas have always had large and beautiful places to worship, such as synagogues, cathedrals, and mosques. Many believed that these structures only represented the physical presence of religion, and not a spiritual or participatory one, as people in urban areas simply had lost, somewhere during the urban experience, most of their conviction and no longer worshiped at them.[39] Urbanism was believed to undermine people's interest in religion and to reduce the part it played in their lives, or the extent to which they subscribed to institutional direction. The urban sociologists argued that the heterogeneity of cities would introduce a whole host of new ideas, and create a new world outlook with a new set of values that would lead people away from the organized religion with which they had traditionally identified. This erosion of religious belief among urbanites would affect members of ethnic groups because for many of them religion, through its institutions, had acted as a bastion for the preservation of their respective cultures.[40] In fact, religion has played a major role in Chicano identity. For Chicanos, religious life in Mexico and in the southwestern part of the United States historically has been dominated by the Roman Catholic Church. The Church has been instrumental in providing religious training, secular education, and some social services. In terms of ethnic identity, it was one of the factors that set the Mexican population apart from its rival, the European population, which was for the most part Protestant. Thus, on the one hand, Chicanos come to the city with a strong orientation toward Roman Catholicism in both belief and practice, and, on the other, city life provides a strong secular orientation that acts to reduce an individual's attachment to religion through a general process of changing those beliefs associated with traditional institutions. These two orientations interact on the Chicano youth in this study.

Among the Chicano youth in San Antonio, urban life does not seem to have altered their sense of religiosity, or belief in religion. They were asked to what religion they belonged, and, as expected, 97 percent (321) said that they were Catholic. When asked how often they attended church, 51 percent (166) said that they attended church every Sunday, and 38 percent (124) said that they attended at least two to three times a month. Both of these figures represent high levels of church attendance. Little difference in church attendance was found when social class background was considered, although there was a very slight difference between men and women. Women tended to go to church more often than men, but here again the difference was not great.[41] Urbanism, as measured by length of time in the city, density, and heterogeneity, had some effect, but, like that of the other variables, this effect was not great; thus it can be assumed that living in a city does little to affect the church attendance of these youth in San Antonio.[42]

Table 2.2

Semantic Differential Mean Scores for the Catholic Church, by
City of Residence, SES, and Length of Residence in the City[a]

	Length of Residence in the City						
	0–4 Years		5–9 Years		Over 10 Years		All	
San Antonio	1.89	(60)	2.06	(89)	2.44	(182)	2.13	(331)
Lower SES	1.79	(41)	1.92	(52)	2.01	(104)	1.90	(197)
Middle SES	1.98	(19)	2.20	(37)	2.87	(78)	2.35	(134)
Albuquerque	1.96	(62)	2.16	(84)	2.85	(165)	2.32	(311)
Lower SES	1.90	(45)	2.01	(50)	2.31	(73)	2.07	(168)
Middle SES	2.05	(17)	2.32	(34)	3.39	(92)	2.58	(143)
Los Angeles	1.93	(79)	2.18	(82)	2.90	(167)	2.36	(328)
Lower SES	1.85	(54)	2.17	(51)	2.39	(78)	2.13	(183)
Middle SES	2.01	(25)	2.38	(31)	3.42	(89)	2.60	(145)

[a]Semantic differential scores should be interpreted as positive when they are from
1–3.50; neutral when they are from 3.51–4.50; and negative when they are 4.51–
7.00.

However, simply attending church says very little about how the
Chicano youth view the Church as a religious institution. That is,
how much are they involved in the Church's dogma or view of the
world? Table 2.2 presents the youths' semantic differential scores for
the Catholic Church. Basically, the semantic differential test measures the meaning a person gives to a particular concept or the value
placed on a concept. In this case, the scores measure the youths'
evaluation of the Catholic Church, or the value they place on the
Church in their lives. Specifically, the young Chicanos in San Antonio indicated that the Catholic Church was very important to
them. The importance they assigned to the Church, as indicated by
the scores, was not affected by the character of their urban neighborhood, the length of time they had lived in the city, or their socioeconomic status. In fact, they considered the Church so important
that in other questions included in the general questionnaire, in
addition to the semantic differential tests, they followed the Church's
position on premarital sex, birth control, and abortion.

Eighty-six percent (280) of the Chicanos from San Antonio thought
that a woman should be a virgin before being married, although the

same standard did not apply to males.[43] Seventy-four percent (241) said that they thought birth control was not appropriate and that they based their belief on the position of the Church.[44] Women were more likely to feel more strongly about this, but the statistics for men and women were quite close. Lastly, 91 percent (296) said that they were against abortion for any reason and that this position also was based on the Church's position. Simply stated, the Church has been able to maintain a strong position in San Antonio Chicano society. The fact that Chicanos look to the Church as an institution to satisfy many personal needs also adds to its importance. It remains the strongest formal institution in San Antonio which represents the interests of the general Chicano population. Many, though by no means all, of the social services given to Chicanos are provided by the Church. If Chicano society were more integrated into other institutions in San Antonio, no doubt some of the Church's influence would be reduced. However, little effort has been made by other institutions to integrate Chicanos. The Church has responded to the fact that Chicanos have been uninvolved in other institutions by providing various socioeconomic and cultural services. Of course, the Church's position is not entirely altruistic; it has also responded because of the practical realization that the basis of its strength in San Antonio is connected directly to the Chicano community. It is acknowledged that if it were not for the Chicano community, which is Catholic, the Church would not have as powerful a position in San Antonio as it does because the Anglo community is overwhelmingly Protestant. Thus, to the Chicano community, the Church's efforts have made it appear to be an institution that is responsive to their needs. Two examples of this belief follow.

Frank, 17-year-old son of a golf course attendant:

The Church is real important to the Chicano community. It has relief funds, helps migrants, and has schools for people. It also has a number of cultural events, especially around the traditional religious holidays. The Church is good for the Chicano community.

Rhonda, 18-year-old daughter of a hotel chef:

The Church is important for me and the entire Chicano community. It gives people who are in need things. It also has helped Chicanos politically, like when they are in the Farm Workers Union. And then you have to understand that the Church also is a place where Mexican culture is still important—like during festivals. I would say the Church in San Antonio represents the interests of Chicanos because the Anglos are Protestant.

Thus a mutually dependent relationship between the Chicano community and the Catholic Church has been maintained in San Antonio.

Although the influence of religion through the Catholic Church does not show any signs of decline or breakdown among the Chicanos of San Antonio, as might have been predicted from the theories of the Chicago school, in Albuquerque and Los Angeles there are suggestions that changes are occurring in the way in which Chicanos perceive the role of the Church and of religion in their lives.

In Albuquerque, the Chicano youth view the Catholic Church as important, although both socioeconomic standing and the length of time the individual has lived in Albuquerque are factors affecting its importance.[45] As an individual's socioeconomic status rose, 87 percent (160)[46] of those experiencing this mobility said that other factors (objects, experiences) now influenced their lives more than the Church. Most of the items mentioned were material objects or life experiences such as vacations. Most of these explanations took the following form:

Linda, 18-year-old daughter of a salesman:

Before when we first came to Albuquerque, the Church was very important to me. I mean, I did everything according to the Church and I went to Church every Sunday and sometimes during the week. But as my family became better off we did more, went more places, and had more things to play with like motorcycles, cars, and stuff. I just spent less time at Church or thinking about it.

James, 18-year-old son of a mechanical engineer:

The Church does not mean as much to me now as it once did. I really did have the Church as a major part of my life—I did everything the way they said it should be. I don't know when exactly that changed, but I think the big thing was when my dad was able to make enough money so that we all could go on trips and do a lot more things than we did before. When that happened I just had less time for the Church. I know that sounds bad, but I can't help it, the Church just doesn't mean as much. [James went to Catholic school for eight years.]

Thus, improved economic conditions for the Chicanos of Albuquerque have resulted in a lessening of importance of the Church and of religion in their lives.

As previously stated, socioeconomic mobility does influence attitudes toward the Church, yet, since not everyone experiences socioeconomic mobility, what happens to those who do not? The answer is that, regardless of socioeconomic standing, living in the city of Albuquerque influences everyone's attitude toward the Church's role in their everyday lives. In other words, the longer an individual is associated with the city, the less important the Church becomes.[47] This change in attitude results from the introduction of new ideas, values, and morals which are present in large urban and heterogeneous communities. For example, the Catholic Church is opposed to premarital sex, all forms of birth control other than abstention or the "rhythm method," and abortion. When the Chicanos from Albuquerque were asked questions relating to these issues, their answers indicated that, in general, the Catholic Church has experienced difficulty in either creating or maintaining support for its positions on premarital sex, birth control and abortion (see Table 2.3). The longer the respondent had lived in the city, the more tolerant he/she was of premarital sex, and of those who thought premarital sex was not immoral, 54 percent (ninety-eight) said "if they loved someone" they would have premarital sex.[48] Further, the longer the individual had lived in Albuquerque, the more accepting he/she was of birth control through the use of contraceptives. Here 73 percent (143) of those who accepted contraceptives in principle said that they would use them personally.[49] Finally, the longer the Chicano youth had lived in the city the more tolerant they were of abortion, and of those who were tolerant toward abortion, 43 percent (fifty-five) said that they would, under certain circumstances, undergo an abortion.[50]

As to why the church's position on these issues has been undermined, the Chicanos in this study answered that the Church did not understand the complexity of certain situations. Sixty-eight percent (144) of those who disagreed with the Church's position on one

Table 2.3
Semantic Differential Mean Scores for Premarital Sex, Abortion, and Birth Control, by Length of Residence in the City

	Length of Residence in the City							
	0–4 Years		5–9 Years		Over 10 Years		All	
Premarital Sex								
San Antonio	5.22[a]	(43)	4.89	(88)	4.77	(197)	4.96	(329)
Albuquerque	5.07	(59)	4.21	(93)	3.02	(159)	4.10	(311)
Los Angeles	5.20	(85)	3.97	(92)	2.82	(150)	3.99	(327)
Abortion								
San Antonio	6.28	(43)	5.91	(89)	5.72	(199)	5.97	(331)
Albuquerque	6.31	(58)	5.17	(93)	4.11	(157)	5.19	(309)
Los Angeles	6.25	(84)	4.76	(92)	3.49	(151)	4.93	(327)
Birth Control								
San Antonio	5.17	(59)	4.99	(73)	4.81	(199)	4.99	(331)
Albuquerque	5.09	(58)	4.03	(93)	3.26	(159)	4.12	(310)
Los Angeles	4.98	(85)	3.93	(92)	2.97	(151)	3.96	(328)

[a]Semantic differential scores should be interpreted as positive when they are from 1–3.50; neutral when they are from 3.51–4.50; and negative when they are 4.51–7.00. Positive score means that the respondent assumed a positive attitude toward the concepts; a neutral score indicates that the respondent did not care one way or the other; and a negative score indicated that the respondent assumed a negative attitude.

or more of the issues mentioned above said that the Catholic Church's answers were too simple, that they had come to this conclusion as a result of receiving more information,[51] and that there were other people who saw the issues as they did.

> Pat, 17-year-old son of an engineer:
>
> Well I used to believe everything the Catholic Church said, but that was before I got some other information on things like abortion and birth control . . . besides there are a lot of people who believe that the issues are more complex than what the Church says.
>
> Lola, 18-year-old daughter of a watchman:
>
> I think the Church has ideas that are too simple about these things [birth control, premarital sex, abortion]. . . . I didn't

always think so, but when you live in the city you can read
some other points of view. . . . I don't think I would ever have
been able to go against the Church's position if there were
not a lot of other people around here that think the way I do.

In essence, these respondents perceived there was broader acceptance and tolerance of their attitudes, and they did not feel isolated.
The social environment of Albuquerque, with its tolerance of countervailing ideas, encourages attitudes that affect the Catholic Church's
traditional authority.

Although there are changes occurring in these young Chicanos'
attitudes toward the Catholic Church's role in their lives, the Church
is still seen as important. It is essential, therefore, to understand
what it is about the Church that makes it important to these individuals, but at the same time less influential. The answer is that,
within Albuquerque (and, more broadly, New Mexico) society, the
Church has remained a reservoir of Hispanic, or Chicano, culture.
In New Mexico, as in Texas, the Hispanics/Mexicans who inhabited
the land before the Anglo-Europeans were all Catholic. The ethnic
antagonisms that occurred between Anglo-Americans and Hispan-
ics/Mexicans throughout New Mexico's history involved the Protestant Anglo-Americans and the Catholic Hispanics/Mexicans. The
Church therefore occupied a central position in group identity, and,
as ethnic antagonisms evolved over the years, became a reservoir of
Hispanic/Mexican culture.[52] It still is associated with many of the
festivals associated with this culture, such as *posadas* and *lumi-
narios* at Christmas; the architectural structures associated with the
past history of Hispanic/Mexican culture; art forms such as *santos*
(wood carvings of saints) that are extremely popular; and the use of
the Spanish language at official functions. For all these reasons, 77
percent (221) of the Chicano respondents from Albuquerque still
viewed the Church as important. Thus, for these 77 percent the
basis of the Church's importance is the role that it plays in group
and personal identity and not its functions as a purely religious
institution. Two comments which represent this attitude toward
the Catholic Church are the following:

Miguel, 18-year-old son of a construction worker:

I think the church is important even though I do not believe
a lot of what they say. It still is important because it's part of
Chicano culture; it has festivals, there are Spanish masses,
and there are cultural events. It's part of Chicano traditions.

Alejandra, 19-year-old daughter of an elementary school teacher:

The Church is not so important religiously as it used to be or at least not for me, but it still is important for Hispanics because it is part of our history and it keeps a lot of the Hispanic's culture alive.

Therefore, in Albuquerque the religious role of the Roman Catholic Church in the everyday lives of the Chicanos in this study is reduced with length of residence in the city, and this reduction is accelerated by socioeconomic mobility. However, the Catholic Church is still important as a cultural symbol, even though it has lost some of its power to influence thought and behavior with regard to questions of morality and ethics.

In Los Angeles the lessening of the Church's role in the Chicanos' everyday lives is even more extreme than in Albuquerque. As shown in Table 2.2, the Chicanos who have lived in Los Angeles for a longer period of time and those who have experienced socioeconomic mobility assign less importance to the Church. In examining the semantic differential scores of Chicanos from Los Angeles with regard to premarital sex, birth control, and abortion, as presented in Table 2.3, it can be seen that more of this group have positive attitudes toward each of these concepts than do the Albuquerque respondents. Forty-eight percent (158) of the Chicanos in Los Angeles thought premarital sex was acceptable behavior, and of this group 63 percent (99) said they themselves would engage in premarital sex given the "right circumstances";[53] 61 percent (202) said that they thought the use of contraceptives was acceptable and 67 percent (139) of this group said that they would use contraceptives; and, finally, 53 percent (175) said that they thought abortion was not immoral and should be left up to the individual, while 47 percent (156) said that they would consider it if the situation arose. In addition, the Catholic Church is viewed as a symbol of Chicano culture by only 12 percent (forty) of this sample as opposed to 77 percent of the Albuquerque sample.

What explains the differences between Albuquerque and Los Angeles with regard to the role of the Church? Other than the Church on the plaza near Olvera Street, there are few churches that Los Angeles Chicanos can identify architecturally as historically Chicano/Mexican churches, as can be done in both San Antonio and Albuquerque. While there are parishes that are entirely Chicano, these churches do not have the historical presence that many of the churches in Albuquerque and San Antonio do. Furthermore, the clergy in Los Angeles are overwhelmingly Anglo-American—there is a clear absence of Mexican clergy who could be viewed as symbols of cultural identity. The fact that the clergy is not composed of a significant number of Mexican priests who were trained in Mexican seminaries is also significant with regard to the type of Catholicism that the Church offers to Chicanos. Although Roman Catholicism has certain continuities in its general religious teachings and procedures, the orientation of the Church can make a difference. In southern Europe and in the Iberian peninsula (Spain and Portugal), from which Mexico received its tradition, the Church has been "madonna"-oriented, with an emphasis on Mary the Mother, who represents a compassionate intercessor in the forgiveness of sins. In northern Europe, the Catholic Church has adopted a Trinity orientation, with a strict adherence to the gospel and to Church doctrine and an emphasis on sacrifice and penance for forgiveness. Given that most, although not all, of the clergy with whom Chicanos come into contact in Los Angeles are those trained in the northern European tradition, persons from a Spanish-speaking, "madonna" orientation are made to feel more distant from the Church. This experience is remarkably similar to that of Italian Americans who found themselves alienated for the same reasons when they first arrived in large metropolitan centers.[54]

Clearly, the fact that Chicanos feel removed from the Church has implications for the Church's position as a cultural symbol, and creates a situation in which other factors, such as the countervailing values found in the city's social environment, act to reduce attachment to the Church. The Catholic Church simply does not have the image of a cultural reservoir for the Chicanos in Los Angeles, as it does for those in Albuquerque. What is important here is not whether the Church in fact functions differently in Los Angeles than in Albuquerque, but rather that the Los Angeles Chicanos in this study perceive it as being different. Because the Church is not seen as a cultural institution by the Chicanos in Los Angeles, it is reduced to a purely religious institution, and, as such, it becomes vulnerable to the ideas that permeate a socially heterogeneous community. Views on premarital sex, birth control, and abortion are much more permissive in Los Angeles than in either San Antonio or Albuquerque. It is therefore not surprising to find the Chicanos from Los Angeles much more tolerant concerning these issues than those from San Antonio or Albuquerque. In fact, many values, attitudes, and norms that are deviant from those of the prevailing society are tolerated to a much greater extent in Los Angeles. In comparing answers to a question concerning the Chicanos' perception of their city's overall tolerance of deviant behavior and ideas, the study data show that 38 percent (126) of the respondents in San Antonio think that their city is a tolerant environment, 74 percent (230) of those in Albuquerque think that it is a tolerant place, and 95 percent (312) of those in Los Angeles think that it is tolerant.[55] The following response is typical:

Irene, 17-year-old daughter of a postal worker:

I think Los Angeles is a tolerant place and I think I have become more tolerant of all kinds of different people and what they think the longer I have lived here. I had to learn to be more tolerant because I am sure people are tolerant of me and if people were not tolerant of each other in Los Angeles there would be a lot of conflict because there are a lot of different people in this city.

It is therefore not surprising to find the Chicanos from Los Angeles much more tolerant of premarital sex, birth control (contraceptives), and abortion than the other respondents. The existence in Los Angeles of a variety of values, attitudes, and norms works to challenge those held and promulgated by traditional institutions such as the Catholic Church. Additionally, the fact that the Catholic Church is not viewed by the Chicanos from Los Angeles as a haven and/or defender of Chicano culture, as it is by those from San Antonio and Albuquerque, works further to reduce its influence on the lives of the Chicanos living there. In the final analysis, the Catholic Church's influence on the Chicanos of both Los Angeles and Albuquerque lessened the longer the respondents lived in the city. Both these cases would tend to support Wirth's and Park's assertions, along with those of the Chicago school, that traditional values diminish with city life. Results from these cities are also consistent with Fischer's findings in studying the contemporary effects of city life on individuals: the urban experience does have the effect of creating more tolerant attitudes toward deviant beliefs and behaviors with regard to issues that have concerned the Church.[56]

Conclusion

This chapter presents some interesting findings. On a theoretical level it is apparent that city life does have an effect on the attitudes of the Chicanos in the study, but that it does not have the effect predicted by the Chicago school of causing a linear process of ethnic assimilation; that is, the longer an individual lives in the city, the more he/she will assimilate to the prevailing norms of the larger community. What the data presented clearly show, however, is that, regardless of the fact that the sample was taken from the same ethnic group, the Chicanos who live in San Antonio, Albuquerque, and Los Angeles do not think or act the same concerning their traditional cultural institutions. The data give a picture of three different cities, although Albuquerque and Los Angeles are somewhat similar, each with its own set of social agents that influence the way the Chicano respondents think about culture. San Antonio is a city that reinforces traditional Chicano/Mexican cultural institutions. The Chicanos of San Antonio have maintained their traditional cultural institutions, and there seem to be no signs of a substantial change in that pattern. There is no indication that San Antonio society as a whole is maneuvering the Chicano segment of that society to abandon its culture and assimilate into Anglo-American culture. On the contrary, it would appear, by virtue of the evidence on the strength of Chicano cultural institutions within the Chicano community, that San Antonio society seems to encourage the maintenance of these cultural institutions. The result has been the strengthening of two relatively strong, self-contained, and stable communities, one Chicano and the other Anglo.

Los Angeles is a city that is completely opposite of San Antonio in that the socioeconomic conditions there encourage, perhaps force, its inhabitants to assimilate to the norms of the community as a whole. Thus, the Los Angeles Chicanos in this study were assimilating at various speeds to the norms, or some variations thereof, of the larger Anglo-American society. Los Angeles society as a whole and Chicano society in particular are in a state of relatively rapid social change. This makes Los Angeles an exciting place to live, but also a difficult one because there is usually, at least on the individual level, some anguish in being involved in the process of change. One particular effect of Los Angeles' environment, with its rapid change and pressure to assimilate, has been manifested in the longing of Chicanos for cultural nationalism.

Albuquerque is a city whose social character is dominated by social class standing. Those Chicanos who have experienced socio-economic mobility and are now middle-class have become assimilated into Anglo-American culture. They are not involved to any degree with traditional cultural institutions such as *compadrazgo*, the Spanish language, or the Catholic religion. Those who have not experienced socioeconomic mobility and have remained lower-class also have become assimilated, but at a much slower rate and to a much lesser extent. What has retarded the assimilation process has been their lack of success in becoming economically mobile, which has worked to reinforce an identification with primary group institutions such as *compadrazgo*, the Spanish language, and the Church. Thus in Albuquerque the ethnic urban experience of Chicanos is in line with the premises of the neighborhood solidarity theorists. In fact, the lower class in Albuquerque is not like the lower class in Los Angeles, which is much less active in traditional Chicano/Mexican culture. All that is needed in Los Angeles for an individual to be less active in traditional culture is for that person to spend more time in the city; social class standing does not have the mediating effect that it does in Albuquerque.

Cultural institutions and the degree to which people participate in them are the life blood of any ethnic group in the United States, or in any ethnically pluralistic society, because of their impact on the group identity and/or the personal identities of the individuals who comprise the group. The data in this chapter have provided a snapshot of the ethnic environments in which political learning also occurs. The chapters that follow examine the ways in which the ethnic, political, and economic environments of these three cities have influenced the formation of political attitudes among the Chicanos in this study.

3

Political Attitudes

THE PREVIOUS CHAPTER provided a glimpse of the way in which the Chicanos in this study view their cultural world and are affected by it. This chapter begins to analyze how they view their political world and, again, are affected by it. This analysis starts by investigating the youth's attitudes toward political ideology. Merelman, in his studies on the development of political ideology among adolescents, nicely describes the properties of a political ideology and the factors that make it important. He states that an ideology involves a set of ideas that (1) are in some way constrained (i.e., if one idea changes they will all change), (2) set forth a statement of political preference, (3) are persistent over time, (4) are applicable globally and have logical consistencies, and (5) have activist directives.[1] Thus, what makes ideology important to politics is its function in structuring a person's political world. In this regard, it acts as a foundation for attitudes concerning the whole range of political issues.

The study described in this work investigated whether the Chicano youth identified with the ideology that is dominant in the United States, namely liberal democracy/capitalism, or with a contending ideology, such as socialism, communism, or Chicano nationalism. In addition, it examined the factors influencing the development of their ideological allegiances, particularly the impact of the urban environment, as well as social class background and cultural orientation (level of cultural assimilation).

Each of the theories concerning urban life and social structure presents some general hypotheses to test regarding the urban environment's impact on ideology. For the Chicago school, especially for Wirth, the impact of urbanism on ideology was an important issue. Wirth, like many of the other Chicago school theorists, was interested in building consensus in the society. He argued that the city had the ability to break down the divisions in a society that were based on kinship and traditional values and to replace them with a more broadly based set of values representing the community as a whole. The end result of this process was a rational society that was devoid of particularistic ideologies. Hence, to Wirth the city, because of its size and heterogeneity, had the potential to bring about positive change by breaking down specific interests, although he also recognized that it had the potential, for the same reasons, to stimulate interest groups to develop ideologies which rationalized their own behaviors in an effort to cope with the abandonment of custom and tradition.[2]

Thus it might be expected that city life would have a profound influence on this study's sample of Chicano youth, particularly in Albuquerque and Los Angeles where a great deal of change was occurring in traditional cultural institutions. In those cities it might be anticipated that a variety of ideologies would be competing with one another because a variety of interest groups would result from the breakdown of traditional culture. On the other hand, more consensus might be expected in San Antonio precisely because there is not as much disorganization occurring, to use Wirth's phrase.

From the teachings of the "neighborhood solidarity" theorists, very little would be expected on the part of the respondents in the way of support of formal political ideologies. Ethnic residents would be too intent on maintaining control of their neighborhoods and therefore skeptical of any ideology being promulgated by someone from outside their community and ethnic group. As Gans and Suttles have argued, people who live in stratified ethnic neighborhoods are almost completely mistrusting of all persons, particularly political leaders, who are not from the community.[3]

The following discussion, guided by these theories, examines how ideological the youth in these three cities are, i.e., what do they know about political ideologies in general, what ideologies do they support, and what are the determinants of that support? Before beginning the analysis of these questions, a brief methodological point should be made. This chapter uses a path analytic model (see Figure 3.1) in order to clarify some of the complexities. In this recursive model there are three exogenous variables: length of urban residence (X_1), measured by the number of years the youth has lived in the

FIGURE 3.1
Path Model Representing Urban Contextual Variables,
Socioeconomic Variables, and Political Variables*

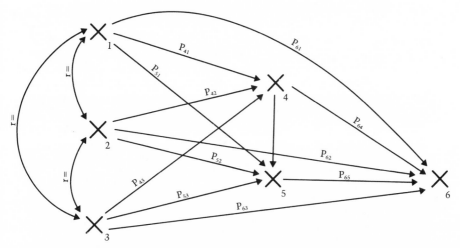

* =   All coefficients are significant at the .05 level or beyond on
       a two-tailed "t" test
X_1 =   Length of residence in the city
X_2 =   Population density in neighborhood
X_3 =   Ethnic homogeneity in respondent's neighborhood
X_4 =   Socioeconomic status
X_5 =   Traditional cultural values (retention of)
X_6 =   Dependent political variable

city; neighborhood population density (X_2), which is the number of
people per four block square; and ethnic homogeneity of the community (X_3), which is measured by the percentage of Chicanos living
within the neighborhood. There are also three endogenous variables,
the first two of which are socioeconomic status (SES) of the youth's
family (X_4), determined from the income of the family, the occu-
pation of the head of household, and the education of the head of
household; and traditional cultural values (X_5), which is a measurement of the extent to which the Chicano adolescents have retained
the values associated with traditional Chicano culture. This latter
variable is an index of four cultural variables: (1) the level of pro-

ficiency in Spanish; (2) the degree to which *compadrazgo* is valued; (3) the degree to which *curanderismo* is valued; and (4) the degree to which the Catholic Church is valued. The various political orientations that will be analyzed comprise the dependent variable (X_6).

The Scope of Ideological Knowledge

The first issue to be addressed is related to the scope of ideological knowledge among the sample of Chicano youth. Four ideologies were presented to the youth both in the questionnaire, in which they were presented with the four labels and asked what they thought, and in the in-depth interviews: (1) capitalism/liberal democracy; (2) Chicano nationalism (separatism); (3) communism; (4) socialism.[4] The study attempted to determine what the youth knew and understood about these ideologies, as well as their sources of information.

In San Antonio, the respondents had some knowledge of each of the ideologies presented to them, but they were most knowledgeable about capitalism/liberal democracy. Eighty-one percent (269) had some basic idea of what constituted a capitalist system. Below are two representative examples.

Gloria, 17-year-old daughter of an insurance salesman:

Well, capitalism is where private people own the businesses of the country and they make the decisions about how the business will be run. Like what kind of product they will make and how much to pay the workers. The owners of the businesses also decide how much to charge for their product and how much profit they should make.

Frank, 17-year-old son of a bartender:

In a capitalist system, there is private ownership of business and property. That's like, the government doesn't control things like who owns land, and it doesn't tell people what to make and how much to charge for it. It's like, whoever owns their own business can make as much money as they can, and they can invest the profits the way they want. Oh, another thing is that in capitalism, trade is supposed to be free, but today that doesn't happen 'cause the government regulates a lot of trade.

In addition to having some basic knowledge about the capitalist system, 52 percent (173) were able to say something concerning the fundamental laws governing the system. Two illustrative examples are as follows:

Josefina, 18-year-old daughter of a truck driver:

In capitalism the thing that controls the market is the supply and demand of things in the economy. You know, like how much of a product there is and how much people want to buy it.

Gerald, 18-year-old son of a brewery worker:

Supply and demand is what runs capitalism, like in the United States. It sets the prices of things too. Let's see, and it's the competition in prices that sets how much of the things will be made.

Not only did the youth know most of the fundamentals of capitalism, but they were also aware that it, along with liberal democracy, is the governing ideology in the United States.

Seventy-three percent (242) mentioned that the United States was governed by a type of democracy and a capitalist economic system. Two examples follow:

Cynthia, 17-year-old daughter of a printer:

In the U.S. our economy is basically capitalistic and our government is a democracy, not a full democracy, but a limited one where you know we have representatives.

Matty, 18-year-old son of an electrician:

I like the U.S. system because it is capitalistic and the government is modified democracy where we have people to represent us. What's so good about this system is that the capitalism and the democracy we have just go together good.

There are a number of reasons for the widespread knowledge about capitalism. First, social studies teachers in the schools examined seemed to be quite positive in their classroom presentation of capitalism. Thus, the youth not only had been introduced to the concept, but had been given a considerable amount of positive information.[5]

Probably the most important factor influencing the youth's knowledge of the basic economic principles of capitalism is the fact that most have taken a course on the free enterprise system. This course is designed to teach the students some of the basic principles governing a capitalist system. In past years, the state of Texas by regulation required the course for all high school students, but more recently it has become an elective, and thus optional to students. However, in two of the three schools studied in San Antonio the scheduling was arranged so that most of the students (79 percent, or 261) found it most convenient to take this course as a sequel to American government. The following comment is representative:

Barbara, 18-year-old daughter of a shoe salesman:

I learned most of what I know from the course I had on American government and the course on the free enterprise system. . . . I took the course on the free enterprise system because it fit into my schedule better because it was the same time as the American government class—I really didn't think I would like it but I learned a lot.

Knowledge of the other three ideologies among the Chicanos in San Antonio was rather limited. What was known has been influenced primarily by the courses that they had taken in school. Most of the youth identified socialism as a system in which the government owns all of the large industry. England was cited most often as an example of this type of system. Seventy-nine percent (262) said that they would not like to live in this type of system because they believed that the services they would get from such a system would not be as good as those of a capitalist system such as the United States. When asked why they thought that the services would be inferior, most said that it was because people who work for the government are not as productive as those in private enterprise because there are not enough incentives.

James, 18-year-old son of a construction worker:

I wouldn't want to live in a socialist country like England because nothing works as good there. I mean in England the government runs everything and they don't know how to do things as business does. So people don't get things and the things made ain't as good as here 'cause the government just can't do it as good as business; because people who work for the government don't work hard 'cause they know they can't get fired.

They also thought that government was not as efficient as private business, but when asked why, only 40 percent (133) could give an answer. The most common answer was that because private business had to make a profit it also had to be efficient, whereas government was not required to make a profit and, therefore, less emphasis was placed on efficiency. Many said that England was going bankrupt for precisely this reason.

Communism to the Chicanos of San Antonio was associated with Russia and/or China and was viewed as the most evil of all possible systems. In their view, the people who lived under a communist system were living in a prison. The government owned everything and the residents had no rights—if they said what they wanted to, they faced the possibility of imprisonment and/or execution. Also, it was believed that communism loomed as a constant threat because communists in general, and Russians in particular, wanted to take over the United States.

Laura, 17-year-old daughter of a waiter:

Communism is where the government owns everything and if a person does anything that the government does not like they imprison you or in a lot of cases kill people. Russia and China are communist systems and look at what happens there. . . . The things that worry me is that the communists will take over America and we will be ruled by Russia.

The concept of Chicano separatism was understood in San Antonio only in its simplest form.[6] The respondents recognized that some people would like to separate and form a country for Chicanos, but they knew of no formal organization that openly supported this policy, nor did they know any other details. Any information that they had about separatism had been obtained from people speaking in the community or from family members and friends who had talked of it occasionally. In fact, their conception of separatism was rather provincial. For example, virtually all of those interviewed thought that any country established for Chicanos would be in Texas. It did not occur to them that a separate Chicano country might include other parts of the Southwest that have large settlements of Chicanos.

Luis, 18-year-old son of a short order cook:

I hear some people talk about a separate Chicano country or something like that. I don't pay too much attention 'cause it's just talk. I don't even know where in Texas this country they're talking about will be. . . . Most of the talk about this will come from people in the neighborhood. . . . I haven't heard of a group that says it wants its own country.

With the exception of separatism, the youth's knowledge of ideologies other than capitalism was dependent on the schools. In the interviews with social studies teachers, nearly all said that they tallked about socialism and communism only briefly, using their discussion of these topics to highlight the advantages of a capitalist system.[7] They also said that they completely avoided any discussion of Chicano nationalism precisely because questions of national identity were so sensitive and the topic of nationalism was so volatile in both the Anglo and the Chicano communities.

The information that is given by the schools regarding the undesirable aspects of socialism, communism, and separatism, as reported by the teachers, is reinforced by the extremely conservative political climate of San Antonio. The city's media reflect this climate and tend to report events in a conservative fashion. The newspapers are perhaps the most conservative form of media, but radio and television reporting are also conservative, especially in the editorials.[8] Given the conservative nature of politics in San Antonio, it is not surprising that little information exists on these other ideologies—socialism, communism, and nationalism—nor is it surprising that the information that does exist presents them in a negative light.

What one finds among the Chicanos of San Antonio is a generally conservative view of politics. One important example concerns attitudes toward labor unions. The attitude toward labor unions in Texas is generally unfavorable (Texas is a right-to-work state), and 79 percent (262) of the Chicanos in this study were also negative toward them. Further, 71 percent (235) said that they thought that the Texas Farm Workers Union should not organize in the Rio Grande Valley of southern Texas, although many were from this area and had worked in the fields for very low wages. Of this 71 percent, 61 percent (144) said that they opposed the Texas Farm Workers Union because they thought unions infringed on the free enterprise system. The others said that they were opposed to the attempts of the Texas Farm Workers to organize because the union caused too much violence and they disliked violence. These sentiments are rather surprising when one considers that the Texas Farm Workers are led by Chicanos and that the majority of the union's membership is Chicano. Yet these attitudes are consistent with the overall conservatism found among the San Antonio respondents.

These youth from San Antonio have adopted a conservative view of political life because, for the most part, they are afraid of negative reprisals from the Anglo community. These reprisals can take the form of economic sanctions, such as loss of a job or difficulty in finding one, and even physical sanctions, such as police harassment or physical threats.

Tony, 18-year-old son of an airport worker:

Hey, can you imagine being a commie in this town [San Antonio]? You would never get a job nowhere, and what's worse is to be a Chicano nationalist, because that would really get the Anglos upset. They'd use the police against Chicano nationalists like they have in the past with the [Texas] Rangers. Those people kill people, especially Mexicans, so I don't need that. I'm going to mind my business 'cause I got to live here.

Maria-Paz, 17-year-old daughter of a sales clerk:

I support the American system of government and economics. If I didn't, and I am not saying I don't, I think I would be in trouble because in San Antonio the people, especially Anglos, would stop you from getting a job. They could make things real tough on you if you were a communist or socialist or something like that.

The combination of fear of reprisal with limited information causes these respondents to perceive that there are limited political options.

In Albuquerque and Los Angeles, knowledge concerning the different ideologies varies. The degree to which capitalism is understood in Los Angeles and Albuquerque in no way approaches that found in San Antonio. Some differences are dependent on social class background. For the most part, the middle-class Chicanos in the study were able to identify capitalism as involving private ownership of property and competition among those in businesses, but were not able to discuss its more particular characteristics, as was done by the youth in San Antonio.

Diana, 17-year-old daughter of a Los Angeles lawyer:

Capitalism is where you have private ownership of businesses . . . and where businesses compete with each other. No, I really can't talk about the specifics, though.

Among the lower-class youth there was even less of an understanding of capitalism. They simply associated the term with the present system in the United States. When questioned further they were unable to say anything more, either about what capitalism was or about how it worked.

Ron, 18-year-old son of an Albuquerque gardener:

I really don't know what capitalism is exactly, I just know the U.S. has it.

Joan, 18-year-old daughter of a Los Angeles maid:

Capitalism is what we live under today, but I don't know how it works or anything specific.

Eighty-three percent (530) of the respondents in both cities said that they had not been taught about capitalism itself, and although brief mention had been made of it by various teachers, this consisted of little more than references associating it with the present system in the United States. One reason for this lack of attention to capitalism is that social studies curricula have been developed to emphasize other aspects of the American system, such as the manner in which the government functions, rather than its economic structure. Thus, most of the youth from both Albuquerque and Los Angeles were able to describe in some detail how the U.S. government runs.

Jason, 18-year-old son of an Albuquerque truck driver:

The U.S. government is a representative democracy where the citizens elect people to make decisions for them.

Roberta, 18-year-old daughter of a Los Angeles accountant:

The government of the U.S. is a constitutional government that has a separation of powers so there is protection against one branch getting too much power. Also, instead of everybody voting on all the issues we elect people to vote for us.

Another reason for the inattention to capitalism concerns the variation in the teachers' ideological outlooks. In interviewing the teachers, it was found that those who were more conservative paid more attention to the economic aspects of capitalism, while those teachers with more liberal attitudes toward politics chose not to emphasize it as much.

Another factor contributing to the Albuquerque and Los Angeles youth's lack of ideological knowledge is the media. In contrast to San Antonio, there is little reference made in television programs to questions concerning the free enterprise system or related topics, so one potentially important source of information is absent. There are some newspapers in both cities that are conservative in their political views, but only 7 percent (forty-five) of the youth in the sample said that they read these newspapers, and of these youth nearly all said that they read sections that were not related to the news, such as the comics.

Thus, the extent of knowledge about capitalism among the youth of Albuquerque and Los Angeles consisted of identifying it with the present system in the United States. Therefore, as becomes evident in the next section, their evaluations of capitalism, whether positive or negative were based on how they felt about their present living conditions, physical as well as socioeconomic, rather than on an understanding of capitalist ideology.

Knowledge of socialism and communism in Albuquerque and Los Angeles varied, but it was generally limited. Seventy-six percent (fifty-one) of the respondents in Los Angeles and 79 percent (fifty-two) in Albuquerque said that communism was a system where the government owned everything and the people had few rights. Nearly all mentioned Russia and China as having such a system.[9] They identified their sources of information as being primarily school and television, but some mentioned the Church and members of their immediate families, such as brothers who had been in the service. Information provided by the schools consisted of references to communism when describing the political systems of Russia, Eastern

Europe, China, and Vietnam. Seventy-six percent (fifty) of the youth interviewed in depth in Albuquerque and 61 percent (forty-one) in Los Angeles said that they could not remember hearing anyone say anything positive about communism. The youth who mentioned the Church said that the priests emphasized that communists were atheists who did not believe in God and that people who lived in communist countries were prohibited from going to church. The Chicanos (sixty-one) who cited their brothers as sources of anti-communist information said that their brothers had described the communists as robots. Almost all (95 percent, or fifty-eight) of their brothers had been to Vietnam, and used the Vietnamese communists as their examples. In point of fact, the youth in Los Angeles and Albuquerque, like those in San Antonio, associated communism with foreign countries, so that any thought of communism coming to the United States was equated with Russia or China assuming political control. Thus, because communism was not seen as a set of ideas about the structure of society, it assumed the character of foreign interventionism.

Carolyn, 18-year-old daughter of a social worker:

Communism is where there are few freedoms, I mean people can't say much or own very much. Russia and China have a communist system, and I was told in school that the communists, Russia and China, want to take over the U.S.

Socialism is no better understood by the youth from Los Angeles and Albuquerque than is communism. Eighty-seven percent (117) of the youth in both cities said that they were confused concerning the differences between communism and socialism; in fact, most thought they were the same. Thirty percent (forty) thought that socialism meant that the government owned the big businesses and that you could receive free medical care, and of this number, 55 percent (twenty-two) gave England as an example.

Reynaldo, 17-year-old son of a clothing factory worker:

Socialism is where the government owns the big businesses, and you can get free doctors [medical care] like in England and Sweden. I don't know more than that. . . . Well, one reason I don't know more [about socialism] is that it's hard to get information.

The vast majority of the youth interviewed reported that little information on socialism had been available to them. Those who had received some information most frequently mentioned the school they attended as the source, although a very small number mentioned that they had obtained their information from the literature of various socialist parties.[10] Regardless of whether information had been available to them or not, none of the youth possessed a clear understanding of the concept.

Of the four ideologies presented to the youth in Los Angeles and Albuquerque, the concept of political separatism, or Chicano nationalism, was the best understood. Seventy-four percent (ninety-nine) of those interviewed in both cities identified separatism as the establishment of a separate country for Chicanos—independent of both Mexico and the United States. This country would be located somewhere in the southwestern part of the United States and would be governed by Chicanos. The official language of such a country would be Spanish, with English spoken only when addressing Anglos who were in the country.[11] Although the overwhelming majority were able to articulate the points mentioned above, there were some variations as well. First, some offered a name to this mythical country, "Aztlan,"[12] while others gave precise definitions of where the country would be and reasons why it should be there. For example:

Eileen, 18-year-old daughter of an auto mechanic:

A free Aztlan would be the five states of Texas, California, New Mexico, Arizona, and Colorado, 'cause this used to be our land before the Mexican war, and most of the Chicanos still live in these states. You know, this is historically our land, so this is where a Chicano country should be. . . . Spanish would be the official language and English would be for visitors—like in Mexico.

Tino, 17-year-old son of a janitor:

Well, a separate Chicano country would be the land in New Mexico, Arizona, Texas, and California and Colorado. This land is where the old Mexican land grants were, and so we should own the land which was taken from us. But also, most Chicanos live in this area, and so culturally it would be important, too. I mean, we would speak Spanish all the time and not have to worry about learning English.

Information about nationalism does not come from conventional sources such as the school or the media. These two institutions have tended to ignore the concept completely in the hope that eventually it will wither away. Their rationale has been that coverage would only serve to intensify ethnic conflicts; thus, there is no social benefit to be gained from it. As a result, information about nationalism has come from within the Chicano culture itself. There are a number of nationalist political groups that have stressed the need for more community autonomy as a first step toward an autonomous Chicano country. Thirty-two percent (100) of the youth in Albuquerque and 33 percent (108) in Los Angeles reported that they had been made aware of the separatist position by listening to speakers from these groups, reading the literature they passed out, or talking to members of some of these groups. Others (26 percent, or eighty-one, in Albuquerque and 23 percent, or seventy-six, in Los Angeles) attributed the majority of their information on nationalism to their parents. In the case of Albuquerque, many said that their parents had talked about separatism as a result of the continuing land grant controversy in New Mexico.

Orlando, 18-year-old son of an Albuquerque lumber yard worker:

My parents, well, mostly my dad, would talk about the need of the Hispanic people in the Southwest to form their own country because only that way would they get their land back. He would talk about how the land was stolen by the Anglos and how they wouldn't give it back, even though the Hispanics had a legal right to it from the land grants.

Others, primarily those from Los Angeles, mentioned that their fathers had simply made reference to separatism in relation to something that was in the news, that was going on in the community, or that had happened to them in the past.

Tina, 18-year-old daughter of a Los Angeles hardware store clerk:

My father mentions that we should make our own country, separate from the U.S., every time he reads about discrimination against Chicanos, and then he always adds that we would only be taking back what was ours anyway.

However, many of the Chicanos in these two cities (42 percent, or 131, in Albuquerque and 44 percent, or 144, in Los Angeles) said that they could not identify the source of their information on separatism. These youth explained that their information had come from what they knew about Chicano culture and how the Chicano had related to Anglo society. For example:

Claudia, 17-year-old daughter of a Los Angeles factory worker:

Nobody told me about separatism. I just figured separatism would be best because Chicanos have more in common with each other than with the Anglos and there has always been a conflict, so I thought it was best. I figured the best place to have a separate Chicano country would be in the Southwest where the Chicano culture is the strongest and people speak a lot of Spanish.

Hugo, 17-year-old son of an Albuquerque construction worker:

Well, I just thought separatism was the best answer to the conflict between Anglos and Chicanos; and, well, nobody has to think too much about where the country should be, 'cause it sort of is obvious that most of us Chicanos live in the Southwest, so like in terms of language and culture that's where it should be.

What is important here is that, in contrast with the other ideologies, information about Chicano nationalism does not depend on outside sources such as the school or the media; it emerges from what is already known about Chicano culture. Therefore, the cultural components shared by a particular ethnic group greatly facilitate nationalism because they provide a necessary awareness of the political and cultural distinctiveness of one ethnic group in relation to others.[13] Probably the most important of the cultural components is language. Language is important not only because it transmits information, but also because it has the power, as Doob has pointed out, to accept or reject foreign words and to make people "think in a particular way."[14] Language becomes so important that it comes to be personified. It is little wonder that issues surrounding language are usually at the forefront of any separatist demand for an independent nation.[15] The scope of any separatist, or nationalist, ideology is therefore broadened because it is based on what Isaacs has called "basic group identity."[16]

Finally, returning to Merelman's position that an ideology involves a set of ideas that (1) are in some way constrained (i.e., if one idea changes they all change), (2) set forth a statement of political preference, (3) are persistent over time, (4) are applicable globally and have logical consistencies, and (5) have activist directives;[17] it must be concluded that only 1 to 2 percent of the present sample of Chicano youth are pure, "ideal-type" ideologues, which is close to what generally has been accepted as the percentage of such ideologues in the population of the United States as a whole.[18] Despite this, 88 percent (915) were prepared to support an ideology on the basis of what they knew about it and about its relation to their present social condition.[19]

Determinants of Support for Political Attitudes

The last section concerned itself with what the youth sampled understood about the four political ideologies presented to them. The scope of their knowledge about these ideologies having been identified, this section discusses the ideologies with which these youth identify and the determinants of their support. At this point, some clarification is in order. As mentioned in the last section, whether the youth in the study understood the fundamentals of capitalism or not, they associated capitalism with the United States; for them, capitalism/liberal democracy and the American system were conceptually the same. Therefore, their positive or negative identification with capitalism should be understood as a positive or negative attitude toward the operation of the United States economic/political system. Thus the use of the concept "capitalism/liberal democracy" in this work is interchangeable with that of the concept of "the American political system."

As Table 3.1 clearly indicates, the youth in this study divided their identification between support for capitalism/liberal democracy and support for Chicano separatism/nationalism. Of the other two ideologies, socialism and communism, only socialism was given some support, all of it directly related to Chicano separatism. All of those respondents who supported socialism (fifty-four) also supported Chicano separatism. All these youth indicated that they wanted a separate Chicano country that was also socialist. The analysis that follows attempts to identify the determinants of the youth's support for the present system of capitalism and liberal democracy, as well as the determinants of their support of separatism.

Table 3.1
Summary Number of Youth Attitudes toward Capitalism/Liberal Democracy, Chicano Nationalism/Separatism, and Socialism

	Capitalism		Chicano Nationalism/ Separatism		Socialism	
	Positive Toward	Negative Toward	Positive Toward	Negative Toward	Positive Toward	Negative Toward
San Antonio						
0–4 Years						
in City	36	7	7	36	7	36
Lower Class	26	7	7	26	7	26
Middle Class	10	0	0	10	0	10
5–9 Years						
in City	71	18	13	77	4	85
Lower Class	40	7	5	42	3	44
Middle Class	31	11	8	35	1	41
10 or More						
Years in City	160	39	30	168	8	191
Lower Class	73	21	17	77	5	89
Middle Class	87	18	13	91	3	102
TOTALS	267	64	50	281	19	312
Albuquerque						
0–4 Years						
in City	24	35	33	26	13	46
Lower Class	19	22	30	11	12	29
Middle Class	5	13	3	15	1	17
5–9 Years						
in City	51	42	36	57	4	89
Lower Class	19	30	29	20	2	47
Middle Class	32	12	7	37	2	42
10 or More						
Years in City	97	62	25	134	4	155
Lower Class	17	39	19	37	3	53
Middle Class	80	23	6	97	1	102
TOTALS	172	139	94	217	21	290
Los Angeles						
0–4 Years						
in City	62	23	18	67	3	82
Lower Class	42	19	16	45	3	58
Middle Class	20	4	2	22	0	24

Table 3.1 (continued)

	Capitalism		Chicano Nationalism/ Separatism		Socialism	
	Positive Toward	Negative Toward	Positive Toward	Negative Toward	Positive Toward	Negative Toward
5–9 Years in City	56	36	38	54	0	92
Lower Class	22	19	23	18	0	41
Middle Class	34	17	15	36	0	51
10 or More Years in City	54	97	85	66	15	136
Lower Class	11	49	53	7	9	51
Middle Class	43	48	32	59	6	85
TOTALS	172	156	141	187	18	310

Note: The numbers in this table are derived from the semantic differential raw scores. Those who were positive toward an ideology (i.e., those who scored the concept 1, 2, or 3) were included in the positive category, while those who scored the concept 5, 6, or 7 were included in the negative category. It should be noted that there is a space (labelled "4") for respondents to check if they do not care one way or the other, but no one checked this category. Neither did any of the respondents check the box provided for anyone who did not know what a particular concept was. Therefore every respondent is accounted for in this table. For a description of how social class standing was assigned, refer to Table 2.1.

First, it must be determined whether the urban environment, particularly the urban ecological environment, is an important factor, as hypothesized by Wirth, in influencing Chicano youth to identify with the United States' system or with Chicano nationalism.[20] The data for San Antonio indicate that the urban environment has no direct effects on support for capitalism/liberal democracy (which the youth perceive as the present U.S. system) that are statistically significant (see Figure 3.2). It is safe to assume that in San Antonio the urban ecological environment, involving length of time in city, neighborhood density, and neighborhood heterogeneity does not play a major role in influencing the views of the youth with regard to capitalism/the present U.S. system. Any impact that can be determined is mediated completely by socioeconomic status, a relationship which will be discussed next.

FIGURE 3.2
Path Model of the Effects in San Antonio of Urban
Contextual Variables and Personal Variables on Student
Attitudes Toward Capitalism*

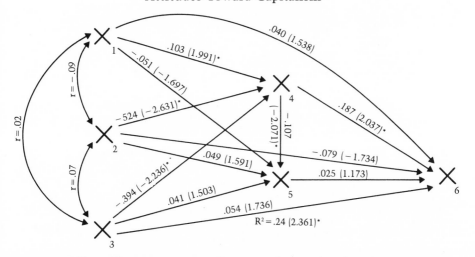

* = All coefficients are significant at the .05 level or beyond on
a two-tailed "t" test
X_1 = Length of residence in the city
X_2 = Population density in neighborhood
X_3 = Ethnic homogeneity in respondent's neighborhood
X_4 = Socioeconomic status
X_5 = Traditional cultural values (retention of)
X_6 = Support for capitalism

However, in Albuquerque and Los Angeles, various aspects of the
urban ecological environment do produce negative feelings toward
capitalism/the present U.S. system. For example, in Los Angeles the
youth who have lived in the city longer are more negative toward
capitalism than are the residents who have arrived more recently
(see Figure 3.3, P_{61} = − .336; also consult Table 3.1 for the raw numbers). This finding can be attributed to two factors. First, there is
optimism among recent migrants because their hopes for a better
future are tied to the continuance of the system. Second, the frustrations felt by many of the long-term residents with regard to various aspects of city life seem to increase the longer they reside in
the city. For example, many of the interviewees in Los Angeles said

FIGURE 3.3
Path Model of the Effects in Los Angeles of Urban Contextual Variables and Personal Variables on Student Attitudes Toward Capitalism*

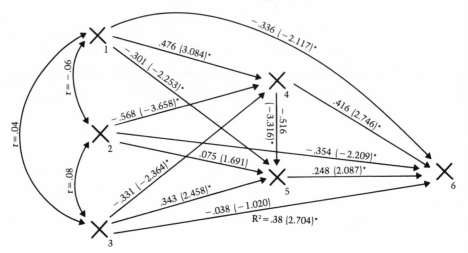

* = All coefficients are significant at the .05 level or beyond on a two-tailed "t" test

X_1 = Length of residence in the city
X_2 = Population destiny in neighborhood
X_3 = Ethnic homogeneity in respondent's neighborhood
X_4 = Socioeconomic status
X_5 = Traditional cultural values (retention of)
X_6 = Support for capitalism

that they were tired of air pollution, of having to fight crowds every time they wanted to go anywhere, of having to tolerate the city's inadequate transportation system, etc. The youth conceivably might have taken a position that was simply negative toward Los Angeles. Instead, they blamed their frustrations with the city on the entire American system.

Alex, 18-year-old son of an auto mechanic:

This city is a drag to live in, with pollution and all the people and cars, and if you are Chicano and poor you have it worse, 'cause the living conditions are worse. The problem with this city is the whole system is terrible, and I don't mean just in Los Angeles, it's the whole country, the whole system, 'cause there are the same problems for minorities and the poor in every city. The system is just set up in a way to make conditions worse for minorities like Chicanos and blacks.

The length of urban residence in Albuquerque has had an impact on the youth's attitudes toward capitalism/liberal democracy. The longer these youth have lived in the city, the more positive they have become with regard to the system. This is a result of the fact that most of the recent immigrants to the city of Albuquerque have come from the northern part of the state, where economic strain has forced many to give up their traditional occupations as small ranchers and move to the city. Many of these same immigrants have fought what was happening to them and have become political, directing their frustration and hostility toward the system, which they perceive to be Anglo-oriented. Thus, many of them have come to Albuquerque quite hostile politically toward the American system, but the longer they have lived in Albuquerque the more their hostility has subsided and the stronger supporters they have become of the system. Of course, the overwhelming majority of these migrants have been able to secure jobs within the Albuquerque economy.

Unlike the differing effects of length of residence on support for capitalism, the ethnic composition of the neighborhood has had a consistent effect on whether these youth support capitalism (the present system) or not. The youth who live in neighborhoods with higher percentages of Chicanos are more negative toward capitalism than those who live in ethnically heterogeneous neighborhoods (Fig. 3.4, $P_{63} = -.176$). This may be considered to be a function of the fact that the majority of the youth who live in predominantly Chicano communities are from lower SES families, and the lower SES youth, in general, are more negative toward capitalism. Certainly, this is a significant factor, but it is neither the only nor the most important explanation of this relationship. Of equal importance are feelings of group discrimination. The youth who live in these predominantly Chicano areas feel that the dominant Anglo society rejects them and their culture and, because of this, discriminates against them. There is a tendency among these youth to associate capitalism with Anglo dominance and, therefore, to react negatively toward it. They

FIGURE 3.4
Path Model of the Effects in Albuquerque of Urban
Contextual Variables and Personal Variables on
Student Attitudes Toward Capitalism*

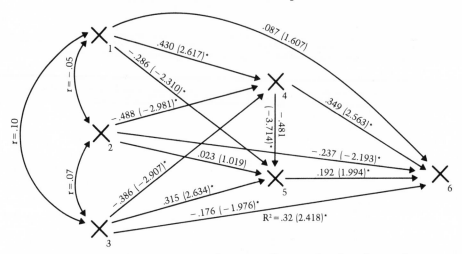

* = All coefficients are significant at the .05 level or beyond on
a two-tailed "t" test
X_1 = Length of residence in the city
X_2 = Population density in neighborhood
X_3 = Ethnic homogeneity in respondent's neighborhood
X_4 = Socioeconomic status
X_5 = Traditional cultural values (retention of)
X_6 = Support for capitalism

view the problems that capitalism has created for them in terms of
a culture conflict, rather than one that involves primarily class antagonisms. Thus, the ethnic neighborhoods tend to reinforce in-
group/out-group perceptions, serving to intensify discontent regarding ethnic inequality and the political/economic system's inability
to correct this problem adequately.[21]

The one urban variable in both Los Angeles and Albuquerque that
uniformly affects the youth's attitudes toward capitalism is the population density in their neighborhoods (Fig. 3.3, P_{62} = −.354; Fig. 3.4,
P_{62} = −.237). In both of these cities, there is a sense of frustration
among the youth regarding what they describe as the social condition
of their neighborhoods. Their complaints include poor housing, in-

adequate services for the community, high crime, and strained police/community relations. These complaints are translated into negative feelings toward capitalism because they believe that it is this system which has either created their undesirable living conditions or failed to correct them.[22]

Catrina, 18-year-old daughter of an Albuquerque construction worker:

Look at the conditions in this section of town; would you say a system that lets this happen is good? I wouldn't. The bad houses and high crime and then we get bad services, too. I don't think I could say this is a good system in this country.

The number of people from these areas who are negative toward the American system is 127.[23] Although this is not an overwhelming number, neither is it insignificant. It represents almost 20 percent of the combined Los Angeles and Albuquerque sample. It should be noted that this is one group of Chicanos who support Chicano separatism.

It also must be emphasized that the negative attitudes toward capitalism expressed by these youth are independent of socioeconomic status. The middle-class youth who live in high-density neighborhoods are equally frustrated with the social conditions which they confront. They, too, are exasperated by the political system's efforts to ameliorate the problems in these high-density areas. Frustration with the social conditions of the neighborhood and the system's performance with regard to these conditions are not the only causes of the middle class youth's negative attitudes toward capitalism. The fact that their primary social contact is with lower-class youth who are extremely negative toward the system, for reasons other than those associated with living in a high-density area, is undoubtedly a contributing factor.

Insight into this problem was provided by a young male from a middle-income family who lives in a single-family house directly across from a large housing project in Los Angeles:

Q: How did you score capitalism?
A: Low [negative].
Q: Why?
A: Because the conditions in this community are real bad
    and nothing is done to make them better. I don't think

the system works for everybody. It only works if you
have a lot of money and live in a nice neighborhood.

Q: Were your negative feelings toward capitalism influenced
by anyone?

A: Well, I wouldn't say I was influenced by anybody, but me
and my friends talk about politics a lot, especially the
things that concern Chicanos and this community. And
we all agree that the system doesn't work.

Q: Where do most of these friends whom you discuss these
problems with live?

A: Most live in —— [deleted to protect anonymity].

Q: The housing project?

A: Yes.

Q: Why don't you think the system works?

A: Well, if you look at the way Chicanos and other
minorities live. You know, like my friends who live in
—— [the housing project]. I go to their houses and
it's nothing inside. The places are clean as you can get,
but there are too many people for the places. My
friends' families try to move, but nobody can find a job
to pay enough. Then the Anglo looks at you and puts
you down for being a poor Mexican. Hey, this system is
no good, man.

Thus, to middle-class youth who live in these densely populated
neighborhoods, social interaction with more disadvantaged Chicanos is an important factor in their dissatisfaction with capitalism.[24]

One of the most important factors influencing the youth of these
high density areas to be negative toward capitalism is police/com-
munity relations. In both Los Angeles and Albuquerque, the police
were given extremely negative evaluations, as can be seen in Table
3.2. Furthermore, 94 percent (119) of the youth interviewed from
these high-density areas mentioned the police when asked what they
disliked about the capitalist system. The most common complaint
against the police was that they were prejudiced and therefore harassed Chicanos and blacks. The respondents cited the fact that the
police used more physical force on the residents in their areas than
they used on the residents of more wealthy, "white" neighborhoods.
They mentioned that the police were patrolling their neighborhoods
constantly, but when needed for something such as burglary, they
did not come for hours. To these Chicanos, the police were simply
a harassment.[25]

Table 3.2
Semantic Differential Mean Scores for the Evaluation of
the Police, Controlling for Socioeconomic Status
and City of Residence

	Lower Class	Middle Class
San Antonio	3.62 (182)	2.98 (149)
Albuquerque	5.58 (159)	3.22 (152)
Los Angeles	6.01 (173)	5.37 (155)

Note: Scores should be interpreted as positive when they are from 1–3.50; neutral when they are from 3.51–4.50; and negative when they are 4.51–7.00.

Joaquín, 17-year-old son of a hotel worker:

The police are terrible. They just try to keep Chicanos down; they don't help. If you need something, they are never around. They only are around to bother you if you are Chicano. They only support the rich and the Anglos.

In Los Angeles, the charges of harassment leveled against the police were sharper than in Albuquerque. This is due to the general police practice of enforcing the juvenile curfew law. The police routinely stop youths on the street after ten o'clock, and sometimes ask for identification. Very often, they will search individuals for possible drugs or weapons. Generally, the police in these areas behave in a manner described by Wilson as a "legalistic style":

A legalistic department will issue traffic tickets at a high rate, detain and arrest a high proportion of juvenile offenders, act vigorously against illicit enterprises, and make a large number of misdemeanor arrests even when, as with petty larceny, the public order has not been breached. They will act on the whole, as if there were a single standard of community conduct—that which the law prescribes—rather than different standards for juveniles, Negroes, drunks and the like.[26]

Thus, the police enforce the curfew to keep juveniles off the street and control the various youth gangs that form in most of these areas. The "stop and frisk" procedure is an extension of the general policy of gang control, aimed at cutting down on the number of illegal weapons circulating within the gangs.

In practice, the tactics of the police have served to alienate Chicano youth of both sexes. Fifty-one percent (thirty-one) of the young
women from the high-density areas report that they have been searched
by police, and 85 percent (fifty-seven) of the young men report the
same. The most bitter feelings toward the police are held by youths
who have been stopped while they were on a date. They felt that it
was belittling to be stopped and, in most cases, felt that their sense
of honor had been offended. To them, the police were merely trying
to antagonize them personally. Such contact with the police has
caused these young people to be negative toward the overall sociopolitical system. They believe that the police represent efforts by
the Anglo community to maintain the status quo by controlling
them.

Gustavo, 18-year-old son of a bus driver in Los Angeles:

You know the police will pick you up and frisk [search] you
at any time. They did that to me while I was on a date. It
was really belittling what those pigs [the police] will do. Let
me tell you, the police want to keep the Chicano in his place
so the Anglo can stay on top. We need to change the system
that keeps the Anglo on top.

If the urban environment has a negative impact on support for
capitalism, at least in Albuquerque and Los Angeles, does it affect
the young people's evaluations of socialism, or of nationalism? Do
the frustrations associated with urban living influence the youth
not only to reject capitalism, but to identify with one of these other
ideologies?

There is no evidence in any of the three cities that the urban
environment affects the youth's evaluation of socialism. All of the
coefficients in the path model approach zero, and the information
from the interviews also indicates no impact. Thus, the findings of
this study are similar to those of the studies of urban squatters in
the Third World, in that any negative effects that the urban environment has on support for the existing political system do not lead
automatically to support for socialist or communist ideologies.[27]

However, the urban environment does affect the youth's evaluations of nationalism, although this was found to be true within the
scope of this study only in Albuquerque and Los Angeles. The urban
ecological environment had no impact on the attitudes of San Antonio youth towards nationalism (see Figure 3.5), just as it had no

FIGURE 3.5
Path Model of the Effects in San Antonio of Urban
Contextual Variables and Personal Variables on Student
Attitudes Toward Chicano Nationalism (Separatism)*

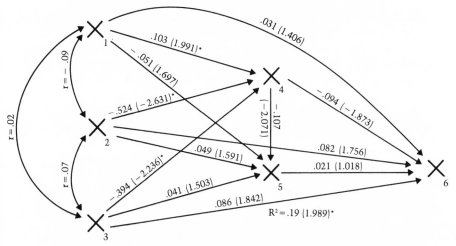

* = All coefficients are significant at the .05 level or beyond on a two-tailed "t" test
X_1 = Length of residence in the city
X_2 = Population density in neighborhood
X_3 = Ethnic homogeneity in respondent's neighborhood
X_4 = Socioeconomic status
X_5 = Traditional cultural values (retention of)
X_6 = Support for Chicano nationalism (separatism)

impact on their attitudes toward capitalism. This is not surprising, since the urbanism present in San Antonio, as we found in Chapter 2, is not like that envisioned by Wirth. What we do find is that the youth of San Antonio, as is evident from the data in Table 3.1, overwhelmingly support capitalism/liberal democracy and are negative toward any ideologies that present a challenge to the system in the U.S. Thus, as the data in the prior section of this chapter indicated, it is the conservative political environment of San Antonio, nurtured by the city's socioeconomic structure, that has the most influence on the youth's attitude toward political ideologies.

In contrast to San Antonio, the urban environments of Albuquerque and Los Angeles did affect the youth's attitudes toward nationalism. First, the length of time they lived in the city affected their evaluations of nationalism. However, the effects were opposite for each city. In Los Angeles, the longer the youth had been a resident, the more positive he/she had become about Chicano separatism (Fig. 3.6, P_{61} = .325; also see Table 3.1 for the raw numbers). In the case of Los Angeles, many of the same factors that produced negative feelings toward capitalism were associated with support of Chicano nationalism, especially the sense of being ethnically discriminated against by the dominant society. The longer their residence in the city, the more contact the respondents reported having had with various forms of discrimination. This sense of out-group discrimination is clearly a critical factor leading to support for a separate Chicano country. It seems to have provided the impetus for these youth to begin to identify more strongly with their own ethnic group rather than with the larger society.[28] Furthermore, it has intensified their negative feelings about other aspects of the city. For example, many respondents thought that they would not have had to endure heavy air pollution, bad housing, or poor services if it were not for the fact that they were prohibited, because of Anglo discrimination, from moving to better areas of metropolitan Los Angeles. There is, of course, discrimination in rural areas, and most of the Chicano youths in the study reported that they had experienced it there as well. Thus, the question of why discrimination is such an important factor in encouraging nationalistic feelings remains.

The answer may be found in the expectations that these youth have for their futures. Varying degrees of optimism exist among these young people from Los Angeles concerning their prospects for obtaining a good job and having the luxuries enjoyed by the Anglo society. The most optimistic are those who have migrated recently to the city. They view the city as a place of unlimited opportunity, and believe that through hard work they will be successful. Perceived obstacles such as discrimination, coupled with setbacks in attaining the material rewards desired, have led those with longer experience in the city to believe that their needs could be satisfied better in a separate Chicano nation, where there would be no cultural antagonisms and where the opportunities for attaining socioeconomic wellbeing would be greater.

In Albuquerque, nationalism also is affected by length of urban residence, but here longer urban residence produces negative attitudes toward a separate Chicano country (Fig. 3.7, P_{61} = - .201; also see Table 3.1 for the raw numbers). The explanation of this finding

FIGURE 3.6
Path Model of the Effect in Los Angeles of Urban
Contextual Variables and Personal Variables on Student
Attitudes Toward Chicano Nationalism (Separatism)*

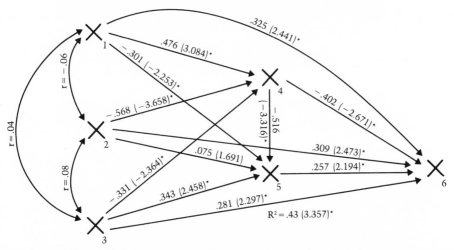

```
* =     All coefficients are significant at the .05 level or beyond on
        a two-tailed "t" test
X₁ =    Length of residence in the city
X₂ =    Population density in neighborhood
X₃ =    Ethnic homogeneity in respondent's neighborhood
X₄ =    Socioeconomic status
X₅ =    Traditional cultural values (retention of)
X₆ =    Support for Chicano nationalism (separatism)
```

$X_1 =$ Length of residence in the city

$X_2 =$ Population density in neighborhood

$X_3 =$ Ethnic homogeneity in respondent's neighborhood

$X_4 =$ Socioeconomic status

$X_5 =$ Traditional cultural values (retention of)

$X_6 =$ Support for Chicano nationalism (separatism)

involves the political orientation of recent migrants from the northern part of New Mexico, who have come to Albuquerque highly politicized and very nationalistic. For the most part, their politicization has been caused by the continuing decline of the area's economy because of the changing pattern of ranching there. The area's economic problems derive from the fact that a growing number of small Chicano ranchers have found it impossible to stay in business because of the constantly shrinking amount of land available to them for grazing. The origins of this scarcity of grazing land are complex, but, for the most part, the problem dates back to the Spanish/Mexican land grants and the question of who owns the land.[29] As more of the small ranchers have been forced to quit ranching, the econ-

FIGURE 3.7
Path Model of the Effects in Albuquerque of Urban Contextual
Variables and Personal Variables on Student Attitudes
Toward Chicano Nationalism (Separatism)*

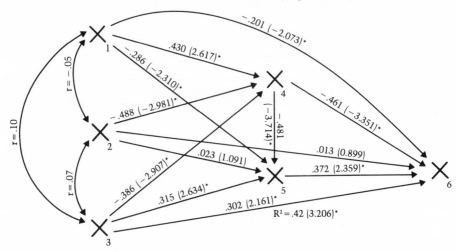

* = All coefficients are significant at the .05 level or beyond on
      a two-tailed "t" test
X_1 = Length of residence in the city
X_2 = Population density in neighborhood
X_3 = Ethnic homogeneity in respondent's neighborhood
X_4 = Socioeconomic status
X_5 = Traditional cultural values (retention of)
X_6 = Support for chicano nationalism (separatism)

omies of the small villages and towns of the region that supplied
services and equipment for the ranchers have also declined, com-
pounding the area's economic problems and forcing many of the
residents of these towns and villages to move to the city. Most of
the Chicanos involved in this process of change view the problem
as one of Anglo vs. Chicano, because in most cases their land either
has been bought by Anglo ranchers or has been taken over by the
federal or state government as forest land.[30]

Numerous political groups have emerged seeking to regain the
land that most Chicanos feel was taken from them unjustly. The
best known was the *Alianza Federal de Mercedes* (The Federal Al-
liance of Land Grants), led by Reies Lopez Tijerina, a folk hero who

led an armed raid on a courthouse in Tierra Amarilla, New Mexico.[31] The Alianza's efforts in the courts to win back the disputed land have been unsuccessful for the most part, although some cases are still pending. Other organizations that emerged during this struggle were even more militant in their separatist position. Thus, many of the youth who have migrated to Albuquerque from the northern part of the state not only have been introduced to separatist, or nationalist, ideology, but have participated in political organizations that espoused this ideology. It was not surprising, therefore, that 89 percent (forty) of the recent migrants from the north were strong supporters of separatism. In contrast, migrants to Albuquerque from other areas of the state, and also from Texas, who had lived in the city for the same length of time were negative toward separatism.

As the coefficient in the path model indicates, however, the longer their residence in Albuquerque, the less supportive the youth were of separatism. The issues that were important in producing separatist sentiments in the villages of northern New Mexico are simply not as salient in Albuquerque, and as these migrants have become more integrated into Albuquerque society, separatist ideology has had less meaning. What is particularly interesting about this finding, as well as the one in Los Angeles that length of time in the city produces more anti-system attitudes, is that they provide examples of the two dynamics that Wirth has hypothesized about the city. One is that the city, through its disorganizing effect, causes anomie and a propensity in individuals to seek shelter in an anti-system ideology. The other is that the city has an integrating effect, assimilating individuals into the general social framework, as in the case of Albuquerque. The longer the Chicano youth in this study have lived in Albuquerque, the more positively they have identified with the ideology governing the system.

Only in Los Angeles does the degree of population density in the youth's immediate neighborhood affect evaluations of separatism. The effects there are positive (Figure 3.6, $P_{62} = .309$), indicating, as noted earlier, that it is in the more densely populated areas that support for separatism is greatest. The support for separatism in these areas is a result of disillusionment with the general living conditions in the neighborhood, including high crime, poor housing, and inadequate services, and frustration with the political system's inability to take positive steps to correct the situation. What seems particularly disturbing to these youth is their belief that the system does not lack the capabilities to correct the situation, but that it refuses to do so because the people who control it are prejudiced against Chicanos. Eighty-five percent (fifty-seven) of the youth interviewed in Los Angeles believe that Chicanos are given the least opportunity for advancement—even less than blacks. In fact, intense rivalries have developed between blacks and Chicanos, especially those who live in the housing projects. These rivalries have generated antagonisms that have served to strengthen feelings of separatism. Some Chicanos clearly believe that what is needed to relieve the tensions associated with their contact with two antagonistic groups (blacks and Anglos) is isolation from them, and that the best way to achieve that is through the formation of a separate Chicano country.[32]

Guillermo, 18-year-old son of a Los Angeles painter:

Yes, I think separatism is necessary and I support those who want it. Take the blacks, we are always fighting with each other—I get into fights all the time; and the Anglos, they never liked us, so the only way for us Chicanos to live in peace is to separate.

Another factor that contributes to separatist attitudes in the more densely populated neighborhoods of Los Angeles is the police. The youth seem keenly aware of the fact that most of the police are Anglos, and 73 percent (sixty-nine, or 21 percent of the total sample) report that the police with whom they have had contact have been insensitive and heavy-handed with them. When asked if Chicano patrol officers were any different, 76 percent (seventy-three, or 22 percent of the total sample) said that there was a slight difference. Chicano patrol officers were described as being more polite, but also willing to harass them in the same ways. There is a slight difference between male and female adolescents in their attitudes toward Chicano police officers. The young women from densely populated neighborhoods tended to give the Chicano police the benefit of the doubt, saying that they were a little better than the Anglos or that they were only following orders.

Rosa, 18-year-old daughter of a food processing worker:

The Chicano police are a little better than the Anglos; they are not as disrespectful. . . . When they do something bad it is usually because they are following orders—or that is what they say, and I believe them.

On the other hand, the young men were overwhelmingly critical of the Chicano police, saying that they did the dirty work for the Anglos and that they were "sellouts." These negative feelings about the police, which help to produce negative attitudes toward capitalism (the system), are also instrumental in reinforcing political separatist feelings.

Richard, 17-year-old son of a clothing worker:

Hey, I hate the LAPD [police] and I hate the whole system they represent, I mean the whole system. The system that has police to control Chicanos is the system we got and that's why I support Chicano separatism.

In Albuquerque, population density had no effect on the youth's evaluations of separatism, although it was associated with a negative opinion of capitalism. The problems faced by the youth who lived in densely populated neighborhoods were not critical enough to make them turn to separatism as an answer. They were much more reform-oriented than were their Los Angeles counterparts. Most believed that the present system could be changed sufficiently so that many of the problems that plagued them would be solved. Two factors seem to differentiate the youth from densely populated neighborhoods in Albuquerque from those in similar neighborhoods in Los Angeles. First, the environmental characteristics of a high-density area are different in the two cities. In Los Angeles, the degree of density is much greater than that in Albuquerque, and the housing patterns are quite different. In Albuquerque, high-density neighborhoods are composed of small, single-family homes. There are fewer public housing projects, and each project has fewer units than those in Los Angeles. Second, the problems associated with these neighborhoods are sufficiently different, if not in kind, then certainly in degree, to cause a different response toward separatism. For example, in Albuquerque, services are not as good in high-density neighborhoods as they are in other areas, and crime is higher, but neither of these problems reaches the level that they do in Los Angeles. Also, among the Albuquerque youth, experiences with the police have been different. Police do have a reputation for being unduly harsh, especially with Chicanos and American Indians. But the prevalent attitude is that if one stays out of trouble, one will not have a problem with the police. It is true that the police are constantly patrolling high-density areas populated predominantly by ethnic minorities, but rarely do they stop youths just to check their identification or to send them home because it is after curfew. Only 8 percent (twenty-five) of the youth interviewed in Albuquerque said that they had been harassed by the police.

In addition, the relationship between black residents of these neighborhoods and Chicanos is different for Los Angeles and Albuquerque. There simply is not as much antagonism between the two groups in Albuquerque as there is in Los Angeles. To be accurate, there is prejudice toward blacks among the Chicano youth of Albuquerque, but the Chicano youth in these neighborhoods do not view the blacks as threats, as they do in Los Angeles. This may be due to the fact that blacks have constituted a very small percentage of the Albuquerque population as compared to Chicanos. This lack of black/Chicano conflict has served to minimize the feeling among Albuquerque Chicanos that a separate Chicano country is needed to alleviate ethnic tensions.

The last element of the urban environment to have an effect on support for separatism is the ethnic composition of the neighborhood. In both Los Angeles and Albuquerque, there is strong support for separatism from youth who live in neighborhoods that are predominantly Chicano (Fig. 3.6, $P_{63} = .281$; Fig. 3.7, $P_{63} = .302$). Similar reasons were identified for this result. First, it is in these communities that the symbols of ethnic culture are the strongest, which tends to reinforce ethnic identity and lay a foundation for nationalist sentiment. Secondly, organizations intent on developing a political following based on nationalist principles are more active in these neighborhoods; thus, the exposure to separatist ideology is greater. In addition, the existence of these organizations provides the youth who have separatist sympathies with the opportunity to feel less politically isolated.[33] Lastly, the youth who live in more ethnically homogeneous neighborhoods have less contact with the Anglo community, which makes the ideology of political separation less of a radical divergence from their everyday lives than it would be for those who live in more integrated neighborhoods. Acceptance of separatism, therefore, is contingent only on whether the ideology is consistent with the youth's political goals. On the other hand, those youth who live in more integrated neighborhoods experience much more difficulty in dealing with what they project that life would be like for them in a separate Chicano country. This clearly represents a life style considerably different from their present one, and causes a great deal of uncertainty, which increases their skepticism toward separatism as a viable alternative.[34]

Bob, 18-year-old son of a Los Angeles mail carrier:

I really don't like the way Anglo society has treated Chicanos and kept them poor, but separatism is too radical for me. I don't know why, but separatism just seems difficult for me to accept; I don't know, maybe it's 'cause it would be so different from the way I live now, I don't know.

Socioeconomic Status and Ideological Support

In the last section, it was demonstrated that conditions within the urban environment have a significant impact on the ideology which the youth from Albuquerque and Los Angeles support, although they do not have an effect in the case of San Antonio. Other factors have an important impact as well. This section will discuss one such variable, socioeconomic status. Although the discussion here will concentrate only on the direct effects of these variables in Albuquerque and Los Angeles, although not true in San Antonio, each of the urban variables in the model indirectly affects the ideological orientation of the youth through its impact on socioeconomic status as well as on the retention of traditional culture, which will be examined in the next section.

Support for capitalism is affected by the youth's SES in all three cities. In Los Angeles and Albuquerque, the effects of social class background are quite strong. As expected, the degree to which the youth identify with the present capitalist/liberal democratic system in the United States depends on their socioeconomic status. The higher the socioeconomic status, the greater the degree of identification with the system (see Fig. 3.3, $P_{64} = .416$; Fig. 3.4, $P_{64} = .349$). Middle class youth see capitalism as providing opportunities not only for themselves, but for the entire Chicano population. They believe that any inequalities that do exist can be remedied best by working within the capitalist system. These youth are quite happy with their class position and with the political system responsible for it.

Francesca, 18-year-old daughter of a Los Angeles lawyer:

I know the system has been difficult for Chicanos to get
ahead in, but what is needed is for Chicanos to continue to
work hard to make it and slowly the system will change and
all Chicanos will be better off. To me, what the U.S. has is
the best system in the world.

Frazier's classic study on black Americans who had achieved high
socioeconomic status found that these individuals were also quite
positive toward the entire American political-economic system. Thus,
this study's findings for Chicanos of upper SES are not unique. They
seem to follow an established pattern.[35] However, the lower-class
youth in Albuquerque and Los Angeles, although not in San Antonio,
were, on the whole, more negative toward capitalism than were their
middle-class counterparts. Fifty-eight percent (178) of the youth from
lower SES families in both Los Angeles and Albuquerque stated that
capitalism did not give poor people an equal opportunity to make a
good living, and they included themselves in this category. The most
negative element within the lower class were those who had resided
in either city for eight years or more and who had not experienced
much socioeconomic mobility. They not only were disillusioned
with capitalism because their families had remained poor, but also
were disillusioned with regard to prospects for improving their socioeconomic status.

Marisa, 18-year-old daughter of an Albuquerque metal pipe
cleaner:

I don't think this system works very well, especially for
Chicanos. My family has worked very hard to try to improve
ourselves and have gotten nowhere. It only tells you that it is
not really a matter of if you work hard, but luck and who you
are. That's not a good system I can support.

Most of the respondents in this study were within five months of
entering the job market themselves, and the overwhelming majority
(83 percent, or 256, from both Los Angeles and Albuquerque) said
that they had no job prospects.[36]
Despite the predominance of negative feelings toward capitalism
among the lower classes in both cities, there was a segment of the
lower class in Los Angeles that did support capitalism as strongly
as did the middle class. This element comprised the lower-class
migrants who had arrived just recently. As mentioned earlier, they

came to the city with high expectations for a better life, and they tended to identify strongly with the existing system. However, the data clearly suggest that this optimism with regard to capitalism will continue only if the high expectations they have are satisfied and they achieve some socioeconomic mobility.

The effects of SES in San Antonio are slightly different from those found in Albuquerque and Los Angeles. Although the data do show a small positive effect (Fig. 3.2, $P_{64} = .187$), there are no major class cleavages concerning support for capitalism, as there were in the other two cities. An examination of the distribution of scores (see Table 3.1) indicates that capitalism receives positive scores in San Antonio regardless of SES. The only difference that does exist is in the degree to which the youth of different socioeconomic standings express positive opinions. Youth from lower SES families are inclined to be slightly less positive, but they are positive nonetheless. This occurs despite the fact that most of them are from extremely poor areas because San Antonio is a politically conservative place. Success in San Antonio is seen as a product of not resisting the system, but accommodating it. While the interviews revealed disappointment among the lower class respondents, there was still a resistance to thinking about the system in negative terms. The respondents seemed to be hopeful that things would change, although they saw no way to promote change without incurring negative sanctions from the Anglo community, and they were concerned about the consequences of such sanctions. The threat of physical violence concerned them, as did the threat of being prohibited from securing a good job.

Turning to the effects of SES on support for separatism, the study found that in both Los Angeles and Albuquerque (here again, there was no effect in San Antonio), Chicanos from upper SES families were more negative toward separatism, whole those from lower SES families were more positive. Upper SES Chicanos could see little advantage to separating from the United States since they had achieved a considerable amount of economic success. In point of fact, these middle-class Chicanos were adamantly opposed to separatism. They saw the concept of separatism and its supporters as personal threats, not so much because they believed that there was a possibility that separation would occur, but rather because they felt that support for separatism would create a backlash from the Anglo community, causing them and their families to be discriminated against and any socioeconomic gains they had made to be reversed.[37]

Victor, 17-year-old son of an Albuquerque businessman:

I hate those people who support separatism because they are
ruining it for all Chicanos. A lot of Anglos will now try to get
back at Chicanos and they will just not help all Chicanos.
My father worked hard to get where he is, and these [profane
name identifying the separatists] will ruin it for us and a lot
of other people.

More lower-class youth in both Albuquerque and Los Angeles supported separatism than did middle-class youth, although the lower-
class support in Los Angeles was slightly stronger. Separatism ap-
peals to the lower class in each of these cities because it represents
a system in which they will have more opportunity for a better life.
The prevailing attitude among these Chicanos is that they have not
been given the opportunities that the majority of American citizens
enjoy because of racial discrimination. These perceptions of racial
discrimination have affected them deeply, and they believe that separatism is the only answer because it will remove the principal factor
keeping them poor.[38]

Carmelita, 18-year-old daughter of a Los Angeles food
processing worker:

The system we live under here, capitalism, discriminates
against Chicanos so they can't get ahead. The Anglos only let
their own get ahead and a few from other groups. That's why
I don't like Anglos or their system and why I say we should
form our own country so we don't have to worry about
Anglos discriminating.

Within the lower class there are some variations with regard to
the degree of support for separatism. In Los Angeles, those who had
been in the city the longest were the most militant separatists, as
well as those who lived in housing projects or predominantly Chicano neighborhoods. Among the lower class in Albuquerque, the
most supportive of separatism were the recent arrivals from the
northern part of New Mexico, the same youth who were the most
negative toward capitalism.

The evidence presented thus far indicates that there are clear class
cleavages in both Albuquerque and Los Angeles between those who
identify with the existing capitalist system in the United States and
those who would like to alter it radically. Yet the lower-class Chi-

canos do not look upon their middle-class counterparts as political antagonists. Instead, it is the Anglos in the society who are considered not only their opponents, but the adversaries of Chicanos in general. Consequently, class consciousness does not exist; it has been submerged by an ethnic view of politics derived principally from the fact that clashes of interest have occurred along ethnic lines in the past. It is not surprising, therefore, that among these lower-class youth nationalism has emerged as the radical political ideology.[39]

The Relationship Between Ethnicity and Ideology

The degree to which the youth in this study have retained traditional Chicano culture is another important factor influencing their evaluations of capitalism, but only for those who live in Los Angeles and Albuquerque, as no relationship was found between the two for the youth in San Antonio. In the former two cities, the Chicanos who have retained traditional culture were more positive toward capitalism (Fig. 3.3, $P_{65} = .248$; Fig. 3.4, $P_{65} = .192$), although this relationship is rather weak. In order to understand more fully the support of capitalism, or the present system, in terms of this relationship, the indirect effects of SES and length of residence in the city must be considered. Those respondents who tended to support capitalism were generally from high SES families who had managed to retain traditional culture. For this group, nothing had been lost through the process of socioeconomic mobility, and they viewed the system as functioning quite well. One exception was in Los Angeles, where support also came from the sons and daughters of lower SES parents who were recent arrivals in the city because they hoped that capitalism would create a good life for them and their families in the future.

Chicanos from both middle and lower SES families were found to be negative toward capitalism for reasons associated with traditional culture. First, the middle-class youth who no longer retained much traditional culture, especially those from Los Angeles, were extremely negative toward capitalism, in terms of the way that the system was working in relation to their own lives. Their alienation from the system was associated with their struggle for personal identity. They did not possess many of the attributes, such as fluency in Spanish, that they considered important to Chicano identity; while

115

they identified themselves as being Chicanos, at the same time they felt inadequate. The blame for these feelings of inadequacy was directed at the entire system, which, they argued, had put immense pressure on their parents not to raise them in a traditional cultural milieu.

Kim, 18-year-old daughter of a small businessman:

I don't like the system we live under in this country and so I answered all the questions about capitalism in a negative way. The reason I don't like the system has to do with my parents and the fact that they did not teach us about our Chicano culture. They spoke Spanish and would not talk to us, so none of us know it. I am Chicano and proud of it, I only wish I had the language and things. I don't like the system because it pressured my parents not to teach us about our culture.

Thus, their alienation because of identity is quite similar to the alienation expressed by many of the white middle-class youth of the early 1960s–70s, as discussed in the works of Roszak and Kenniston;[40] they are struggling to establish an identity within a complex industrial society. The process of economic mobility creates two different effects simultaneously. As socioeconomic mobility occurs, it produces positive attitudes toward capitalism, or the system. On the other hand, socioeconomic mobility also tends to affect the retention of traditional culture negatively, and when the possession of traditional culture is considered important (and often it is not), it acts to produce negative feelings toward the system because of issues related to the establishment of a personal identity.[41]

Negative attitudes directed toward capitalism/the U.S. system caused by cultural alienation were also present among Chicanos from lower-class families. It was most prevalent among those who had lived in Los Angeles and Albuquerque for a considerable period of time, usually for their entire lives, and who had retained very little of their traditional culture. Many of these parents had tried to raise them in a non-traditional manner (which usually consisted of not speaking Spanish to them) in the hope that they would have a better opportunity to become upwardly mobile. Yet, for reasons associated with the parents' own inability to make socioeconomic gains, these youth found themselves still lower-class and without the benefit of possessing many of the traits associated with traditional culture. The result was an extreme hostility toward the system, which these youth believed had taken everything and given nothing.[42] This group of youth is most prevalent in Los Angeles, and is the same group that was identified as being culturally marginal in Chapter 2.

Lorenzo, 18-year-old son of a private sanitation company worker:

I hate this system we have in the United States, capitalism. It takes everything from you if you are Chicano. It takes your money, it takes your culture away from you, and it gives you nothing. I really hate it, I can't tell you how much I hate it. I'll tell you one thing, I won't do anything to help keep it going.

As one might expect, traditional culture is a major factor affecting attitudes toward separatism. In Los Angeles and Albuquerque, the Chicanos who have the most positive attitudes toward separatism are also those who have retained more of the traditional culture (Fig. 3.6, $P_{65} = .257$; Fig. 3.7, $P_{65} = .372$). Clearly, those less assimilated into the American system are much more at ease with the concept as a political alternative. Of course, SES has an impact here. Lower-class youth are more apt to retain traditional culture; therefore, support emerges from lower-class Chicanos who have maintained this culture. These Chicanos believe that their possession of traditional culture is what gives their personal identities definition. In many cases, it is all they have to be proud of. Fifty-six percent (170) of the lower class in both cities believe that Anglo society is actively attempting, through schools and other institutions, to take their traditional culture away from them. Consequently, culture has become a salient political issue, and, in the opinion of many of the respondents, separatism is the answer to these cultural intrusions.

Felipe, 17-year-old son of a Los Angeles gardener:

Anglo society is always trying to put you down because of your culture [Chicano]. They want you to speak English all the time and act like them. That is why the schools don't teach you about Chicano culture. If we had our own country we wouldn't have to fight to speak Spanish and we could act the way we want. Like we wouldn't have to protect our culture. It would just be easier to live. That's why we need to get our own country.

Maurilia, 17-year-old daughter of an Albuquerque night watchman:

I think if Chicanos had their own country it would be better for them 'cause they could live the way they want. Right now American society tries to take your culture away. They [the Anglo society] don't like us speaking Spanish and things, so I think we should be separate from them with our own country, then we can have our own culture.

On the other hand, middle-class Chicanos thought that maintenance of traditional culture was important, but they did not consider it important enough to become a political issue, and certainly not an issue over which to separate from the United States.

Charles, 17-year-old son of an Albuquerque realtor:

We should definitely keep our culture because it's important, but separatism is no good. I mean culture is not important enough to separate. If some Chicanos want to separate they should go to Mexico.

One of the more interesting findings concerning the retention of traditional culture and support for separatism is that the middle-class Chicanos in Los Angeles and Albuquerque who were negative toward capitalism (the U.S. system) because they felt deprived of their culture did not support separatism. These Chicanos were frustrated with the American system, but separatism seemed much too radical for them. They were inclined to believe that major reforms within the system were better than creating a new structure.[43]

Wilma, 18-year-old daughter of a Los Angeles insurance salesman:

I don't think to separate from the United States would be good. It's not that I don't think Chicano culture is important or anything, but I think we can still have our culture within the United States. Other nationalities do it, like the Jews and the Chinese.

Paul, 18-year-old son of a Los Angeles businessman:

I really think what the system does to Chicano culture is wrong, or what it does to other cultures too. I think there is something wrong with the system and it needs to be changed, but I don't believe separatism is the answer. It's just too radical for me. I think the system can be changed without going that far.

The importance of traditional culture in developing a political ideology is directly related to the youth's attitudes toward traditional culture. When youth see (1) traditional culture as a vital part of group identity, (2) their own identity associated with group identity, and (3) their own identity associated with the retention of cultural traits, then, in an ethnically diverse society, the social and psychological conditions exist for culture and its retention to make their way into the political arena. In this study, the net effect of the retention of traditional culture proved to be the production of generally critical attitudes toward the political system. Sometimes these attitudes engendered such a cynicism that they produced radical solutions to the problem of cultural retention, such as support for a separate Chicano country, a response analogous to that found among other ethnic groups who live in multiethnic countries throughout the world.[44]

Conclusion

Although the youth in each city cannot be considered ideologues, they do, in spite of everything else that is happening in their young adult lives, think about their relationship to the political system. In fact, they have developed a number of interrelated attitudes toward politics that present an idea of their political views. Basically, there are two views about politics in the United States, and these are: (1) that the present system in America (capitalism and liberal democracy) is working well, or at least well enough to identify with and be supportive of; or (2) that the system in the United States is not working well enough to identify with, and that a new political arrangement, in the form of a separate Chicano country, is necessary.

Whether the youth in this study had positive attitudes toward the system existing in the United States depended on their perceptions of what the future looked like for them. When the youth were living in physical comfort, and/or had a positive outlook with regard to their futures, and/or had a positive sense of their own identities (influenced by ethnic identity), then they had positive attitudes toward the system, identified with it, and supported it, in that they thought that it was the best political/economic system in the world. Conversely, if the youth were living in poor physical conditions, did not have an optimistic view of their future, or were not satisfied with who they were, then they displayed negative attitudes toward the American system and identified themselves with the political alternative of a separate Chicano country.

Whether the youth were happy, satisfied, or prepared to identify with an alternative political arrangement was influenced by the city in which they lived. Those who lived in San Antonio perceived the system to be working well and were very supportive of it. Their positive attitudes toward the system were predicated on the fact that they lived in a politically conservative environment, an environment that has had a history of conflict between Mexicans and Anglos and an Anglo community that has been ever vigilant for signs of Mexican identity becoming a political force. The youth understood the prevailing view of politics in San Antonio, and saw that this prevailing view was reinforced in the schools and the media. Thus, the youth were aware of the values of the area, and knew that these values were strongly entrenched and that they must accommodate them in some way. When the youth in San Antonio did express attitudes indicating that they were not happy with the way the system was operating, there was nearly always an accompanying attitude that, although the system was out of synchronization, it was only temporary, and all that was needed were some reforms and not any substantive changes in the structure. Thus, San Antonio presents an interesting paradox. It is the system most closed to Chicanos; even Chicanos perceive it to be extremely closed, and yet the Chicanos identify with and are the most supportive of (as compared to Los Angeles and Albuquerque) the political/economic arrangements. With regard to the issue of urbanism and its impact on political attitudes, the data from San Antonio do not support the hypotheses of Wirth and the Chicago school that urbanism and increased exposure to it will have an effect on people's attitudes toward ideologies. None of the urban ecological variables, such as the density of a person's neighborhood or the ethnic heterogeneity of the neighborhood, produced any effect on attitudes. What proved to be most influential in affecting the youth's attitudes was the political-economic character of San Antonio and the youth's perceptions of their position within the city.

On the other hand, the data on the youth in Los Angeles and Albuquerque present general support for the Wirth/Chicago school thesis that urbanism affects ideological attitudes. First, the urban ecological conditions of urban density/ethnic heterogeneity did have an influence on the youth's attitudes toward the political-economic system in the United States, as well as on their attitudes concerning the formation of a separate Chicano country. Second, the data provide interesting examples of what Wirth theorized would be the two possible effects of urbanism on ideological attitudes. In the case of Albuquerque, the longer the youth had lived in the city, the more they had become supportive of the U.S. system. Even when they came to the city with negative attitudes toward the system, in terms of not liking it and wanting to change it, longer residence tended to produce strong positive attitudes. This happened generally, but was accelerated when economic mobility accompanied longer residence. Essentially, the city worked as an integrating mechanism creating a consensus (in this case, support for the system), much as Wirth hypothesized it would. Albuquerque's socioeconomic and political environment has been able to do this because it can produce opportunities for economic mobility and convince the vast majority of its citizens that a better life is within their reach, and that there are no structural constraints that will either diminish or preclude their chances for mobility.

The data in the case of Los Angeles are even more supportive of Wirth's hypothesis that there would be less ideological consensus in cities where people were experiencing the disorganization accompanying the transition from traditional customs and culture associated with either a rural environment and/or a foreign country of origin to the new urban culture associated with American cities. Hence, the experience of living in Los Angeles for an increasingly longer period of time has had a politically integrating impact of producing general support for and identification with the U.S. system. However, living in Los Angeles for longer periods of time (generally longer than nine years) also has produced the opposite effect, an increasingly negative attitude toward the system and support for a separate Chicano country. This latter result has been observed in Los Angeles when sociocultural assimilation has not been accompanied by economic mobility and when economic mobility has occurred along with cultural assimilation, but personal identity (Who am I? Am I Mexican, Mexican American, or American?) has been left in a vacuum. It is this division along competing ideological lines that constitutes the other consequence of urbanism recognized by Wirth as a possible alternative effect.

In sum, the youth of San Antonio have an attitudinal consensus in their support of the U.S. system. In Albuquerque, there are cleavages within the sample between those who support the system and those who do not. Those who do not support the system are from the lower class and are recent migrants to the city, while those who support it are middle-class and have been in the city for a longer period of time. Lack of support for the system among the lower class in Albuquerque does not mean that these youth support a separate Chicano country. Here the lower class is divided between those who want a separate country and also are recent arrivals to Albuquerque, and those lower-class youth who have lived in Albuquerque more than six years and who are critical of the system, but do not support separatism. In essence, the data for the youth in Albuquerque emphasize the importance of social class background in influencing attitudes about the political system.

In Los Angeles there are also cleavages between those who support the present system and those who support a separate Chicano country. These cleavages are a result of social class and cultural issues engendered by living in Los Angeles. For the most part, the data on the Chicano youth in Los Angeles support the Wirthian notion that identification with, and therefore competition among, a multitude of ideologies will be most intense in cities where people are experiencing the social/psychological disorganization accompanying the transition from one set of cultural norms (traditional/rural) to another (urban/modern). Los Angeles urban society is so large and complex, so "mass-like" in character, that it has an impact on people's political attitudes, regardless of their social class standing. Thus it is that the Chicano youth in Los Angeles experiencing the greatest social disorganization are also the ones who have the strongest attitudes opposing the present American system and favoring separatism.[45]

4

Voting and
Political Parties
Articulating Interests
in the System

Every modern state, regardless
of its political structure, encourages its citizens to identify with the
nation as a whole, and to give allegiance to existing political structures and to the processes that govern them. The United States is
no exception to this, and many studies have attempted to determine
when political learning begins and to identify the specific agents
that are most important in this process.[1] Most of these studies have
concentrated on how young children and early adolescents relate to
the political system. There has been no concerted effort in the literature to date to study youth in the sixteen- to eighteen-year-old
age group.[2] The studies that have been done on this age group have
dealt primarily with white adolescents. These analyses, which have
attempted to incorporate non-white groups, usually have considered
only blacks, and then have generalized their findings to other minorities.[3] It is doubtless true that many of the agents, such as the
family, schools, peers, and media, that socialize and influence black
children and adolescents in the development of their political beliefs
also influence members of other minority groups. However, it is also
true that members of other minority groups, such as Chicanos, are
influenced by different agents as well. This becomes particularly
apparent when one considers the fact that Chicanos are only now
involved in the process of urbanization and are products of a different
historical experience within the United States.

The focus of this chapter is the way in which the Chicano youth
in this study, who form a part of the urbanization process, view their
participation in the formal structures of the American political system. In analyzing the youth's views of their participation in the
American political system, attention is focused on their attitudes

toward voting and on their choice of a political party. These two topics are an appropriate barometer of the way in which Chicano youth in this study relate to the American political system. Voting symbolizes mass citizen participation, and reflects the conviction that those elected to office are extensions of the responsible electorate of the United States. Political parties are important because they are the principal organizations toward which the vote is directed. In this respect, they ultimately serve to fill public offices, make policy, socialize people politically, and act as agents of nation building. In essence, they act to organize and run the government.[4]

It might be hypothesized that the Chicano youth in this study, as members of an ethnic group which has suffered discrimination at the hands of a powerful Anglo-American majority, would be apathetic toward voting.

In addition, it could be hypothesized that, because these Chicano youth are members of a socioeconomically deprived ethnic group living in cities, they are vulnerable to machine politics, and, like other urban ethnic groups who have gone through the process of socioeconomic and political assimilation, are willing to give up, or sell, their votes in return for economic and psychological security. Like other ethnic groups in American politics, these youth would be likely to view voting not as an exercise in civic responsibility, but as a resource to be bartered or simply given away.[5]

It also might be assumed that the youth in this study would be highly supportive of the Democratic Party, since this party has dominated politics in the southwestern United States and has a history of trying to recruit Chicanos into its ranks.[6] Yet, because these youth are products of different urban environments, it is equally possible that the interaction of social class standing with the divergent environmental conditions found in each city would influence these youth to have divergent views toward voting and to identify with different political parties.

Voting

Many studies on voting among minority groups in the United States have shown that voting is related to a sense of political efficacy and that feelings of political efficacy are related to a person's socioeconomic status.[7] The fact that Chicanos, as a group, have experienced a great deal of ethnic/racial discrimination and have found themselves, on the average, in a lower socioeconomic status than most other Americans (particularly white Americans), would suggest that their levels of political efficacy may be low and that they may not view voting as a politically meaningful act. Rather, they may feel alienated from the system and powerless to affect American politics, and thus may feel that voting is a useless act. In the present study, it might seem logical that the youth who have observed their parents' low sense of efficacy and feelings of alienation from the system would be inclined to see voting as a waste of time.[8]

It must be remembered that the youth in this study were all 12th grade students, required in each school system sampled to take a course in civics. Each of the civics courses was visited numerous times. In each of these courses, the teachers stated that the objective of the curriculum was to develop in the students a knowledge and appreciation of the American political system. The act of voting was singularly emphasized throughout the courses. The students were taught that adult citizens were given the right to vote and that it was every citizen's obligation to exercise that right. Given the emphasis on voting as an obligation, it could be hypothesized that the overwhelming majority of the youth would think of voting as part of their civic duty.[9] Thus the question is posed as to whether the youth in this study viewed voting, as previous attitude studies might suggest, as a useless act, or whether they viewed it positively as part of their civic duty.

The answer to this question is that, except for the middle-class youth in San Antonio, Chicano youth in general did not view voting either apathetically or as a part of their civic duty. Nearly all of the youth in each city sampled were positive toward voting. Yet this fact does not say anything about how they actually view voting.

The findings from Albuquerque and Los Angeles were approximately the same. Eighty percent (133) of the youth in these two cities expressed the initial belief that, as Chicanos, they were disadvantaged in comparison with white Americans, and that if they were to overcome this disadvantage, changes were necessary. One area where changes were considered crucial was among those who held political office. The youth reasoned that, if they could vote the candidates they wanted into office, they could effect those changes that had helped other ethnic groups to gain socioeconomic mobility. Two examples of this reasoning are as follows:

Isabel, 17-year-old daughter of a small Albuquerque store owner:

We Chicanos have to vote for people who will help us. I mean, if there are candidates who will help us, we will be given more opportunities to get ahead in life. I mean, look at other ethnic groups, they were able to do it that way—like the Irish and the Italians and the Jews. I could name a lot more. They were all part of groups that were discriminated against and they used politics to get a better life.

Jorge, 17-year-old son of a Los Angeles trucking firm clerk and a nurse:

Hey, Chicanos have to use the ballot to get some power so they can make some changes in those institutions that make it hard for us to get better paying jobs. If we vote correctly, we should be able to get the same high-paying jobs, you know, the ones where there is a lot of status, that the Irish or Jews or other ethnic groups have. After all, they got their jobs through playing politics, by getting all their people to vote a certain way.

However, despite the fact that the youth from Albuquerque and Los Angeles believed that voting could be a powerful tool, there were significant differences among youth from different socioeconomic backgrounds in the importance that they attached to voting. The data show (see Figures 4.1 and 4.2) that the longer a youth's family had been living in the city, the higher the family's socioeconomic status; and the higher the youth's socioeconomic status, the more useful he/she perceived voting to be.[10] This is what might have been expected, and if the evidence from both the questionnaire and the interviews is combined, the following trend is noted. A youth's family migrates to the city, usually in a socioeconomically disadvantaged condition. The longer the family lives in the city, the more economic opportunities become available, and, over time, the family becomes increasingly more mobile. As this occurs, family members become more confident that they can be successful, and gain an increasing sense of political efficacy. Thus, the youth from middle-

FIGURE 4.1
Path Model of the Effects in Albuquerque of Urban
Contextual Variables and Personal Variables on
Student Attitudes Toward Voting*

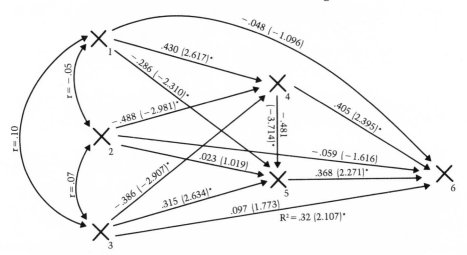

* = All coefficients are significant at the .05 level or beyond on
a two-tailed "t" test

X_1 = Length of residence in the city
X_2 = Population density in neighborhood
X_3 = Ethnic homogeneity in respondent's neighborhood
X_4 = Socioeconomic status
X_5 = Traditional cultural values (retention of)
X_6 = Attitude toward voting

class families thought that, by electing candidates who were in favor
of aiding Chicanos, they would be able to gain a higher socioeconomic status. Two examples of this pattern of thought are as follows:

Juan, 18-year-old son of an owner of a gardening business in
Los Angeles:

I think voting is very important. It can help Chicanos to get a
better chance to have a better life. You see, if we can change
some of the laws that have been used to hurt Chicanos, or if
we are able to pass some laws that would help Chicanos to be
in business or become professionals, like more aid to schools
and universities to train us, Chicanos will be able to have a

FIGURE 4.2
Path Model of the Effects in Los Angeles of Urban
Contextual Variables and Personal Variables on Student
Attitudes Toward Voting*

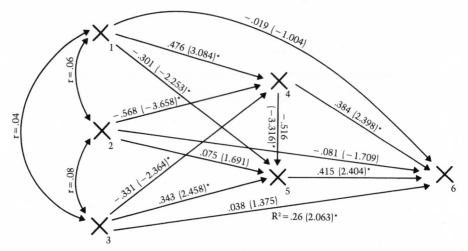

* = All coefficients are significant at the .05 level or beyond on
a two-tailed "t" test
X_1 = Length of residence in the city
X_2 = Population density in neighborhood
X_3 = Ethnic homogeneity in respondent's neighborhood
X_4 = Socioeconomic status
X_5 = Traditional cultural values (retention of)
X_6 = Attitude toward voting

better life. But you see, we have to get all the Chicanos to
vote for the candidate that will help us as a people.

Patricia, 17-year-old daughter of an agent for an insurance
company in Albuquerque:

I believe voting is really important. You see, Chicanos can
use the vote to help themselves. Like, for example, we can
look for candidates that will help change some of the laws or
see to it that we are not discriminated against, and we can
vote for that candidate. When candidates know we will do
this, they will want to be more helpful toward us. As we get
stronger in voting for one candidate or another, we will be

able to get a better education and better jobs. And better jobs is a better life.

There is an unanticipated and interesting secondary effect of socio-economic mobility on the evaluations of voting by the youth from Albuquerque and Los Angeles. The longer a youth's family has been in either of these cities, the more middle-class the family has tended to become, and the more middle-class the family, the less the extent to which traditional Chicano culture is a part of the youth's life (Figures 4.1 and 4.2, $P_{54,41}$). Thus, in Albuquerque and Los Angeles, socioeconomic mobility has had the effect of producing some youth who are assimilated into the dominant American culture. These youth do not speak Spanish, nor do they know or practice many of the customs associated with the traditional cultural institutions. Where mobility has occurred and the youth have been able to maintain cultural ties, and therefore identity, voting is seen as a very important tool for them to achieve their goals—goals they have identified in socioeconomic terms. However, where mobility has occurred and the youth have not maintained cultural ties, voting is not viewed as the most appropriate form of participation to address their interests—interests they have defined in terms of cultural identity.

Among this culturally alienated segment of the middle class in Albuquerque and Los Angeles, voting is considered less important than among those middle-class youth who have not been culturally assimilated. The interviews revealed that these youth are not negative toward voting but, in contrast to the other middle-class youth, they do not view voting as either the only or the most effective form of political participation to effect political change. Other forms, some of which were more violent in nature, are thought to be appropriate. To understand this result, one must look at the backgrounds of these youth. As a consequence of the families' socioeconomic mobility, these youth have enjoyed many of the material comforts of middle-class life—but they also have experienced cultural alienation. All of these youth express anxiety and anger over the fact that they did not know very much about their ethnic heritage. They expressed feelings that the system had deprived them of their culture. Most of these youth felt left out of both the Anglo and the Chicano cultures. They wanted to belong to the Chicano culture, but their feelings of inadequacy with regard to both language and Chicano customs inhibited them from achieving a sense of belonging. They were caught between two cultures and were struggling for personal identity. Most were aware that it was their parents who had neglected to teach them about their Chicano culture, but emotional attachment, as well as an understanding of their parents' motivations and constraints, led them to direct their frustrations at the system rather than at their parents. Two examples of this reasoning are as follows:

Andrés, 18-year-old son of an owner of a trucking company in Albuquerque:

My parents never spoke Spanish to me at home even though they would talk to each other in it; and they never taught me anything about my culture. They said they did it for me, because they wanted me to have a good life. . . . I don't blame them, though, 'cause they were only doing what the system forced them to do. That's why I don't like the system, 'cause it takes away our culture.

Gloria, 18-year-old daughter of an owner of a shoe store in Los Angeles:

The system, you know, like the school and everything, makes you speak English. They [the Anglo society] tell you that the Anglo way is the best, so everybody learns it. You know your parents don't teach you about your culture 'cause they are afraid you won't get a job. So I don't think the system is so good.

Thus, in the eyes of these youth who are culturally alienated, the American system not only should produce opportunities for socioeconomic mobility, but ought also to provide for the maintenance of ethnic culture and identity. The feeling that the system has failed them has influenced these respondents to see a need to participate in more ways than simply by voting. It was the opinion of 96 percent (eighty-one) of these youth that what was needed was more direct confrontation politics, such as protest activity. Voting was useful, but was not seen as a method that could change the system sufficiently to compensate for their lack of cultural identity. Only protest activity could do that.

Randy, 17-year-old son of a bank loan officer in Los Angeles:

Voting is important, but it is not the only important political act to get involved in. Protest stuff, like walkouts in school,

FIGURE 4.3
Path Model of the Effects in San Antonio of Urban
Contextual Variables and Personal Variables on Student
Attitudes Toward Voting*

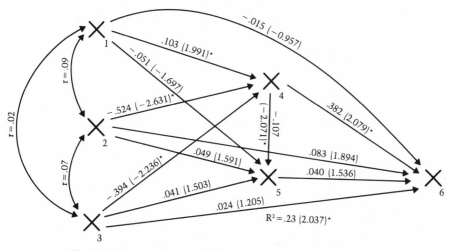

* = All coefficients are significant at the .05 level or beyond on
    a two-tailed "t" test
X_1 = Length of residence in the city
X_2 = Population density in neighborhood
X_3 = Ethnic homogeneity in respondent's neighborhood
X_4 = Socioeconomic status
X_5 = Traditional cultural values (retention of)
X_6 = Attitude toward voting

strikes, and sit-ins are more important to change things like
strengthening Chicano culture and language—things I want to
change. Because without protest the system won't change
enough to strengthen Chicano culture.

Margarita, 18-year-old daughter of a district court clerk and a
school teacher:

I think voting can be important to get some things, but I
don't think changes to help Chicanos keep their culture could
happen just by voting. I really believe the only way to get
these changes is to pressure the system through protest.
In San Antonio, social class standing is also a factor affecting

attitudes toward voting: the higher a particular youth's socioeconomic status, the more positive he/she is toward voting (see Fig. 4.3; P_{64}). Although this follows the general pattern established among the middle-class youth in Albuquerque and Los Angeles, with the exception being those who are culturally alienated, there is a difference between the middle-class youth of San Antonio and those of the other two cities with regard to the meaning they attach to voting. Whereas in Los Angeles and Albuquerque the middle-class youth see voting as a tool to bring about the social change necessary to improve their socioeconomic position, among the Chicano middle-class youth in San Antonio, voting is seen in the classic perspective as a citizen's civic duty. Middle-class San Antonio youth feel that voting is a part of a citizen's obligation, as in the following examples:

Enrique, 18-year-old son of an investment analyst for a bank:

Voting is important to keep democracy. I would vote every election because that is what a good citizen should do. It is kind of an agreement a citizen has with his government.

Julia, 17-year-old daughter of a restaurant owner:

I think voting is important because it shows how good citizens run the country. It shows how a democracy is supposed to be—it allows its citizens to participate. It is part of being a good citizen.

The reason that middle-class youth from San Antonio see voting differently than do those from Los Angeles and Albuquerque is revealed in the youth's perceptions of socioeconomic and political conditions in San Antonio. In San Antonio, the nature of the economy—the fact that it is based predominantly on services and not on industrial production—limits the overall number of high-paying jobs, since service jobs are generally much lower on the wage scale. In addition, the cultural/social prejudice toward Chicanos in San Antonio acts to reduce the availability of high-paying jobs to Chicanos. The result is that Chicanos are provided limited opportunities for socioeconomic mobility. Throughout the interviews, these youth from middle-class families were both appreciative of, and insecure about, the socioeconomic status that their parents had achieved. Their attention focused on the fact that their families had attained a certain position in a rather tough economic environment, and that because of this difficult economic environment they felt vulnerable.

Jacobo, 18-year-old son of the owner of a cleaning service:

I'm lucky to be where I am. When my grandfather and father were growing up, it was difficult for Chicanos to get good-paying jobs or own their own business. There was a lot of prejudice against Chicanos. I know compared to other Chicanos in San Antonio I am pretty lucky, because my family has been able to get this business.

Alicia, 18-year-old daughter of an office manager for a small company:

My father makes good money, and I guess I am fortunate compared to other people. My dad was really fortunate to get the kind of job he has. He told me that my grandfather would never have had the chance because there was a lot of discrimination against Mexicans, and even now there is a lot, so I guess I have to feel lucky because there are a lot of Mexicans in San Antonio who don't have much.

The middle-class youth's insecurity is due to their awareness that San Antonio's economy is controlled almost exclusively by Anglo-Americans and to their belief that if Chicanos become problems for the Anglo community, this community is capable of reducing the socioeconomic position that their own families now enjoy. Therefore, these young people do not want to draw attention to themselves as troublemakers or radicals. They view voting as a person's civic duty because this lets them be seen as loyal citizens and thereby reduces the potential threat both to the Anglo community and to themselves.

Paul, 18-year-old son of a salesman:

I feel voting is what a citizen should do. I don't believe in any of the other things that Chicano radicals have talked about, like protesting or voting only for Chicanos. I mean, I don't know how to put this, but if I were a radical, maybe I could cause my father to lose his job. Everything he worked for could be lost; that would be awful.

Louisa, 17-year-old daughter of an accountant:

To me voting is something you do to be a good citizen. There are Chicanos around here that want you to vote for Chicanos only. They say that is the way to change things, but I don't agree. My father says that these radicals won't get a job, or they will get fired, or they might get their parents fired. I would never do that to my father and my family. Anyway, I will just vote to vote and there won't be any trouble.

What is interesting about the views of voting among the middle-class youth of San Antonio is that they, like the middle-class youth of Los Angeles and Albuquerque, see voting as a means to improving their own socioeconomic positions. However, in Los Angeles and Albuquerque voting is viewed as a tool to create a new order, while in San Antonio this conceptualization is avoided for fear that the Anglo community would view proponents of this point of view as threats and invoke some form of retribution, resulting in a loss of their present socioeconomic positions.

Until now, the focus of discussion has been on those Chicano youth from middle-class families. But what of those youth from families with lower socioeconomic standing? In all three cities, youth from lower-class families were positive toward voting, but less positive than their middle-class counterparts. Voting, for these lower-class youth, was a resource to create some positive change in their lives. They wanted to have the same material possessions enjoyed by the middle class, and they saw politics as a means of securing a better lifestyle. This is, of course, the same attitude that prevailed among most of the middle-class respondents, except for those respondents from San Antonio, but the responses in the interviews with the lower class indicated a belief that voting alone could not accomplish this, and that other forms of politics must be used in order to bring about the changes necessary for improved living conditions among Chicanos. In Los Angeles and Albuquerque, the lower-class youth believed that in addition to voting, some protest and political violence would be needed to bring about the changes they desired.

David, 17-year-old son of a truck driver in Albuquerque:

We need changes so that Chicanos are given more opportunities. Voting can help some, but other things will have to happen, like the use of protest and even some violence. No one thing can bring about changes alone.

Veronica, 17-year-old daughter of a mechanic in Los Angeles:

Voting can't help us [Chicanos] alone, it just can't. The only way we can get some of the changes is to use some protest and even some violence. All these things will be necessary.

In San Antonio, the lower class's perception of voting was quite different from that of the middle class. Members of the lower class saw voting as a method of creating changes that would help them socioeconomically. Members of the middle class saw voting as a way to preserve what they had already achieved by portraying it as a citizen's civic duty.

To recapitulate the findings concerning the youth's attitudes toward voting, no sense of apathy toward voting was found among the youth in any of the three cities. The differences noted were found among the youth of different social class standings. Members of the middle class were more positive with regard to the potential of voting in making an impact on their lives than were youth from families of lower socioeconomic status. Yet the factor that was most important in influencing all the youth's ideas about voting was the city of residence. In San Antonio, where the economy is low technology/service-oriented, there is little opportunity for rapid and extensive socioeconomic mobility. In addition, a history of ethnic/racial discrimination has resulted in limited access to middle-class occupations for Chicanos. These factors, together with a political system that traditionally has been operated by influential businessmen from the Anglo community who have been anxious to preserve existing socioeconomic arrangements, have combined to yield the unsurprising result that the youth from San Antonio are more conservative in their views of voting than are the youth from the other two cities.

In Los Angeles and Albuquerque, opportunities for socioeconomic mobility are more readily available because the cities' respective economies are more diversified among the service, commercial and industrial sectors. The ethnic composition of these two cities is more varied than that of San Antonio, as is the political system. There are differing sources of political power, and this creates a more complex political arena. Therefore, a more heterogeneous economic and political condition has produced more diverse views among these youth concerning the political participatory alternatives available to them.

Chapter 4

Political Parties

The preceding section has presented evidence indicating that all of the youth in this study, with the exception of the middle class of San Antonio, viewed voting as an act to benefit their economic interests. The youth in this study are similar, in a sense, to what Popkin et al. have called the "investor-voter."[11] This section asks the logical follow-up question: If these youth see their vote as a type of investment, in what political party are they prepared to invest their vote, and what factors influence their choice?

Jennings and Niemi, in their important study of the political character of adolescents, focused their analysis primarily on white and black adolescents. Their sample of adolescents did include a small number of Puerto Ricans and Chicanos, but they decided to include these groups in their category of "black." Their rationale was that, ". . . while every racial group or sub-group is to some extent distinctive, our judgment is that in many politically relevant circumstances, Puerto Ricans and Mexican Americans share many of the characteristics ordinarily associated with the black population."[12] Thus, from their point of view, Chicanos and Puerto Ricans would share the same political disposition as "blacks." Given their assumptions that Chicanos are like blacks, and that blacks are extremely supportive of the Democratic Party, the Chicano youth in the present study should be expected to be overwhelmingly supportive of the Democratic Party as well.[13] This was not the case. The Chicano youth divided their support between two political parties; however, it was not between the Democratic and Republican parties, but rather between the Democratic and Raza Unida parties.

At the time of the research involved in this study (1977) the Partido de la Raza Unida (PRU, Party of the United Race) was still a competing political party in Texas, New Mexico, California, Colorado, and Arizona, and despite its subsequent demise, which will be discussed later, the party played a significant role in the lives of Chicano youth at that time. The organization of the party began in 1968–69, and it officially entered elections in three south Texas counties in 1970.[14] The immediate success of the party in Texas stimulated organizational efforts in other states. The party's objectives were not always completely clear, partly because of ideological cleavages. There was constant friction between those who wanted the party to concentrate on issues that would benefit Chicanos and those who wanted the party to be a nationalist/separatist party like the Parti Quebecois in Quebec, Canada. Despite these rather important ideological cleavages within the leadership, there were points of general agreement that allowed the party to function effectively. These were: (1) that the party should concentrate on state and local politics and not become involved at the national level; (2) that an effort should be made to promote bilingual/biculturalism throughout the Southwest; (3) that support should be given for national health insurance; and (4) that emphasis should be placed on the redistribution of wealth within the United States.[15]

The Raza Unida Party was relatively successful in its first attempts at having its candidates elected to various offices at the state and local levels, but the strength of the party varied from state to state and from time to time. At the time of the research for this study the party was still running candidates, although it was not nearly as competitive with the other parties as it once had been. This was due to a deficient organizational structure, leadership cleavages, and insufficient financial resources. Since that time, the party has ceased to operate as a competitive political party because of its inability to raise sufficient financial resources and various legal entanglements resulting from its ten years of political struggle.

In discussing the party preferences of the Chicano youth in all three cities, one must start with the impact of social class standing. Support for the Democratic Party in all three cities comes primarily from middle-class youth. As the data in Figures 4.4, 4.5, and 4.6 (P$_{64}$) clearly show, the higher the youth's socioeconomic status, the more positive he/she is with regard to the Democratic Party. If one considers that the Democratic Party has been the traditional party of Chicanos, this finding is not unanticipated. The middle-class youth of all three cities fully understood the Democratic Party's traditional appeal to Chicanos. For example, 87 percent (905) of the youth in all three cities mentioned the fact that the Democrats had supported issues such as civil rights and economic programs for minorities that had helped Chicanos to gain increased access to better-paying jobs.

Jaime, 17-year-old son of a business manager for a laundry company in San Antonio:

The Democratic Party has helped my family. I mean, they supported civil rights and a number of economic programs for

FIGURE 4.4
Path Model of the Effects in San Antonio of Urban
Contextual Variables and Personal Variables on Student
Support for the Democratic Party*

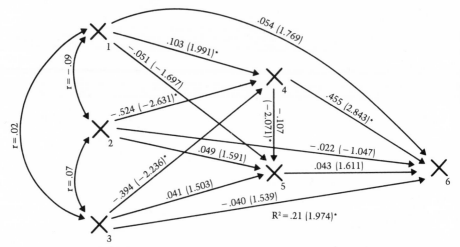

* =   All coefficients are significant at the .05 level or beyond on
       a two-tailed "t" test
X_1 = Length of residence in the city
X_2 = Population density in neighborhood
X_3 = Ethnic homogeneity in respondent's neighborhood
X_4 = Socioeconomic status
X_5 = Traditional cultural values (retention of)
X_6 = Support for the Democratic Party

blacks and Chicanos, and this helped Chicanos get jobs. It
also helped Chicanos get better schooling. Chicanos would
not have gotten any of these without the Democratic Party.

Andrea, 17-year-old daughter of a lawyer in Albuquerque:

I think most Chicanos have been helped because of the
Democratic Party's support for civil rights. I think my family
has. Who knows if my father would have been allowed to get
a good education and go to law school if he didn't get an
equal chance. The Democratic Party supported that, so I
support them.

FIGURE 4.5
Path Model of the Effects in Albuquerque of Urban
Contextual Variables and Personal Variables on Student
Support for the Democratic Party*

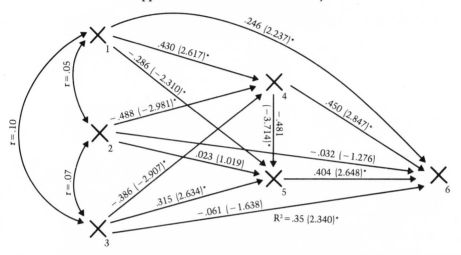

* = All coefficients are significant at the .05 level or beyond on
     a two-tailed "t" test
X_1 = Length of residence in the city
X_2 = Population density in neighborhood
X_3 = Ethnic homogeneity in respondent's neighborhood
X_4 = Socioeconomic status
X_5 = Traditional cultural values (retention of)
X_6 = Support for the Democratic Party

Elena, 18-year-old daughter of an insurance salesman and
nurse in Los Angeles:

I support the Democratic Party because they were for better
education for blacks and Chicanos so that we could get into
better colleges and be able to get good-paying jobs. They also
were for equal rights, you know, against racial discrimination,
and this helps Chicanos who have good qualifications to get
an opportunity they would never get, and this will help me in
the future.

In addition, the interviews and other data from the questionnaires

FIGURE 4.6
Path Model of the Effects in Los Angeles of Urban
Contextual Variables and Personal Variables on Student
Support for the Democratic Party*

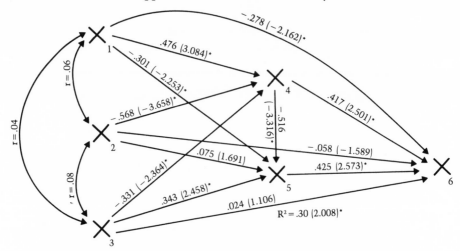

* = All coefficients are significant at the .05 level or beyond on
a two-tailed "t" test
X_1 = Length of residence in the city
X_2 = Population density in neighborhood
X_3 = Ethnic homogeneity in respondent's neighborhood
X_4 = Socioeconomic status
X_5 = Traditional cultural values (retention of)
X_6 = Support for the Democratic Party

indicate that the middle-class youth are aware of the structure of
their local economies and how the Democratic Party has affected
it. Therefore, in San Antonio, where the town is economically dependent on the military bases, the youth of middle-class status are
not only aware but appreciative of the Democratic Party's efforts to
sustain the military bases.[16]

Hector, 18-year-old son of an electrical engineer in San
Antonio:

The Democratic Party is the most important party for me
because they provide jobs for people. Like, they want the

military bases here, and my dad works on the base, so it
helps our family.

Juanita, 17-year-old daughter of a small tool and dye company
owner in San Antonio:

Well, a couple of years ago the Congress wanted to shut down
some of the military bases, but Congressman Gonzalez
[Henry B. Gonzalez, D-San Antonio] worked hard to stop it,
and that was good for my dad, because his company makes
parts for all of the bases. So I think the Democratic Party is
real important.

In Los Angeles and Albuquerque, where the local economies are
much more diversified, the middle-class youth's support of the Democratic Party is related to the party's efforts to aid business and
maintain programs of financial aid to residents of the *barrios* who,
it is hoped, will spend this money on minority businesses. This
directly helps many members of the Chicano middle class, and therefore support for the Democratic Party is a result of economic self-
interest.

Lisa, 17-year-old daughter of the owner of an automobile
dealership in Los Angeles:

My dad got a loan to start his business, and he said the
Democratic Party was the party that put up the bills
[legislation] that help minority businesses to get loans. So I
support it [the Democratic Party] 'cause it helped my dad and
other Chicano businessmen.

Raymond, 17-year-old son of the owner of a hardware store in
Albuquerque:

The Democratic Party has supported loans for minorities and
they [the party] are for pouring more money into the *barrios*. I
know a lot of programs have put money into the *barrio* and
so the people were able to build or repair things they couldn't
do before. They came to my dad's store to buy, and this
helped him out. So I feel strongly about the Democratic
Party—they seem to be the best for Chicanos.

What is particularly interesting about the support of the middle
class for the Democratic Party is their use of different criteria to

calculate the benefits and costs of supporting the Democratic rather than the Raza Unida Party. In San Antonio the Raza Unida Party was perceived to be radical by both the Chicano and the Anglo communities. Despite the Raza Unida Party's attempt in Texas to present itself as simply a third party, its platform position of redistributing wealth was understood as a desire to alter present economic arrangements. Since the Anglo community controlled the economy in San Antonio, these middle-class Chicanos perceived that the Raza Unida Party's position might provoke economic sanctions from the Anglo community against those who supported the party. If sanctions were imposed on them, it could make it difficult for their parents to maintain the socioeconomic status they had achieved. Given the fact that their families had become mobile while the Democrats were the only party in town, in the solidly Democratic south, they were not about to jeopardize their socioeconomic gains by identifying with a radical political party, even if that party had the potential to provide future benefits to them. For them, the risks associated with Raza Unida were too high; the Democrats did not offer as much, but they were a safer choice.

In Los Angeles and Albuquerque, the middle-class youth's support of the Democratic Party derived from the fact that their families, like those of their counterparts in San Antonio, had achieved middle-class status at a time when the Democratic Party was the only party supporting policies beneficial to Chicanos. Even though the Raza Unida Party was competing for the Chicano vote, the middle-class youth of Albuquerque and Los Angeles did not believe that it had the power to win or the ability to become a permanent competing party. Accordingly, for these youth, support for the Democratic Party was based on their calculations that it was the Democratic Party that was more likely to win consistently and thereby to aid them.

On the other side of the class spectrum, the lower classes in each of the three cities were negative toward the Democratic Party. Here, as was mentioned previously, the economy of the local community was a critical factor in influencing the lower-class youth's negative attitude toward the Democratic Party. In looking at the results from the path model concerning urban environmental conditions and socioeconomic status, and supplementing these results, based on the questionnaire data, with data from the in-depth interviews, a clearer picture of the origins of the lower class's negative attitude toward the Democratic Party emerges. Negative feelings toward the Democratic Party are associated with inability to achieve socioeconomic mobility within the local economy. In all three cities, those youth whose families have been in the city for a long time and have achieved very little economic mobility (some have even seen their status decline) have given up on the political system. One should bear in mind that the vast majority of these lower-class youth come from families who have come to the city with great expectations of making a better life. They came to the cities and settled in extremely homogeneous (Chicano lower-class), high density areas, not dissimilar to those areas in which other ethnic groups lived when they first immigrated to the cities. However, having been in the city for a considerable time and having observed the economic mobility of others, these same youth had negative feelings toward the system and the Democratic Party. The lower-class youth all said that they had supported the Democratic Party for a considerable time, but that it had done nothing to help them. The fact that their hopes for a better future were slowly being left behind had led them to disappointment and bitterness.

Their negative feelings toward the Democratic Party, then, stem from their perception of the Party as an organization that has been indifferent and/or inept in aiding them to achieve a better life.[17]

Ernesto, 17-year-old son of an unskilled laborer in Albuquerque:

Our family has worked hard to make a better living since we got to Albuquerque, but we can't make ends meet. My father works hard, but he can't get a job that will keep him for a long time, so he is out of work a lot. The Democrats are supposed to be for the working man, but they haven't helped our family or a lot of other families. I don't believe they want to help—they just say they want to, that's why I hate them.

Melina, 17-year-old daughter of a clothing worker in Los Angeles:

The Democrats say they help workers and unions, but they don't. My family has worked for this clothing company for a long time, and they don't pay good wages. They [the workers] have tried to get a union in, and the union wants to come, but there are all these laws. They [the workers] asked the Democrats for some help and they got no response at all. What good is the Democratic Party? I think they are on the side of business and are trying to fool workers.

In Albuquerque there is an interesting corollary to the lower class's negative feelings toward the Democratic Party. Within the Albuquerque sample the more negative attitudes toward the party came from those who had just arrived in Albuquerque. In contrast to the lower-class youth in the other cities, they did not go through a process of first identifying with the Democratic Party and then becoming disillusioned with it. The recent Chicano migrants came to the city with an extremely antagonistic attitude toward the Democrats. The reason for this is that nearly all came from northern New Mexico where economic conditions, such as livestock prices, taxes, and the availability of grazing land, had forced many of the Chicanos who owned small ranches to sell their land and move to Albuquerque. The struggle to save their ranches had become a highly political issue. The Raza Unida Party became integrally involved on the side of those being dispossessed, while the Democratic Party did not take an official position. As a consequence, these youth came to Albuquerque highly politicized and opposed to the Democratic Party. Once in Albuquerque, they faced the same conditions as did other lower-class families. If their families did experience socioeconomic mobility, their political views became more moderate and they became supporters of the Democratic Party. However, if they suffered the plight of many other lower-class families and stayed in roughly the same socioeconomic position, they became even more radical. It is this segment of the sample that was the most militantly nationalistic and separatist.

Issues concerned with economic mobility were not the only issues causing a negative evaluation of the Democratic Party. The issues of cultural retention and personal identity also elicited negative attitudes toward the party. Those youth (mostly the middle class from Albuquerque and Los Angeles, but some from the lower class as well) who found themselves having difficulty with cultural identity, because they no longer practiced many of the customs of Chicano culture, such as maintaining the ability to speak Spanish, were extremely negative toward the Democratic Party. They felt that the Democratic Party did very little to support bilingualism/biculturalism, and that its policies were actually designed to promote assimilation, which to them would mean that Chicanos would be like other ethnic groups in the United States—ethnic in name and history only. In the interviews they kept referring to those policies aimed at ethnic assimilation as cultural genocide, and repeated that they could not support a political party that did not take an active part in promoting bilingualism/biculturalism.

As has been apparent, issues surrounding cultural retention have arisen exclusively among the youth of Albuquerque and Los Angeles. In San Antonio, all but a few of the youth still maintained strong cultural ties, and this was true regardless of the length of time the youth's family had lived in the city. One reason for the high levels of cultural retention is that Chicanos constitute a very large percentage of the population of San Antonio. Another reason is that the Anglo community has been discriminatory in its relations with Chicanos, and this has created residential and social patterns which have acted to maintain relatively strong cultural ties. In the other two cities, the Chicano population is not as large a percentage of the total population, and there are numerous other ethnic groups in these cities, which serves to promote the concept of pluralism. Finally, the media and social systems in both Albuquerque and Los Angeles tend to promote cultural adaptation and accommodation. These factors work to influence Chicanos who live in these cities toward an ideology of acculturation, which creates problems with regard to cultural retention for some individuals.

The rise of the Raza Unida Party is the result of the Democratic Party's inability to deal with the problem of economic mobility and other problems that plague the Chicano community. Had the Democratic Party been able to bring about more economic development and had it taken a strong position on acculturation as a model for Chicano cultural identity, there would not have been a significant number of people who supported the Raza Unida Party. However, in none of the cities in the study did the Democratic Party advance and support policies that would alleviate the problems associated with these two issues. The Raza Unida Party directed its attention to the problems associated with lack of economic mobility for Chicanos and ethnic pride in Chicano culture. Ultimately, it was those youth who were disillusioned with the Democratic Party who formed the basis of the Raza Unida Party's support.

Social class background (P_{64}, Figs. 4.7, 4.8, 4.9) is probably the most important factor in predicting whether the youth would support the Raza Unida or the Democratic Party. The Raza Unida in general drew its support in each city from those youth who were from lower socioeconomic backgrounds. In Los Angeles and San Antonio, support for Raza Unida came from those among the lower

FIGURE 4.7
Path Model of the Effects in San Antonio of Urban
Contextual Variables and Personal Variables on Student
Support for the Raza Unida Party (PRU)*

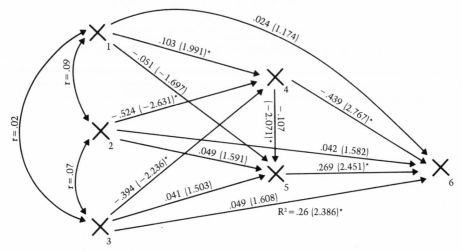

* = All coefficients are significant at the .05 level or beyond on
a two-tailed "t" test
X_1 = Length of residence in the city
X_2 = Population density in neighborhood
X_3 = Ethnic homogeneity in respondent's neighborhood
X_4 = Socioeconomic status
X_5 = Traditional cultural values (retention of)
X_6 = Support for the PRU

class who had lived in the city for at least five years and had not
achieved any economic improvement. These youth were nearly always from high-density areas that were highly homogenous. In other
words, these youth's families were trapped in densely populated
areas that were entirely Chicano. Thus a party like the Raza Unida
that addressed the question of economic inequality among Chicanos
was quite popular among the downtrodden within the Chicano community.

Lita, 18-year-old daughter of an unemployed laborer:

The Raza Unida wants to change the economic system of the
city and the country. They want to redistribute all the money

FIGURE 4.8
Path Model of the Effects in Albuquerque of Urban
Contextual Variables and Personal Variables on Student
Support for the Raza Unida Party (PRU)*

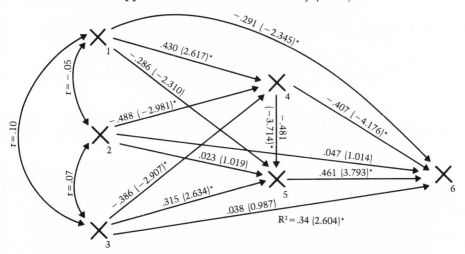

* = All coefficients are significant at the .05 level or beyond on a two-tailed "t" test

X_1 = Length of residence in the city
X_2 = Population density in neighborhood
X_3 = Ethnic homogeneity in respondent's neighborhood
X_4 = Socioeconomic status
X_5 = Traditional cultural values (retention of)
X_6 = Support for the PRU

more evenly. I support them [the Party] because until that is done, Chicanos won't have a fair chance to get ahead.

Carlos, 17-year-old son of a gas station attendant:

I know I'm for the Raza Unida Party because they want to make major changes in the economic system. Chicanos won't be able to improve until there is a major change in the way business is done in this country.

There is a difference, however, in the way in which the lower-class youth in San Antonio perceived the Raza Unida Party as compared to those in Albuquerque and Los Angeles. In San Antonio, the

FIGURE 4.9
Path Model of the Effects in Los Angeles of Urban
Contextual Variables and Personal Variables on Student
Support for the Raza Unida Party (PRU)*

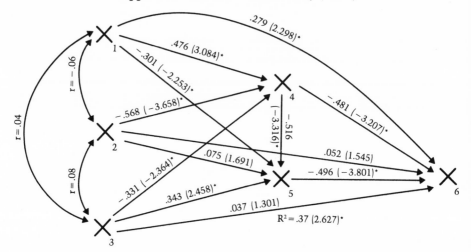

* =   All coefficients are significant at the .05 level or beyond on
a two-tailed "t" test
X_1 =   Length of residence in the city
X_2 =   Population density in neighborhood
X_3 =   Ethnic homogeneity in respondent's neighborhood
X_4 =   Socioeconomic status
X_5 =   Traditional cultural values (retention of)
X_6 =   Support for the PRU

lower-class youth were prepared to support Raza Unida, which they
saw as just another political party within the American tradition of
third parties. However, in Albuquerque and Los Angeles, the lower
class saw it as a nationalistic party with aspirations to separate from
the United States. Their notions as to how this could be done are
the subject of the chapter on ideology. Briefly, the Raza Unida was
viewed by these Chicanos in much the same manner that the Parti
Quebecois, a party that entered provincial elections in Quebec with
the intent of separating from Canada and forming an independent
country, was viewed by the French in Quebec.[18]

If the youth from Albuquerque and Los Angeles saw the Raza
Unida Party as a separatist party, why did the youth from San An-

tonio not think the same? There are probably two related reasons. First, the party leaders in Texas presented the party simply as a third political party that articulated the interests of Chicanos. Second, and this is probably the reason behind the party's rationale as well, these youth were fearful of Anglo-American reprisal if they supported a separatist party. Ninety-two percent (eighty-one) of those lower-class youth who supported Raza Unida in San Antonio said that they would never have supported it if it were a separatist party. They believed that economic and physical reprisals were possible if they supported a party that advocated separation, and they were anxious about being identified with such a party. Following are two representative comments:

Rudy, 17-year-old son of a clothing worker:

I wouldn't support the Raza Unida if it wanted to separate at all. Are you kidding? All hell would break loose—Anglos wouldn't give me a job and my father could lose his. I can tell you, the Anglo community would be mean.

Laura, 17-year-old daughter of a recreational parks ground keeper:

If Raza Unida became a separatist party, I really couldn't support it. In fact, I would really oppose it because it would jeopardize everything Chicanos have been able to gain. All you have to do is think what the Anglos would do. They would do everything to hassle supporters of such a party, like fire them from jobs and get the police to harass them. It would be real bad.

Here is an excellent example of the local political culture shaping the character of a new political party, as well as influencing how people relate to it.

In Albuquerque, the most intense support for Raza Unida came from those lower-class youth who had just arrived from the northern part of the state. As discussed earlier, this is the same segment of the lower class that was extremely negative toward the Democratic Party. These youth were from families who not only were lower-class, but who had been forced, because of economic and legal issues surrounding land tenure, to give up their land and homes and move to Albuquerque. Most had not done this without a fight. The Raza Unida had joined the fight on the side of those who were being forced out. In fact, many of the party's workers were people whose land had been lost. The result was that these lower-class youth came to Albuquerque extremely distraught at having had to move from their ancestral homes, highly politicized, and strongly supportive of the Raza Unida Party—the only party that they felt had represented their interests. In fact, in addition to electorally supporting Raza Unida, about 30 percent (eighteen) of these youth reported being Raza Unida activists, doing various jobs for the party that included advertising and fund raising activities.

As noted earlier, however, once these youth arrived in Albuquerque, their support for a particular party depended on how well the local economy was able to provide opportunities for their families. If no improvement occurred, these youth became even more politically radical, adopting a more militantly separatist position than they had had when they arrived. However, if their families' economic position improved, they moved to supporting the Democratic Party. This switch in party allegiance was brought about by the realities of their new socioeconomic status. They knew that the Democrats were a much stronger party than the Raza Unida in Albuquerque, and they reasoned that the Democrats had a much better chance to win elections and to effect policies that could benefit them in their new middle-class status. In other words, a change in social class status altered their conception of their interests, which dictated a shift in their party allegiance.

The last segment of the Chicano youth to support the Raza Unida Party was that segment which had been culturally assimilated. These youth were predominantly from the middle class in Albuquerque and Los Angeles, but there were some from the lower class as well. As mentioned, these youth were socially alienated because they wanted to regain those aspects of Chicano culture that they had lost. Since Raza Unida was a strong advocate of bilingualism/biculturalism, it is not difficult to understand why this particular segment of the sample supported the party. For these youth, Raza Unida represented both a symbol of the Chicano cultural renaissance, a reaffirmation of pride in Chicano culture, that was occurring at the time and a vehicle through which they would be able to regain some of the culture that they had lost.[19]

Finally, the lower-class youth in all three cities who came from densely populated Chicano areas were extremely positive toward Raza Unida. Not only were these youth disgusted by the lack of services provided to their neighborhoods, but the fact that the Raza

Unida Party's workers and candidates were drawn from and still lived in these areas affected their level of support. These lower-class youth were given the impression that the Raza Unida Party's workers and candidates had not abandoned them for the suburbs, and this elicited great respect and allegiance.[20] In sum, it was discontent over the ineffectiveness and/or reluctance of the Democratic Party to address the problems plaguing various segments of the Chicano community that influenced the youth to switch allegiance to Raza Unida.

Discussion up to this point has focused only on the Democratic and Raza Unida Parties. Briefly, attention will now be given to the Republican Party, which was discounted by the youth in this study as a party that they realistically could support.

In each of the three cities, the Republican Party received negative evaluations. Such results are not surprising, since the Republican Party has not enjoyed a great deal of support from Chicanos. One reason for this is that in Texas and New Mexico, the Democratic Party has always been dominant in the past and has made an effort to recruit Chicanos into its ranks. Chicanos have responded to the Democrats because of a general recognition that the Democratic Party controls local government in these two states and that benefits are more likely to be gained through supporting it. In addition, the Republican Party has not, in most elections, offered an attractive alternative. Eighty-eight percent (274) of the youth in Albuquerque and 93 percent (308) in San Antonio felt that the Republicans offered no alternative to the Democrats.

Anthony, 18-year-old son of an insurance salesman in San Antonio:

The Republicans are always for the same things as the Democrats, but the thing is they never win, either. So I wouldn't vote for them because there is no difference and they won't win. There is nothing I can get if I vote for the Republicans.

Mario, 18-year-old son of a bartender in San Antonio:

The Republicans are useless, and it is useless to vote for them. They never say anything new, they always say the same thing as the Democrats, and they hardly win any election, so there is no reason to vote for them. I mean, what could you get if you vote for the Republicans? They won't win, so they can't help you get a job or something like that.

In Los Angeles, the Republican Party's relative lack of support stems from the political situation in California. There the lack of Chicano support is the product of differences over policy issues, whereas in the cases of Texas and New Mexico, lack of support is related to instrumental concerns—can they win and will I benefit? Not only has the Republican Party in California made little effort to recruit Chicanos, but it very often has recruited people and nominated candidates who have taken stands opposed to the interests of the Chicanos. For example:

Donna, 17-year-old daughter of an architect:

I don't care if the Republican Party exists or not. I know I would not vote for them. They supported the growers in the grape boycott and the lettuce boycott. They were also against the Mexican nationals coming here to work; they all want to use their [undocumented workers'] labor and pay them almost nothing for wages.

Ramón, 18-year-old son of a construction laborer:

I hate the Republican Party. They don't help Chicanos. They only help Anglos. They don't even like Chicanos. Like Chief Davis [L.A. Police Chief Ed Davis, a prominent figure in the California Republican Party]. All he wanted to do was to put more police in the *barrios* to harass us. The rest of the Republicans are the same way; they supported the bosses in the grape boycott. They are just no good.

The Chicano youth in this study very clearly see nothing to be gained—and perhaps even something to be lost—from supporting Republican candidates.

Ideology and Political Party Support

Numerous studies have been undertaken to determine whether the American electorate's support of a particular political party is related to ideology. The evidence generated from these studies, as well as the conclusions drawn, are conflicting. Some of the studies

Table 4.1
Pearson Correlation Coefficients of Political Party Support and
Ideological Orientation by City of Residence

	Democratic Party		Raza Unida	
San Antonio				
Capitalism	.435*	(251)	.390*	(248)
Socialism	−.385*	(261)	−.284*	(209)
Communism	−.421*	(280)	−.371*	(227)
Separatism/Nationalism	−.368*	(233)	.083	(58)
Albuquerque				
Capitalism	.416*	(270)	−.310*	(244)
Socialism	−.112	(87)	−.283*	(194)
Communism	−.307*	(253)	−.338*	(260)
Separatism/Nationalism	−.374*	(258)	.458*	(267)
Los Angeles				
Capitalism	.436*	(261)	−.344*	(255)
Socialism	−.248*	(197)	−.108	(91)
Communism	−.371*	(263)	−.295*	(205)
Separatism/Nationalism	−.341*	(258)	.414*	(269)

*P<.05

conclude that only a small percentage of the population has a set of attitudes on issues and policy that could be considered ideological, and that party choice is affected only by attitudes toward candidates.[21] Still another body of research argues that not only does a large portion of the American electorate have attitudes on various issues and policies, but that these attitudes, as measured on a liberal-conservative continuum, have been so structured as to be ideological in nature, and that in certain elections party choice has been related directly to those ideologies.[22] Data from this study indicate that a relationship exists between a youth's political party choice and his/her ideological orientation (see Table 4.1). In all three cities, it was found that Chicanos who were favorable toward capitalism/liberal democracy, and toward the U.S. system as a whole, were also supporters of the Democratic Party. These Chicanos believed that capitalism/liberal democracy could be beneficial to them and that the Democratic Party, because of its well-established organization, was the party most likely to achieve the socioeconomic goals they desired. On the other hand, in looking at the correlations between capitalism/liberal democracy and the Raza Unida Party, some interesting variations appear. In Albuquerque and Los Angeles, where the relationship is negative, a relatively large number of the youths who are positive toward the present system and supportive of it do not support the Raza Unida Party because they view the party as attempting to change basic political and economic relationships in the United States. For these youth, this party is much too radical. Yet as the low correlations tend to suggest, this is not completely true for the entire Los Angeles and Albuquerque sample. In analyzing the scores for this bivariate relationship on a scattergram, it was discovered that a number of the respondents supported both capitalism and the Raza Unida Party. These Chicanos viewed the present system as having the ability to satisfy all of the needs that they considered important, and their support for the Raza Unida Party was based on their belief that the party's candidates would represent their interests better than would the candidates of the Democratic Party. Thus, in the case of these youth, the Raza Unida Party was not considered radical.

In San Antonio, there is a positive correlation between capitalism/ liberal democracy and the Raza Unida Party ($r = .390$). For the most part, the youth of San Antonio, like those of Los Angeles and Albuquerque, consider Raza Unida as merely an additional political party competing for their patronage. The Party does not assume the character of a radical party attempting to change the system fundamentally.

> Rosalie, 18-year-old daughter of a San Antonio food processing worker:
>
> I like the Raza Unida Party because I think it gives Chicanos more of a choice. It also helps Chicanos because it gets the Democratic Party to do things for Chicanos. . . . Because the Raza Unida is not radical, I don't see anything wrong about being for it and being positive toward the U.S. system of capitalism.

Therefore, the youth's party choices were not particularly related to whether or not they supported capitalism. Rather, these choices were based on specific issues affecting them within the general ideology of capitalism and liberal democracy.

The relationship of socialism and communism to party support is negative for all three cities. As indicated earlier, the overwhelming majority of the respondents were negative toward both of these ideologies. Consequently, it is not surprising that those who supported each of these parties did not consider themselves either socialists or communists.

The data concerning Chicano nationalists indicate that the youth in Albuquerque and Los Angeles, although not in San Antonio, who supported the concept of a separate Chicano country also supported the Raza Unida Party. This is interesting, given that the Raza Unida Party's platform has nothing in it that even hints that one of its goals is to achieve a separate Chicano country. Eighty-eight percent (182) of the youth interviewed from both these cities who consider themselves separatists said that they knew that the Raza Unida Party was politically moderate and that most of those who worked in the Party were opposed to separatism. However, they also went on to say that in light of the fact that there was no political party that did incorporate separatism into its platform, they chose to support Raza Unida because, as an ethnic party, it came closest to their beliefs.

Juana, 17-year-old daughter of an Albuquerque pipe fitter:

Well, I'm for separatism and I support the Raza Unida because it is closest to what I believe even though it [the party] doesn't support separatism.

There was a small percentage (26 percent) of these youth who went even further. They thought that the Raza Unida could be transformed into a pure separatist party in the future. Their opinions were based on the fact that there were already some Chicanos, albeit a small number, in the party who had separatist sympathies, and they believed that these individuals could act as a nucleus to restructure the party.

Julio, 18-year-old son of a Los Angeles painter:

Hey, I support the Raza Unida Party because there is nothing else I can do for a political party—it's the best there is. I know it's not for separatism, but there are people in the party who support separatism. Plus the party is for Chicanos and Chicano problems, so it's good in that way. It is the best we got, so you got to go with it, and change it to a separatist party. I think that can be done and so do other people I know.

In both Los Angeles and Albuquerque, those who viewed themselves as separatists, or nationalists, were negative toward the Democratic Party. To these Chicanos the Democratic Party represented "assimilationist aspirations"—that is, the desire to identify with and become a part of the dominant society, and they no longer held these to be important goals. Their abandonment of the Democratic Party as a vehicle for assimilation and a better life was due primarily to three factors: (1) their past support of the Democratic Party had resulted in little success in gaining political power or influencing policy; (2) even when the Democrats had won elections, they had not delivered economically as much as was expected or promised; and (3) they no longer felt that giving up their culture for the sake of socioeconomic advancement was worthwhile. To these Chicanos, the Democratic Party was seen simply as a contributing factor in keeping them in a disadvantaged state.

The relationship in San Antonio between separatism and both parties is negative. This was expected because in San Antonio neither party is believed to represent separatist aspirations. As noted earlier, the Raza Unida Party is understood to be simply another small third party, much like the American Independent Party (the party whose presidential candidate was at the time George Wallace), which had run in a number of earlier elections. Thus, because the youth in San Antonio are generally not radical, support of either the Democratic Party or the Raza Unida Party produces the same negative reaction toward the radical politics that separatism represents.

Denise, 18-year-old daughter of a hotel worker:

I like the Raza Unida Party, but I'm not for separatism and the rest of the radical things that those people talk about and want. I support the Raza Unida because they want to help Chicanos get better jobs in the system we have.

Whether issues constitute an important factor in the youth's party choice seems clear. The youth who supported one party over another did so on the basis of how the party related to their political ideology, but a vital element of their ideology was related to specific issues affecting them. The issues most often referred to were: (1) educational opportunities, (2) employment opportunities, (3) housing conditions and crime, and (4) bilingualism/biculturalism in the schools and in society as a whole.

Conclusion

One of the most important findings in this chapter concerns the attitudinal patterns that emerged among youth from different social class backgrounds as they considered political participation through voting and their allegiance to a particular political party. In general, both middle and lower classes saw their vote as an investment that they hoped would bring them economic benefit. However, the middle class relied on voting as a way to create the changes they deemed necessary in order to receive more economic benefits; the lower-class youth thought that voting was important, but they did not think of it as more effective than other forms of political participation, such as protest. In fact, many thought of it as less effective. In terms of political parties, support for either the Democrats or Raza Unida was influenced by whether or not the youth were satisfied with their own lives, either socioeconomically or culturally. If they were, they were usually middle-class and supportive of the Democratic Party. If they were not, they were predominantly lower-class and supportive of Raza Unida. The exception to this middle-class pattern of allegiance to the Democratic Party is a portion of the middle class in Los Angeles who felt they had lost the values and practices of their cultural heritage, were also discontented, and supported Raza Unida with its policies of strengthening Chicano culture through promoting bilingualism/biculturalism.

Given that the Raza Unida Party is no longer competing, one may question whether the data presented on this party are dated and irrelevant to an understanding of Chicano politics. As mentioned in the introduction, a follow-up study was conducted in the fall of 1982 to determine what attitudes had changed among the youth in the original study over the five years that had elapsed from the time it was undertaken. One of the areas of greatest concern was the Raza Unida Party. What did the youth, especially those who had supported the party, think of the party now that it had ceased to operate? The follow-up study included in-depth interviews with some 300 of the original 1,040 young people who had participated in 1977. It was found that 94 percent (168) of the youth in the follow-up study who had supported the party in 1977 still were sympathetic to what the party had stood for, and they all said that they would support the party, or another party like it, if it emerged again. In other words, the factors that had influenced them to support the party in the first place still influenced them to support its goals in 1982. Thus, special attention should be given to the conditions that originally influenced the youth to support one party over another, because these conditions were important enough to have sustained these party identifications for five to six years. It is also important to point out that the follow-up study suggests that a proportion, and perhaps a significant one, of this generation of the Chicano electorate has been placed in a position, with the demise of Raza Unida, of having to choose between two political parties to which they have no allegiance. At the time of the follow-up study, 46 percent (seventy-eight) of these youth said that they refused to vote and 54 percent (ninety) said that they voted reluctantly for the Democratic Party as the lesser of two evils.

The overall findings related to social class differences in attitudes toward voting and political parties are significant because to date social class differences within the Chicano population or, for that matter, any non-white ethnic groups, have been overlooked. Chicanos, like other non-white ethnic groups, are usually treated as a homogeneous group and compared only to whites. This approach obscures not only the social class basis of politics within the Chicano community, but the general nature of American politics as well.

This chapter has shown that the interaction between an individual's social class interests and the perceived constraints on expressing and acting on them within the city in which he/she lives, explains the youth's attitudes toward voting and support of a particular political party. The next chapter moves to an analysis of the extent to which various aspects of the urban environment influence attitudinal support for political protest and violence.

5

Political Protest
and Violence
Attitudes Toward
Pressure Politics

Following the urban riots of the 1960s, political scientists and sociologists in the United States became acutely interested in protest and violence. The primary concern of analysts at the time was determining what caused urban riots to occur. The most basic question that interested them was whether there was something peculiar about the black urban experience that led to large-scale protest movements and/or the use of violence.[1] Interestingly, the questions they addressed were very similar to those asked by Wirth and Park; that is, is there something about the urban experience that causes the individual to become alienated and discontented to such a degree that he/she begins to have positive attitudes toward physically aggressive political acts as a remedy for these conditions? Both Wirth and Park feared that it was quite possible that urban life could produce such a reaction.[2] Many analysts of the urban riots of the 1960s and 1970s in fact did attribute the cause of riots to the urban life of blacks—more specifically, to the deterioration of socioeconomic conditions in cities and a general climate of racism that blocked socioeconomic mobility and forced blacks to live a life of poverty.[3]

This chapter is concerned with determining the Chicano youth's attitudes toward political protest and violence, and the factors, particularly those associated with urban life, that have influenced their attitudes. At this point, it is appropriate to define the terms "political protest" and "violence," which are political facts and must be understood as part of the spectrum of political behavior. Within the context of this work, protest and political violence are not considered to be any more inherently irrational than other political acts, as some social scientists have argued. Whether they are or are not irrational is, as Arendt has suggested, dependent on a number of contingent factors.[4]

Some analysts of American politics have tended to combine violence and protest and label the result political protest.[5] They have viewed riots as political acts that demonstrate a symbolic form of protest. Other violence, especially that associated with opposition to the Vietnam War, was considered a form of protest against the foreign policy of the United States.[6] However, these views of violence and protest confuse two potentially independent acts and can lead to errors in the analysis of the causes and motives for an individual's participation in such acts, as well as possible errors in predicting his/her future use of these tactics. For this reason, protest activity and political violence will be treated separately here. Protest activities will follow Lipsky's definition:

> A mode of political action oriented toward objections to one or more policies or conditions characterized by showmanship or display of an unconventional nature and undertaken to obtain rewards from political or economic systems while working within the system.[7]

It is the "working within the system" that constitutes the major element of protest. One can think of few instances, although there are some, where protest activity has had the intent of changing the fundamental structure of the government. For the most part, protest movements in the United States, especially the more recent ones, have endeavored to create changes within the system.

Political violence, however, has a different character. It can be either a form of political protest, as in the case of a riot, or an act that intends to create revolutionary changes in the political structure, such as urban guerrilla warfare. Whatever its form, it must be, as Arendt has argued, "instrumental" to be considered political violence. She has stated:

> Violence . . . is distinguished by its instrumental character. Phenomenologically, it is close to strength, since the implements of violence, like all other tools, are designed and used for the purpose of multiplying natural strength until, in the last stage of their development, they can substitute for it.[8]

This definition is at odds with that of Lupsha and MacKinnon, who have argued that it is a much too stringent definition of political violence. They believe that the fatal wounding of a police officer in a ghetto, or the bombing of a branch building of the Bank of America, must be considered aspects of political violence, but they contend that any definition that requires that the act be "instrumental" would prohibit this determination.[9] It is easy to agree with Lupsha and MacKinnon concerning the violent nature of these acts, but unless some type of political intent were necessary in order for them to be described as political violence, it would be next to impossible to separate random violence from that which is clearly political. Thus, in this study, the youth's support for political violence is considered in relation to its "instrumental" character.

In order to sort out and clarify some of the confusion regarding both protest activity and political violence and who subscribes to what tactic, four questions will be addressed: (1) Is there general support among the youth of this study for protest and political violence as legitimate modes of political activity? (2) What institutions and/or people are mentioned most as possible targets for these tactics, and why? (3) What are the social characteristics of those who support protest and political violence, and are there differences depending on whether a person supports one or the other? (4) Is a person's political ideology a factor in supporting protest and/or political violence?

Political Protest

This section concerns itself primarily with the question: Is there support among the youths in this study for political protest as a tactic? As mentioned earlier in this chapter, protest can be either peaceful or violent, and because of this, each form will be treated separately, with the nonviolent form being considered first.

The youth in the study were all asked to evaluate "economic boycott" as a concept. This concept was chosen because in each of the three communities a number of economic boycotts that directly concerned Chicanos either were in progress or had just recently ended. There was a boycott against table grape growers; there was a boycott against lettuce that did not bear the label of the United Farm Workers Union; there was a boycott against Gallo Wines; there was a boycott against Coors Beer; and, finally, there was a boycott

Table 5.1
Semantic Differential Mean Scores for the Evaluation of Economic
Boycott and Riots, Controlling for City of Residence

	Economic Boycott		Riots	
San Antonio	3.52	(328)	5.01	(331)
Albuquerque	2.41	(309)	3.24	(311)
Los Angeles	2.37	(323)	3.15	(327)

Note: Scores should be interpreted as positive when they are from 1–3.50, neutral
when they are from 3.51–4.50; and negative when they are from 4.51–7.00.

against the Farrah Clothing Company. Obviously, all these boycotts
did not involve one single organization, although the United Farm
Workers Union was responsible for calling most of them.

As Table 5.1 indicates, there was more general support for economic boycotts in Albuquerque and Los Angeles than in San Antonio. Two factors explain this result. The first concerns the nature
of local politics in each of the cities. As Eisinger has noted, in his
study of protest behavior in American cities:

> Protest occurs most frequently in cities where the
> opportunity structure is relatively closed. The protesters are
> people who are unable to gain access to decision-making
> councils by conventional means.[10]

Chicanos in all three cities have had difficulty gaining access to
the decision-making apparatus, so on this count all three cities are
the same. However, Eisinger went on to say that protest was most
likely to occur in cities with a mixture of open and closed factors—
if the system is too closed there will be no protest, while a system
that is too open will produce the same result.[11] Here the difference
between the cities looms large. Both Los Angeles and Albuquerque
have more of the mix that Eisinger noted. On the one hand, there
is the closed part of the system—the difficulty that Chicanos, as
well as other poor groups, have in gaining access to the decision-
making machinery. Yet there are open factors as well. For example,
in Los Angeles there is a general tolerance for protests on the part
of the authorities that is due primarily to the attitude that this type
of behavior is preferable to that which occurred in the Watts riot of

1965 and the East Los Angeles riots of 1970 and 1971, and to the fear that a riot could happen again. Albuquerque is tolerant of protests for similar reasons, even though the disturbances that have occurred there have not been of nearly the same magnitude as those in Los Angeles. Furthermore, the mere fact that there have been a considerable number of protests in both of these cities has acted to reinforce the attitude that protest is a legitimate, and sometimes an effective, political act. In San Antonio, however, there is a closed system. In fact, San Antonio is very much like other parts of southern Texas in that there is a general fear of the Chicano within the Anglo community, primarily because Chicanos constitute such a large proportion of the city's population. Where fear in the other two cities has opened the system, in San Antonio it has caused the opposite reaction. The authorities there have made every effort to discourage protests, and rarely has protest activity produced the positive response that the protesters intended. The result has been fewer attempts at protest and a more generalized feeling of indifference toward protest as an effective political tactic.[12]

The second factor that helps to explain why there is more support for boycotts in Los Angeles and Albuquerque than in San Antonio is related to the first, but has some independent aspects as well. Basically, the organizations responsible for the large national boycotts have been more active in Los Angeles and Albuquerque than they have in San Antonio. For example, the boycotts led by the United Farm Workers Union against various lettuce, wine, and table grape growers have had their largest organizational networks in California and in the midwestern and eastern states; while the boycott against the Adolph Coors brewery, for unfair labor practices, has been most active in the states of Colorado, New Mexico, and California. This has occurred for two reasons. First, the boycotts themselves involved Chicanos in California and Colorado, which necessitated some effort to gather support for their cause in those two states. Second, the markets for the boycotted products were to be found in both of these states and in the East. Therefore, in order for the boycotts to be effective, there was a need to direct most of the activity to these areas. However, it would be incorrect to think that these boycotts have no organizational presence in the San Antonio area. These organizations do exist, but they have not been as visibly active as they have been in the other two cities. As a result, the salience of the economic boycott as a tactic of protest has been minimized.[13]

Chapter 5

Urban Effects on Attitudes Toward Protest

In all three cities, the length of time the youth had spent in the city influenced how they evaluated economic boycotts (see P_{61} in Figure 5.1, 5.2, 5.3). Longer residence produced more positive attitudes toward the concept. Youths who had lived in their present city of residence for more than five years had a great deal of confidence that economic boycotts were an effective means of bringing about needed changes. Much of this confidence was associated with personal experience and with an awareness that such tactics had worked in other cases. The in-depth interviews provided strong evidence that the youth in this study, as well as members of their families, were more likely to be involved in local politics the longer they lived in the city. As they spent more time in the city, they said that they felt less like outsiders and more as if they "belonged." These feelings of belonging were transformed into positive attitudes about becoming involved in local politics. Consequently, many of them had been involved in some type of protest, and 65 percent (676) had been involved in some phase of one of the national economic boycotts.

Those youth who had been in each of the three cities for a relatively short period of time (usually less than five years), appeared to be uneasy about economic boycotts as a tactic. Some 45 percent (sixty-six) felt that they did not want to become involved in this type of politics because it was too risky, while 23 percent (thirty-four) said that they did not believe that this type of tactic was politically effective. This reaction seemed quite reasonable when it was learned that 74 percent (108) were from rural areas where, they said, such forms of political behavior were viewed in extremely negative terms; another 30 percent (44) reported that they had lived in areas where economic boycotts had occurred and had proved to be ineffective.

Whether or not the youth lived in densely populated neighborhoods had no effect in any of the three cities on their evaluations of the concept of economic boycott; but whether or not they lived in more homogeneous Chicano communities did have an impact. In each of the three communities, those youths who lived in less ethnically homogeneous areas gave the concept higher scores (see Figures 5.1, 5.2, 5.3, P_{63}). This should not be interpreted to mean, however, that the youth who lived in predominantly Chicano areas

FIGURE 5.1
Path Model of the Effects in San Antonio of Urban
Contextual Variables and Personal Variables on Student
Attitudes Toward Economic Boycott*

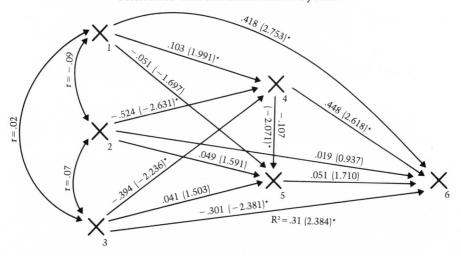

* = All coefficients are significant at the .05 level or beyond on
     a two-tailed "t" test
X_1 = Length of residence in the city
X_2 = Population density in neighborhood
X_3 = Ethnic homogeneity in respondent's neighborhood
X_4 = Socioeconomic status
X_5 = Traditional cultural values (retention of)
X_6 = Economic boycott

were negative toward the concept, which is simply not the case.
Their scores were primarily positive, but they were less positive
than the scores given by those who lived in more integrated neighborhoods. The differences between communities reflect different perceptions regarding the use of economic boycotts. In predominantly
Chicano areas, the prevailing view was that economic boycotts were
good, but that they took a long time to be successful and that this
amount of time could not always be spared without a great deal of
suffering. For these youth, other tactics sometimes seemed more
effective and appropriate. On the other hand, those who lived in
more integrated neighborhoods viewed economic boycotts as ex-

FIGURE 5.2
Path Model of the Effects in Albuquerque of Urban
Contextual Variables and Personal Variables on Student
Attitudes Toward Economic Boycott*

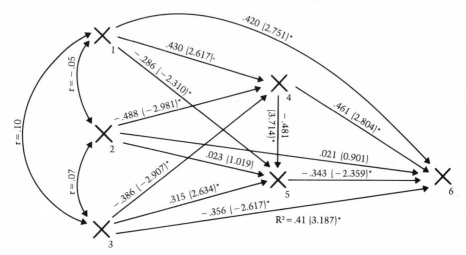

* =   All coefficients are significant at the .05 level or beyond on
       a two-tailed "t" test
X_1 =   Length of residence in the city
X_2 =   Population density in neighborhood
X_3 =   Ethnic homogeneity in respondent's neighborhood
X_4 =   Socioeconomic status
X_5 =   Traditional cultural values (retention of)
X_6 =   Economic boycott

tremely effective, not only because they produced results, but also
because they helped to organize the Chicano community. Sixty-nine
percent (295) of the youth from these neighborhoods said that one
of the most beneficial aspects of this type of political activity was
that it stimulated many people in the community to participate,
and this helped Chicanos to look at themselves as a community.
Thus, it was their opinion that where other forms of political behavior had worked to divide the community, the various economic
boycotts had acted to unify it. What was most important for these
youth was the vitality of the Chicano community, because they
identified with it personally for cultural reasons, even though they
were not a physical part of it. Consequently, any activity that had

FIGURE 5.3
Path Model of the Effects in Los Angeles of Urban
Contextual Variables and Personal Variables on Student
Attitudes Toward Economic Boycott*

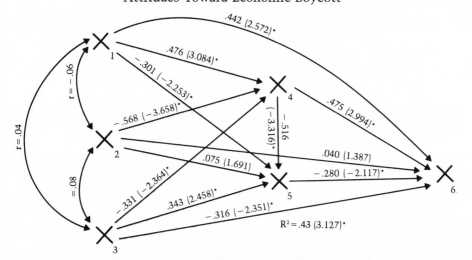

* = All coefficients are significant at the .05 level or beyond on
      a two-tailed "t" test
X_1 = Length of residence in the city
X_2 = Population density in neighborhood
X_3 = Ethnic homogeneity in respondent's neighborhood
X_4 = Socioeconomic status
X_5 = Traditional cultural values (retention of)
X_6 = Economic boycott

the possibility of enhancing community solidarity was considered
very important, while the specific goals of the boycott assumed a
somewhat secondary importance.

Social Class and Attitudes Toward Protest

In all three cities, the youth's socioeconomic status proved to have
had an impact on their evaluations of the economic boycott. In each
case, the higher the respondent's status was, the more positive his/
her score was.[14] Middle-class youths felt that economic boycotts
were effective because they had produced some gains for Chicano

migrant workers in signing union contracts, and some rent strikes had been successful in forcing the landlords to improve the property. In addition, these middle-class youths wanted to become politically involved in helping the poorer segment of Chicano society, and the fact that economic boycotts, at least those involving the United Farm Workers, were legal made them feel that there was not much chance of their experiencing negative repercussions from participation. Interestingly, 86 percent (895) said that they wanted to participate in the economic boycotts that were nationally oriented, such as the lettuce or the Coors Beer boycott, but only 19 percent (198) said that they wanted to participate in local boycotts, such as rent strikes. One reason they gave was that they would have felt awkward participating in most rent strikes, since they were not residents of the places they would have to picket. The other reason most often given was that it was not always clear whether rent strikes and the like were legal, and the authorities were sometimes very forceful in the way in which they dealt with such activities; thus, they did not want to get involved. Reluctance to become involved in protests that had the potential of eliciting negative sanctions from the authorities was the reason that the respondents were so positive toward economic boycotts like the lettuce boycott, which allowed them to participate with a low probability of high personal cost.[15]

The lower-class youths were less positive toward the economic boycott as a tactic. A number of reasons were given for this. First, there was a general dislike of the fact that the success of economic boycotts like the lettuce and Gallo wine boycotts were dependent on the cooperation and support of Anglos. Sixty-eight percent (396) said that they did not like the fact that the United Farm Workers Union had to be dependent on contributions from the Anglo community, especially the large labor unions (the U.A.W. and the AFL-CIO both gave money, and the United Farm Workers are now an affiliate of the AFL-CIO), because they believed that Chicanos, through the United Farm Workers Union, would be indebted to Anglos again. An illustrative example:

Richard, 17-year-old son of an automobile mechanic in Los Angeles:

I really didn't like that Chavez [leader of the United Farm Workers Union] had to accept money from the other bigger unions. Now he will be dependent on them. I mean, if the economic boycotts win, Chicanos still won't have all the

respect and dignity they deserve because they will still owe
these other Anglo unions.

Further, 42 percent (245) said that they did not care for the fact
that in order for the boycott to be successful, Chicanos had to appeal
to Anglos not to eat the products. Not only did they not appreciate
having to rely on Anglos for the success of their protest, but they
considered their appeal to boycott lettuce and Gallo wine to be
begging, and they felt that this was inappropriate.

Another reason mentioned by the lower class in explaining their
dislike of economic boycotts was that they had to work with Anglos.
The United Farm Workers had recruited whoever wanted to work,
and many Anglos, especially the youth, responded by volunteering
their services and time. This tended to alienate some of the Chicanos
from lower-class families. They thought that Chicanos and Filipinos
should do their own work, since it concerned them. In addition, 12
percent (seventy) said that they did not like to work with Anglos
because Anglos always wanted to be the leaders.[16]

> Lydia, 18-year-old daughter of a factory worker in San
> Antonio:
>
> The trouble with economic boycott is that too many Anglos
> are working for it. We Chicanos need to do the work
> ourselves. That way we can become strong as a community
> and show the Anglos we can do things ourselves and that we
> don't need their help.

> Tomás, 18-year-old son of a janitor in Albuquerque:
>
> I guess the main reason I don't think the economic boycott is
> really the best, although it does help some, you know, is
> because the Anglos who come to help always want to run the
> show. I've gone down to work for the lettuce boycott, and
> every time an Anglo is either running whatever we're going
> to do or wants to run it.

The fact that economic boycotts sometimes require a considerable
length of time to accomplish the desired results is a factor in the
lower-class youths being less positive toward them. In discussing
boycotts, these youth often mentioned their frustration at having
to wait for any sort of positive results. Most of this frustration was

directed at the fact that while everyone was waiting, some people were suffering for no good reason.

The last factor influencing the lower-class evaluation of economic boycotts is related to the perception that participation in such activities makes a person physically vulnerable. Many of the lower-class youth interviewed had been personally involved in rural areas with the grape, lettuce, and wine boycotts, while others in the city had been involved with rent strikes. Fifty-two percent (131) of those who had participated in these particular activities said that at times they had had a difficult time with the authorities. Some had even been arrested, and six said they had been physically abused while involved in the boycotts. This experience had caused them to feel somewhat apprehensive about participating in such activities. They explained that they felt that they were vulnerable to the courts' interpretation of the laws concerning the boycott and to police interpretation of enforcement of the law. This, coupled with the fact that many efforts to use economic boycotts to create change had failed, left them feeling cautious about boycotts as a protest tactic.

Cultural Identity and Attitudes Toward Protest

In both Los Angeles and Albuquerque, the less a respondent had retained an involvement in traditional Chicano culture, the more positive his/her scores for economic boycott were (see Fig. 5.2, 5.3, P_{65}). The youth who had not retained traditional culture perceived the economic boycotts as part of the Chicano cultural renaissance. Cesar Chavez and the United Farm Workers Union were looked upon as leaders in Chicano efforts to assert their rights and culture. Respondents cited such phenomena as the *teatro campesino*, or theater of the rural worker, which helped to dramatize both the plight of migrant workers and the union's attempt to organize them, as examples of cultural pride and development.[17] They also made reference to the flag of the United Farm Workers Union as a symbol of Chicano culture, pointing to the Aztec eagle that occupies the flag's center and characterizing it as an object that was distinctly Chicano. Thus, for these young Chicanos, economic boycotts had a positive effect on Chicano identity, and they were positive toward them because they identified strongly with Chicano culture.

It is important to point out that social class background is a factor in the attitudes described above. The youth of upper-status backgrounds who had not retained much of their traditional culture were among the strongest supporters of economic boycotts because of their impact on cultural identity. Youth of lower-status backgrounds who had not retained their traditional culture thought that economic boycotts were important, but not as important in creating political changes as other means of political protest, especially the more violent forms. A discussion of what forms of protest they both supported and their rationales for choosing them will be presented later in this chapter.

The other significant aspect of this relationship is that the youth in Albuquerque and Los Angeles who had retained their traditional culture did not score economic boycotts as high as did those who had not retained many aspects of this culture. Since these youth had retained a substantial amount of traditional culture, the questions of cultural identity and a cultural renaissance were not of primary importance in their evaluations of the economic boycott. Therefore, instead of focusing on the fact that economic boycotts had produced more cultural activities, awareness, and pride, they evaluated the concept in terms of its effectiveness as a political tactic. Their lower evaluations reflect their belief that although the boycotts had achieved some success, they had not been as successful as other forms of political activity such as strikes and riots. It should be kept in mind that most of these youth were lower-class and that their beliefs reflect a lower-class perspective.

Alternative Forms of Protest Activity

Although the economic boycotts of lettuce, grapes, and wine have received the most attention from outside observers, the Chicano youth in this study were involved in other non-violent forms of protest as well. Probably the most frequent target of protest among the youth from Los Angeles and Albuquerque has been the public schools.[18] Protest against the public schools was reported in San Antonio as well, but it was not the most frequently mentioned form of protest. The protests against the schools center on two issues which are not necessarily independent of one another. One has to do with the frustrations involved in being confined for six to eight hours a day in one physical structure.[19] The most common protests related to this issue concerned dress codes, which were considered too stringent; inadequate time to eat lunch; the food served in the cafeteria, which was considered to be of low quality; smoking regulations on campus, which were considered too strict; too little time between classes; and penalties for tardiness and absenteeism, which were considered too harsh. The forms of protest concerning these problems have been varied, but have included formal meetings between the youths, sometimes accompanied by their parents, and the school administration to discuss the grievances; presenting the administration with signatures opposing certain policies or supporting new proposed policies; and picketing the school. Interestingly enough, the lower-class youth appear to have been involved in this type of protest more than those from the middle class; they were much more sensitive than their middle-class colleagues about being confined by the codes of the school. Although there was always a great deal of "grumbling" among these youth about rectifying the situation, protest activity rarely seems to have achieved a very high level of intensity.

Another issue that produced protest against the schools was the educational system's seeming inability to promote the skills necessary for most youth to achieve socioeconomic mobility. The concern here was that Chicano youth be given the best education available so that they would have the same opportunities for advancement as other students, especially those from families with higher social standing. In the past, the schools have been quite negligent in meeting the educational needs of Chicanos and, as a result, there always have been inordinately high dropout rates for Chicanos, as well as very low percentages enrolling in college or professional schools.[20] School administrators have been a focal point for criticism by the Chicano communities in Los Angeles and Albuquerque, which has put them on the defensive. Part of the problem faced by the schools emanates from the structure of the economy, which limits full employment. For example, many of the youth believed that the difficulty that many young Chicanos (most mentioned members of their own families) have had in securing employment was the fault of the high schools because the schools did not prepare Chicanos adequately to compete equally for jobs. Protest activity was directed primarily at: (1) curricula that were considered dated and ineffective in developing necessary skills; (2) teachers who were considered incompetent in their ability to teach new skills; (3) teachers who were considered racist in their attitudes toward Chicanos; and (4) school administrators who were considered disorganized in estab-

lishing clear strategies for quality education and/or who were un-
cooperative with the local community in helping to solve school
problems. The youth reported that they had used various types of
protest tactics, including sit-ins, picketing the schools and central
administration buildings, and staging walkouts at the schools they
attended. It became apparent that the issues raised by the protesters
concerning the structure and quality of the educational system were
quite sensitive for both school and local authorities because they
were difficult to solve completely. In fact, 54 percent of the youth
who were involved in these protests said that there was a great deal
of hostility and tension between the authorities and those protesting.[21]

Sixty percent (257) of the youth from Los Angeles and Albuquerque
who were active in protesting the quality of the educational system
were from the middle class. They were concerned that they be able
to compete with Anglo students for positions in the best colleges,
as well as for employment. For the most part, they aspired to achieve
higher socioeconomic status and were making demands on the educational system to give them the necessary skills.

Jason, 18-year-old son of an architect from Los Angeles:

I was involved in the protest at our school for better
education, especially better teachers. Some of the teachers
were never prepared for class and some didn't like Chicanos.
We needed to get rid of these teachers, but the school
authorities wouldn't do anything, so there were protests. . . .
It is important to have a good education because you need it
to get into good colleges and get good jobs. Up until now the
Anglos have gotten the best jobs because they had better
schools and teachers.

Denise, 18-year-old daughter of an accountant from
Albuquerque:

When we protested, we wanted the schools to have the same
facilities as the Anglo schools. We also said we wanted better
teachers and better courses. You know, the Anglo always
thinks Chicanos are dumb, but that's not true, it's just that
the schools have not been good. Chicanos want good jobs that
pay high just like they [Anglos] do. I know I do. So we need
to get a good education so we can go to college and get these
jobs.

The other 40 percent (172) who were involved in protests concerning the quality of schools were primarily from lower-class families who were in the process of transition. That is, these families' income had increased to a level where they now could be considered lower-middle class, on the basis of purely economic criteria. In 75 percent (129) of the cases, these families had recently (within two years) moved from strictly lower-class housing to housing associated with lower-middle-class incomes. The youth from these families were particularly critical of the school system, and in most protest activity they were much more aggressive than the middle-class students who were protesting. These youth's criticism emanated from the fact that although their families now had incomes that were middle-class, most had not yet developed the values associated with average middle-class families. For example, they wanted to do well in their academic work, and their parents also wanted them to, but the values associated with academic achievement, such as persistent reading and study on the part of the students and constant monitoring by parents to see that their children fully understand and complete their school work, were more often than not absent. The students from these homes wanted desperately to rid themselves of what they perceived as the Anglo society's stereotype that they were "dumb" or "stupid." Therefore, they put a considerable amount of pressure on the school.[22] When grades did not reach the levels expected, the school was blamed because the youth reasoned that since the physical environment was no longer a problem, the school somehow should produce good students.

Protest against the public schools also was reported by the youth in San Antonio, but among a low percentage (19 percent) of those interviewed. The most frequent protest activity in which these youth engaged was working for an organization named Communities Organized for Public Services (COPS), a Chicano citizens' group. This group had protested and lobbied effectively enough to secure a better drainage system as well as more paved streets in poor Chicano neighborhoods of San Antonio. At the time that the research for this study was being conducted, COPS was involved in a battle with the city council over the rezoning of an area of land for the construction of a large shopping mall. The land being rezoned was on top of an aquifer that was the sole source of water for the entire metropolitan area. COPS objected to the construction of this shopping mall because (1) environmental studies had produced evidence that there was a possibility that the underground water system could be seriously damaged, thereby affecting the quality of the water; and (2) an added shopping mall on the outskirts of the city would draw money away from the central city, forcing businesses to close and putting unnecessary pressure on the poorer Chicano community to pay increased transportation costs to shop for simple necessities. Almost all of the youth who had been involved said that they had helped in soliciting signatures for petitions. At the time, COPS was mounting a campaign to get the number of signatures required to put the issue of rezoning the area over the aquifer up for a referendum vote. Some of the tasks in which the youth reported that they had been engaged were standing on street corners and going from house to house in various neighborhoods attempting to solicit the necessary signatures for a referendum. A few also reported that they went to city council meetings to be vocal protesters against the proposed action to rezone the area.

The police and the local public works department were two other institutions against which some of the youth in the study had protested. Again, this was true only for Los Angeles and Albuquerque. No San Antonio youth reported that they had protested against the police, and only two said that they had been involved in any type of protest against the public works department. In Los Angeles and Albuquerque, about one-third of the youth had been involved in protests against the police. This is not very surprising, considering the high level of hostility that exists between Chicano youth and the police. Protest usually has been directed at police procedures that have been considered either too harsh or purely acts of harassment, and also at the lack of quality protection from local crime. All these protests took the form of picketing the police headquarters.

A small percentage of the youth from both Los Angeles and Albuquerque (6 percent, or twenty, and 5 percent, or sixteen, respectively) said that they had participated in a protest against some subdepartment of the public works department. Most of these protests were designed to dramatize the need for better drainage, street maintenance, and garbage collection. The youth often accompanied one of their parents, who usually were more deeply involved in the issues underlying these protests than they themselves were, or so they reported. Holding protest signs and picketing were their primary tasks.

It has been established at this point that some of the youth in this study had participated in nonviolent protest activity. But outside of the economic boycott as a form of protest, as discussed earlier, how much support was there among them for nonviolent protest as a legitimate and effective political tactic? That is, did the Chicano youth in this study, regardless of whether they participated in protests or not, think that nonviolent protest should be used? The evidence indicates that 66 percent (217) in Los Angeles, 60 percent (190) in Albuquerque, and 34 percent (112) in San Antonio thought that protest was a legitimate and effective form of political action that should be used by the Chicano community. The same pattern existed among the cities as was found previously in the evaluation of the economic boycott. This provides further evidence to support the argument made earlier that in San Antonio protest is not a popular form of political expression. Most of the respondents from San Antonio were apprehensive about the use of political protest, even if it was nonviolent. Protest activity, whether nonviolent or violent, simply had not become a legitimate aspect of San Antonio's political culture, whereas it had in Los Angeles and Albuquerque.

Support for Riots as a Form of Political Protest

The evidence in Table 5.1 indicates support for riots among the youth from Albuquerque and Los Angeles, but not among those from San Antonio. In San Antonio, any type of violence is handled forcefully by the law enforcement agencies—the San Antonio police, the Texas State Police and the Texas Rangers—and this has created an atmosphere of fear with regard to participating in riots. The youth's attitudes about riots and their participation in them reflect this political ethos.[23] Sixty-eight percent (225) of those interviewed said that they had been told stories of police brutality against Mexicans, and some said that they had lived in communities where they had seen these acts committed. The Department of Public Safety (the Texas State Police) and the Texas Rangers were mentioned most often as involved in acts of police brutality, and they seemed to evoke the most fear among the youth, although the San Antonio Police were also mentioned. These youth said that riots would produce few meaningful changes for the Chicano community, and that all that they would get out of participating would be getting arrested and/or beaten and killed. The youth from San Antonio simply perceived no personal benefits that could be gained from their participation in a riot. Furthermore, they could not see any advantage to rioting even if they themselves did not participate. Their view was that if people rioted, the authorities would use force to put down the riot and would do nothing to correct the social conditions that had created a climate conducive to riots in the first place. They went on to say that they thought the authorities would simply spend more money on the law enforcement agencies so that they could handle future riots with greater efficiency and effectiveness.

In Los Angeles and Albuquerque there was support for riots, although there is considerable variation in the respondents' scores. The difference between the attitudes of Chicanos in Los Angeles and Albuquerque and those in San Antonio is attributable to the fact that protest activity, including riots, has been more prevalent in Los Angeles and Albuquerque and has been reported extensively through the news media. Some successes also have emerged from protesting and rioting. For example, a great deal of money has come into the rioting communities in an effort to solve some of the problems that have caused the discontent. Eighty-five percent (544) of the respondents from Los Angeles and Albuquerque combined said that they had read or heard a great deal about riots and that they thought some improvements had been made after the riots. Thus, the youth of Los Angeles and Albuquerque were given a relatively positive image of riots. Yet the data indicate that the Chicanos from these two cities were split as to whether riots were a positive or negative form of political participation. They also indicate that the urban environment, as well as the socioeconomic status of the youth's families, influence these perceptions.

As Figure 5.4 shows, the length of time that an individual has lived in Los Angeles does influence his/her evaluation of riots. Those youth who had lived in the city for six years or more felt positively toward riots as a form of political participation. This is due to a number of factors. First, the youth who had lived in the city for six years or more not only had a wider range of contact with various aspects of the city, but also had built up more frustrations as a result. In fact, in the interviews, these youth vocalized at least twice as many grievances with regard to certain aspects of city life—local agencies that provided inadequate service, the police, and various store owners—as did those youth who had lived in the city for a shorter period of time.[24] Second, the longer the youth had lived in Los Angeles, the more they viewed Los Angeles as their permanent home and the more comfortable they felt about participating in local

FIGURE 5.4
Path Model of the Effects in Los Angeles of Urban
Contextual Variables and Personal Variables on Student
Attitudes Toward Riots*

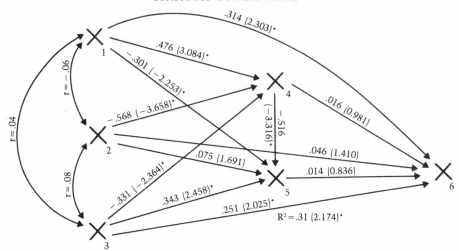

* = All coefficients are significant at the .05 level or beyond on a two-tailed "t" test
X_1 = Length of residence in the city
X_2 = Population density in neighborhood
X_3 = Ethnic homogeneity in respondent's neighborhood
X_4 = Socioeconomic status
X_5 = Traditional cultural values (retention of)
X_6 = Riots

about participating, they also became more frustrated with what they perceived to be their inability to influence public policy, especially policy affecting them. These youths viewed the political system as being prejudiced against Chicanos, and therefore felt that conventional political channels were closed to them. Finally, longer residence had provided more opportunities for them to hear about the Watts riot of 1965, the East Los Angeles riots of 1970–1971, and some of the benefits that had resulted from them.[25] As a number of studies have argued, a type of riot ideology had emerged among blacks in Los Angeles after Watts, which encouraged a general belief that riots were a legitimate form of protest and could be effective

FIGURE 5.5
Path Model of the Effects in Albuquerque of Urban
Contextual Variables on Student
Attitudes Toward Riots*

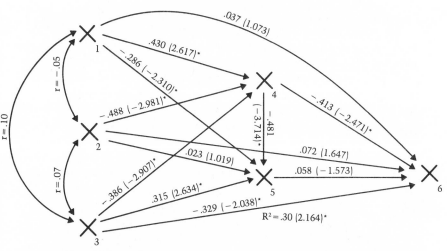

* = All coefficients are significant at the .05 level or beyond on a two-tailed "t" test

X_1 = Length of residence in the city
X_2 = Population density in neighborhood
X_3 = Ethnic homogeneity in respondent's neighborhood
X_4 = Socioeconomic status
X_5 = Traditional cultural values (retention of)
X_6 = Riots

in pressuring authorities to improve conditions.[26] The Chicanos in this study who had lived in Los Angeles for six years or more shared this belief about riots, and used the Watts and East Los Angeles riots as positive examples.

The amount of time that respondents had lived in Albuquerque (Fig. 5.5, P_{61}) had no effect on how they would evaluate riots. Nowhere in the interviews could a pattern be detected whereby simply living in the urban environment produced discontent and/or support for riots as a possible solution. Whether or not these young Chicanos supported riots depended on how a given individual related to other aspects of the urban environment.

In Los Angeles, the youth who lived in areas that were predominantly Chicano were more positive toward riots than those who did not live in such areas. Living in these neighborhoods tended to produce a strong sense of ethnic identity, as well as strong opinions concerning in-group/out-group relations. What has emerged from this situation are feelings that the Anglo community in general discriminates against Chicanos, and that they as Chicanos are relatively deprived vis-a-vis most Anglos with the larger society. Seventy-eight percent (143) of the youth from these neighborhoods believed that they were deprived, and, as has been found in similar studies of blacks with strong feelings of deprivation, they considered riots both an acceptable and an effective method to redress grievances.[27]

As the data in Figure 5.5 indicate, living in predominantly Chicano neighborhoods in Albuquerque has had the opposite effect of the one it has had in the case of Los Angeles. In Albuquerque, the more ethnic the respondent's neighborhood, the lower riots were scored. Seventy percent (125) of the youth who lived in Chicano neighborhoods did not see the need to redress grievances by rioting. It was their opinion that any grievances they had could be handled better by seeking the help of their local political representative. Nearly all of the politicians in these neighborhoods, it should be noted, are Chicanos themselves, and they have worked to establish close personal ties with the electorate in their districts. They have emphasized that if people in their district have problems, they should bring these problems to the politicians and they will be taken care of. These politicians have discouraged the use of riots because riots, by virtue of the fact that citizens take matters into their own hands, threaten their positions as community leaders as well as the entire patron-client system that they have tried to establish. Their efforts seem to have been relatively successful, at least among the youth in this study, because these youth believe that community leaders are effective in solving personal and community problems. This finding may seem to contradict that regarding economic boycotts, since the youth from these areas held positive opinions of economic boycotts as a form of political protest while at the same time holding negative ones of riots. However, the findings are not contradictory in that there is support for economic boycotts as well as for other forms of nonviolent protest because they are legal, and because many politicians have become involved in many of these issues and/or protest activities. Thus, these youth adhere to the general political norm of their community.

Social Class as a Determinant of Riot Support

Banfield, in *The Unheavenly City*, has identified social class as the most critical variable in explaining riot behavior, contending that the lower class is more aggressive and therefore more predisposed to riot. He also has argued that, in most cases, participation in riots has been based on a young lower-class person's search for fun (excitement) and profit (stealing).[28] However, Sears and McConahay, in their study of the Watts riot, refuted Banfield's theory, presenting data that showed the opposite: the youth from relatively high-status families were more active in riots than lower-class youth, and that the youth who did participate felt more aggrieved than did the non-rioters and participated in the riots to protest their grievances.[29] In sum, Sears and McConahay argued that riots were a product of people protesting deeply felt grievances, while Banfield contended that riots were the result of lower-class values and had little to do with grievances.

How do the data in the present study bear on the arguments and data presented by Banfield and by Sears and McConahay? The data for Los Angeles and Albuquerque indicate that there is support for both arguments; first an analysis of the Los Angeles findings follows.

Social class in Los Angeles does not show a direct causal effect on support for riots in this study, but there are, nevertheless, some interesting aspects in the relationship between class status and riot support. An examination of the distribution of scores for riots in relation to social class indicates that there is support for riots at both ends of the socioeconomic scale. The middle-class youth in Los Angeles were found to be as positive toward riots as the lower-class ones. Although these middle-class Chicanos did not feel deprived of the physical necessities of life, 80 percent (119) felt deprived of an equal opportunity to be as socially mobile as Anglos within the larger society. They expected upward mobility because they felt personally competent, but they also had fears that they would be deprived of this mobility because of racial prejudice.[30] Two examples of this thinking follow:

David, 17-year-old son of the owner of a dry cleaning store:

The Anglos in this city or for the country try to put you down just if you are Chicano. They don't even find out if you are smart or not. They just think you are dumb because you are Chicano. Like, I won't get as good a job as I would get if I was an Anglo 'cause they think I'm not as good as they are. I know I am, though. I've got a good education from this high school and I have studied hard, so I know I can do most things, but a lot of Anglos won't give me or a lot of Chicanos a chance 'cause they know some of us are better than they are. I mean, they think they'll lose their jobs to us or their places in college.

Lisa, 17-year-old daughter of an accountant:

I read a lot about discrimination and I feel like I won't be given the same chance as Anglo students. I think I'm as good as anyone, but it doesn't matter because Anglos still discriminate against you. I really think this is bad and I resent it 'cause I work as hard as any Anglo and deserve the same things.

In addition to the fact that these youth saw rioting as a legitimate form of protest, they also thought that it was effective. Most mentioned that riots made the people in power aware of injustices and forced them to take steps to correct the situation. Their opinions were based on the belief that after the Watts riot and the East Los Angeles riots more jobs were made available through various federal relief projects. In addition, they thought that private enterprise hired more minorities because of a number of incentives provided to them by the federal government. Thus, the evidence concerning the middle-class respondents from Los Angeles would tend to support the findings of Sears and McConahay.[31]

Support for riots was also found among the youth of lower-SES backgrounds; however, there are differences within the lower class with regard to reasons for supporting riots. Sixty-five percent (177) of the lower-class youth who scored riots positively said that they did so because they felt that Anglos, especially the police, discriminated against them, and they further believed that riots were a way of communicating that Chicanos were not going to stand for this type of treatment. They wanted to be given the same chances as everyone else. These youth did not think that they would gain anything materially from riots, but they did believe that it was important to stand up for their rights to equal treatment. What rioting symbolized to them was a defense of personal honor, a lashing out at Anglo society, particularly at the police, for not allowing them some personal dignity.[32]

Nancy, 18-year-old daughter of a factory worker:

I mean, riots don't always get a lot of things, but I sort of think they are good because when Chicanos riot, at least the Chicanos I know, they are saying to the Anglo that we are not going to be treated like we're worthless or lazy. Like, they don't give you a chance to get a job and then tell you that you're lazy. Chicanos are tired of that stuff, especially the stuff with the police. They harass you and treat you like dirt.

Mario, 18-year-old son of a cleaning woman:

The Anglo discriminates against you and belittles you. They don't have any respect for us, but when the riots happened in East Los [East Los Angeles] then they knew Chicanos would not back down. They had to give a little more respect then. . . . I think riots can be important because they at least tell the Anglo that we won't be discriminated against for jobs and be made fun of, too.

This evidence would also support those studies that have argued that riots are a form of political protest. However, some of the lower-class youth in this sample viewed riots in the manner described by Banfield. These youth were not only exclusively from the lower class, but nearly all also were identified with one of the many local Chicano youth gangs. Youth gangs in the Chicano *barrios* are an integral part of the Chicano community in Los Angeles as a whole, but particularly among adolescents and young adults. Members of these gangs viewed riots as important because they were able to loot stores for goods that they could resell. Gangs often were involved in theft in order to increase their holdings and their prestige. What the riots represented to these youth were favorable opportunities to accumulate these goods. This view of riots is presented quite vividly in the comments of two gang members.

Julio, an 18-year-old who has been a gang member for four years:

I mean, I think riots are all right 'cause, you know, it's easy to do some jobs [steal]. You don't have to worry about the police 'cause it's kind of confusing for them. I mean, you can get some good stuff real easy and that's nice. . . . There are some "home boys" [gang members] who keep some of the good stuff, but most of the time we try to push it [peddle it off].

Ramon, an 18-year-old who has been a gang member for three years:

I like riots. They've been good to me and my friends. . . . Well, in riots you don't have to worry about the police when you want to get something. And when you get a lot of stuff you can sell it and make some good money.

Illustrating Banfield's second point, some of those interviewed expressed the opinion that riots were just fun to be involved in because there was a great deal of activity that made things exciting.

Juan, an 18-year-old who has been a gang member for three years:

It's a lot of fun when riots are going on. There are a lot of people in the streets, and you can do whatever you want 'cause there is no police.

Aurelio, a 17-year-old who has been a gang member for five years:

Riots are all right because they're fun to be in. I don't know how to say it. There's a lot of things happening and the police can't stop you. I don't know, my friends and me just have a good time.

Yet there is one important difference between the findings of this study and Banfield's assertions. The attitudes expressed by these gang members were not, as Banfield has suggested, representative of the lower class in general because the vast majority of the lower-class respondents thought of riots as a legitimate form of symbolic protest. Rather, these attitudes were representative only of a sub-cultural group of the lower class that has developed unique group values.

In Albuquerque, the data concerning social class standing and support for riots are slightly different from those for Los Angeles, although some of the data involving intraclass differences are similar. First, as Figure 5.5 shows, the middle-class youth are negative toward riots, whereas there is positive support for riots among the lower class ($P_{64} = -.413$). The majority of those in the lower class thought of riots as a form of protest against ethnic discrimination, poor living conditions, and unemployment. Furthermore, riots were considered effective means of communicating this discontent to those policy officials who, it was believed, could make the necessary changes. However, similar to the findings for Los Angeles, there was a small percentage of the lower class who felt positively toward riots because they considered them personally entertaining. What made riots appealing to these youth were the prospects for obtaining material goods illegally. One difference between the youth in Albuquerque and those in Los Angeles is that none of the Albuquerque respondents were members of a gang. Gangs long ago ceased to be an important part of youth culture in Albuquerque. However, many of the same personal characteristics exhibited by gang members in Los Angeles were also found among the youth of Albuquerque who saw rioting as being profitable. They were lower-class, usually very poor; they did not like school; they received poor grades in school; and they were in trouble with school officials and/or the police. They were what school officials often label as "problems." Many wanted to quit school, but they said that they stayed because they could not find a job very easily without a high school diploma. It is necessary to emphasize, however, that the attitudes of these youth with regard to riots were not representative of the entire lower class; they prevailed only among a small part of that class.

The middle class of Albuquerque was negative toward riots. The explanation for this is not at all complex. The Chicanos who were middle-class saw riots as counterproductive. Not only did riots unnecessarily damage property in the *barrios* (some property of which, the youth reported, was owned by their fathers), but they also created a negative image of all Chicanos, whether they had participated in the riots or not. Probably the biggest concern of the middle class was this latter one, because they believed that negative attitudes toward Chicanos caused by the riots had the potential to undermine everything they had achieved.

As is evident from the results presented, the lower-class youth in Los Angeles and Albuquerque had similar perceptions of riots. However, the youths from middle-class backgrounds had slightly different responses, depending on the city they lived in. This raises a question as to what would cause this difference between the middle classes of the two cities. The most important area of difference was in the way in which each middle-class respondent viewed his/her present socioeconomic position and the obstacles to future mobility. In Albuquerque, the youth were comfortable with middle-class living, and although they were interested in social mobility, their expectations did not reach beyond the occupations and living styles of their parents. Their perceptions of the problems facing both the maintenance of their present socioeconomic status and their prospects for future mobility were focused on Anglo attitudes toward Chicanos. Their concern was that Chicanos in general not pose a threat to Anglos that would elicit a negative response, making life difficult for their parents or limiting their own opportunities for higher-status jobs. Thus riots posed a threat to their individual interests.

On the other hand, in Los Angeles the middle-class youth were quite achievement-oriented, with rapidly expanding expectations for future mobility. Their perceptions of the problems confronting their chances for mobility centered on the question of whether the Anglo-dominated socioeconomic and political system would stop discriminating and give them an equal opportunity for achievement. Riots were appealing to some members of this class because they were considered a political resource to pressure the Anglo community for greater opportunities for advancement.

The data presented thus far show support for riots among the youth in Albuquerque and Los Angeles, but do those who support riots also feel that they would actively participate in them? Sixty-eight percent (133) of the lower-class youth in both cities who said that they supported riots also said that they would participate in them. However, nearly all of the middle-class respondents in Los Angeles who supported riots said that they themselves probably would not participate in a riot. This seemed somewhat peculiar, but further probing provided an explanation of their rationale. The middle-class youth in Los Angeles did not want to participate in riots because they did not want to risk being assaulted and/or arrested by the police. Nevertheless, they did want to take advantage of any benefits that might occur as a result of the riots.

Political Violence

The type of acts to be discussed in this section are those which many social observers have labeled as "terrorist." There has been little research on terrorism in the United States, primarily because terrorist acts have not been a common occurrence. Another factor that has contributed to the lack of research on this subject is the assumption that terrorism in the United States only involves a very few people, generally considered mentally unstable, who pose no threat becaue there is virtually no support for such acts among the general public. Yet these may be false assumptions. A considerable number of acts have been reported that were terrorist in character, and there is no way to determine how many such acts have not been reported to the public, either because a lack of evidence left the situation ambiguous, or because the F.B.I. or some other agency simply considered the information classified material. Further, the fact that there has not been a great deal of information on terrorism in the United States leaves the social scientist at a disadvantage to predict if there has been, or might be, support for such acts. The purpose of this section is to begin to provide some additional information. A word of caution is in order concerning the analysis. Although the focus of this study is on youth, the intent here is not, as in the case of political socialization studies, to determine if support for violence has its origins in adolescence. Rather, an attempt will be made to determine what social and environmental factors, if any, influence the acceptance or rejection of terrorism.[33]

The youth in all three cities were asked to evaluate three concepts connoting terrorist acts. These were terrorist kidnapping, terrorist bombing, and urban guerrilla warfare. In San Antonio, all three of these concepts were scored extremely low, and there was little variance in the scores. In addition, only one youth said during the in-depth interviews that he supported any one of the three. A typical comment was:

Raphael, 17-year-old son of a truck driver:

I don't support that kind of thing. I don't think it's right to jeopardize innocent people's lives. These kind of things never do any good; they only bring more hardship to the people they are trying to help. Like for example, say some Chicanos bombed Joskie's [a large department store in San Antonio] and said it was bombed because there was discrimination there. Well, not only did innocent people maybe get killed, maybe even some Chicanos, but the police would probably stop all Chicanos going into the store before being searched. And they would probably search Chicano homes looking for who did it.

I mean they [the police] would harass a lot of Chicanos because of this. So the whole thing would be worse instead of better.

Two themes emerge from this and the other interviews explaining why the youth in San Antonio were opposed to this type of political activity. First, they were opposed on moral grounds—these acts might harm innocent people, and this was not good. Second, they opposed these acts on a more functional basis—the response from the Anglo community, especially the police, would make things worse than they had been before.

In Los Angeles and Albuquerque, however, there was support for some, although not all three, of the terrorist acts. Terrorist kidnapping was scored negatively by nearly all of the youth in both cities, but terrorist bombing and urban guerrilla warfare both received some positive support.[34] Figures 5.6 and 5.7 indicate the causal influences of urban environmental factors, SES, and cultural variables on the youth's scores for terrorist acts. An analysis of the path model as a whole indicates what segment of the sample supports terrorism.[35] In Los Angeles, the length of time the youth have lived in the city has a positive coefficient, as do the population density in their neighborhoods and their social class backgrounds.[36] Support for terrorist acts emerges from those youth whose families have lived in the city for a long period of time, usually more than eight years, and who have not experienced any socioeconomic mobility. These youth are members of families who have simply lingered on for various reasons, being poor or lower-working-class, and usually living in small, undersized homes or in public housing projects. They are extremely frustrated with their situation and very antagonistic toward government and society.[37]

In Albuquerque, a slightly different pattern emerges. The youth who were positive toward terrorism were those who were recent arrivals from northern New Mexico, most of whom had been forced to migrate to the city because of land usage problems, and who were from lower SES families. Like their Los Angeles counterparts, they were very frustrated about their present living conditions and very hostile toward both the state and the federal governments for their complicity in not rectifying the problem.

Thus, respondents in both cities had experienced a high degree of frustration and resentment toward the Anglo society and the government. Still, it is a rather radical move from feeling deprived to

FIGURE 5.6
Path Model of the Effects in Albuquerque of Urban
Contextual Variables and Personal Variables on Student
Attitudes Toward Terrorist Bombing*

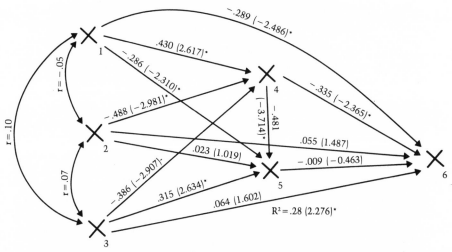

* = All coefficients are significant at the .05 level or beyond on a two-tailed "t" test
X_1 = Length of residence in the city
X_2 = Population density in neighborhood
X_3 = Ethnic homogeneity in respondent's neighborhood
X_4 = Socioeconomic status
X_5 = Traditional cultural values (retention of)
X_6 = Terrorist bombing

supporting terrorism. How is it that these youth perceived terrorism as helpful to them, and how were they able to accept and rationalize violence? Among the youth in Los Angeles who supported terrorism, the vast majority felt that terrorism pressured authorities to meet the demands of moderate political organizations that would not have been met without the presence of an extremely radical group that the authorities considered a "lunatic fringe."[38] An example of this argument is articulated by Rachel, an 18-year-old female whose parents are separated and whose mother is unemployed; she lives in a housing project.

I mean, some groups which use peaceful tactics ask the

FIGURE 5.7
Path Model of the Effects in Los Angeles of Urban
Contextual Variables and Personal Variables on Student
Attitudes Toward Terrorist Bombing*

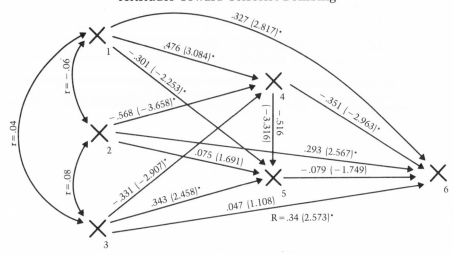

* = All coefficients are significant at the .05 level or beyond on a two-tailed "t" test

X_1 = Length of residence in the city
X_2 = Population density in neighborhood
X_3 = Ethnic homogeneity in respondent's neighborhood
X_4 = Socioeconomic status
X_5 = Traditional cultural values (retention of)
X_6 = Terrorist bombing

government for some help, but the government says they can't do anything because they don't have the money or enough people to work on the problem. But if there is a group that bombs things and makes radical demands, the government turns and gives in to the peaceful group because they think the group bombing is crazy and they don't want people in the community to join that group. So bombing helps, because the community gets something they wouldn't get.

In Albuquerque, the youth view violence as politically helpful because it has the potential to force the government to make changes in its policies regarding land tenure in northern New Mexico. Bombing government buildings in Albuquerque as well as in northern New Mexico was seen as an important harassment technique to pressure the government to make more land available to Chicanos for grazing. With more land available, the respondents thought that their families might be able to move back to northern New Mexico, where they would prefer to be.

The most important fact about these findings on violence is that in both cities the youth who supported terrorism rationalized their support by saying that they only supported it because they believed that there was no alternative; all the other forms of political participation had not produced any changes in their socioeconomic condition. For example:

Homer, 17-year-old son of a short order cook in Los Angeles:

When Chicanos want some changes to happen and they ask for the changes, nothing usually happens. If they try to get the changes a number of other ways, you know, peaceful and all that, nothing happens. We got no choice. So I don't think there is anything wrong with violence.

Anselmo, 18-year-old son of a lumber yard worker in Albuquerque:

Well, violence like bombing is only for when you have tried everything else and you still don't get anything. And in our case, we've tried everything. We got petitions together to have the Forest Service let us graze on more land, we had demonstrations, and, let's see—we took somethings to court to get the government to honor the land grants [Spanish-Mexican land grants]. Nothing helped.

Yet even if these youth were frustrated with the lack of positive action emanating from participation through legitimate channels,[39] other youth were also frustrated, and they did not support terrorism. Consequently, what other factors could explain positive leanings toward terrorism? Some might argue that the economic conditions of these particular youth were so bad that they forced them toward more radical forms of political activity. This is doubtless important, but there seems to be one additional factor, having to do with the youth's personal knowledge of violence. For example, in Los Angeles the acceptance of political violence is made easier for youth from the impoverished segment of Chicano society because violence in some form is not uncommon in their neighborhoods or personal lives. Therefore, the thought of using violence for political purposes is not a radical departure from their own experience. In answer to the question, "Are not bombing and political violence of that type somewhat extreme?", a representative reply was:

Alberto, 18-year-old son of a welfare mother in Los Angeles:

No, I don't think so. Hey, look—there is violence all over the United States. Take the *barrio.* If a dealer wants cash for his dope and you don't give it to him, he uses violence. If you go into the neighborhood of another gang and they don't want you to be there they beat you up or something. Even the police use violence if they want something and you don't want to give it to them. . . . So if Chicanos want something and they couldn't get it using other ways, they should use violence. It's no different.

Albuquerque presents a slight variation of this situation. The youth who supported violence here were predominantly from the northern part of the state, a place where violence had been used before to obtain political goals. Thus the move from feeling politically frustrated to support of terrorism has been facilitated by the respondents' prior introduction to violence as a legitimate political resource.

Tomás, 18-year-old son of a garbage collector in Albuquerque:

The government uses violence to stop Chicanos from using their land. And if you protest, they sometimes use guns to arrest you. I know a lot of Chicanos have used violence to protect their property and stop the Anglos from taking their land. So if you have no choice, I think you should use violence, too.

Support for Terrorism Versus
Terrorist Participation

Does support for terrorism mean that these same youth would participate in bombings themselves? In the interviews, those youth who said that they supported terrorist bombing and guerrilla warfare were asked if they personally would participate in a bombing. Eighty-five percent (199) said that they would not participate; but of this number, 55 percent (110) added the qualifier that although they would not participate now, they might in the future. Their apprehension about immediate participation was based on their perceptions of what was involved in terrorist bombing. The consensus was that one could not just go out and bomb or perform other violent acts, that it was necessary to become involved with a group no matter how small it was. Without such a group, it would be next to impossible to get the equipment necessary for making bombs. Also, someone in the group would have to know how to use the equipment. The majority of the respondents said that they did not know of any such political groups; consequently, they felt that they had no opportunity to become involved. Those who said that they had heard of some groups that used bombs also said that they had no idea how anyone could make contact with them.

The remaining 45 percent (eighty-nine) said that they supported terrorist activities, but that they never could participate in such acts themselves. They stated that they supported terrorism only because they felt that they understood why it was sometimes necessary to use this type of political tactic. Their support was basically ideological support.

Of the 15 percent who were prepared to use terrorism if they were given the opportunity, most (86 percent, or thirty) were from that group of Chicanos whose families had lived in the city for more than ten years, were still poor, and no longer retained traditional Chicano culture. As the group who were the most frustrated and angry, they were also the most extreme in their support of terrorism.

Roberto, 18-year-old son of a Los Angeles hotel maid:

I would participate in organizations that bomb. That's the only way to get what you need from Anglo society. That's the only thing Anglos understand is force. . . . No, I'm not afraid—I don't have anything, nothing at all, man, so I got nothing to lose.

Political Violence and Ideology

As Table 5.2 indicates, there is a relationship between the ideology with which the youth identify and whether they support political violence. The youth who were positive toward capitalism were opposed to terrorism, as might be expected. They perceived terrorism

Table 5.2
Pearson Correlation Coefficients of Ideological
Support and Terrorism

	Capitalism		Chicano Separatism	
Albuquerque Terrorism	−.524*	(286)	.339*	(249)
Los Angeles Terrorism	−.481*	(275)	.395*	(255)

*P<.01

as disruptive, illegal, unnecessary, and immoral. It was particularly threatening to them because it threatened the system upon which their aspirations for the future depended. It was not surprising to find that these youth were advocates of extreme punishments for anyone who was caught participating in terrorist activities. This was particularly true of their attitudes toward Chicanos who were caught. It appeared that they needed to make examples of those Chicanos in an effort to indicate to the majority population that, although they themselves were Chicanos, they should in no way be associated with those who supported terrorism, nor should they be penalized for the actions of these others.

On the other hand, the youth who supported political separatism were more positive toward political violence. Those who were for separatism said that although they might not use terrorism themselves, they were not opposed to its use, especially if there was no other way to gain separation. This opinion was based on their belief that the government would not let them separate unless it was under extreme pressure to do so, and they considered terrorism a useful pressure tactic.

Research involving separatist movements in other areas of the world also has indicated a high level of support for political violence.[40] Basically, what appears to happen when there are separatist sentiments among a subculture of a population is that instead of asking for a larger piece of the socioeconomic pie, which the system is capable of giving, the separatists ask for a whole different kind of pie, which the system is not capable of giving. Thus the structure of the confrontation itself sets the stage for more extensive use of political violence, including terrorism.

Conclusion

The data presented in this chapter are somewhat complex, but some general trends stand out. To begin, the youth from San Antonio were unanimous in their rejection of political violence, including riots, and indifferent toward protest activity as an effective political tactic. These attitudes reflect the political environment of San Antonio, which can be described as conservative. Some of these youth had accepted a conservative perspective on politics out of conviction, believing that this was the proper perspective for themselves and for the community. Others also had adopted a conservative position, but had done so because no realistic alternative seemed available. The authorities were willing to deal harshly with anyone who broke the law or tried to challenge the present system. Thus, their acceptance of a conservative political perspective was based on the fear that they and/or their families would suffer if they tried to alter the present system. The majority in this group came from the families with the lowest SES.

While there was no support for political protest and violence in San Antonio, there was evidence of such support in Los Angeles and Albuquerque. The main reason for this difference between cities is that the political climate in both Los Angeles and Albuquerque is more tolerant of such forms of political participation. This attitude can be attributed to three factors: (1) the historical relationship between Chicanos and Anglos in Los Angeles and Albuquerque has been different from that in San Antonio—the Anglo community has not felt threatened to the same degree, and therefore has not reacted in such a negative manner; (2) Los Angeles and Albuquerque have a more regionally diversified population (many of the inhabitants of both cities have come from the Northeast or Midwest), and these people have infused the community with many new and different attitudes, some of which are understanding of and/or sympathetic to these forms of politics; and (3) protest activity and political violence have occurred more often in these two cities, and this has established a certain acceptance of them as political facts that must be dealt with through a variety of approaches.

However, there are clear divisions as to who will support which form of participation—protest or political violence. The middle class in both cities accepted protest as both a legitimate and an effective means of gaining advantages, although they were only prepared to participate in those protests that were nonviolent. The middle class also was supportive of riots, believing that they were an effective way to pressure the Anglo society to do more for the Chicano community. Yet they were not willing to participate in a riot themselves. Essentially, the middle-class youth wanted to maximize their opportunities for socioeconomic mobility, and considered these tactics to be necessary at times. In spite of their support for protest and riots, members of the middle class were overwhelmingly opposed to the use of terrorism of any type because they saw the use of such tactics as counterproductive to the Chicano struggle to gain socioeconomic mobility.

Like those from the middle class, the youth from lower SES families were generally supportive of protest, with the prevailing attitude being that protest could be helpful in forcing needed changes. Riots also were supported, and it was found that the supporters offered two distinctly different reasons for their support. The vast majority felt that riots were a form of protest communicating to those in power that something needed to be changed. A small minority said that they supported riots because they could obtain (steal) valuable merchandise and/or because participation in riots was simply fun; i.e., it was fun to see everybody in the street doing what they wanted to do. Thus there was some evidence that substantiated both the "rioting as protest" and the "rioting for fun and profit" arguments. It is probably accurate to say that in any riot both of these attitudes are represented, and not just one or the other.

A small percentage of the lower class supported terrorism, seeing it as an alternative to riots and protest in pressuring Anglo society to make their lives better. Nearly all of the youth who supported this form of politics were from extremely poor families, the poorest in the sample.

Two other important findings remain. First, the youth in both cities were influenced by their immediate urban environment. In Los Angeles, the more radical forms of political participation, such as riots and terrorism, were supported by those youth who had resided in the city the longest. The frustrations associated with long residence in the city gave rise to disappointment and to a propensity to support more radical means of securing change. The other urban variables, such as the ethnic homogeneity of the youth's neighborhoods and the neighborhoods' population density, acted to intensify the frustrations of life in Los Angeles and to increase the probability that a long-term resident of one of these neighborhoods would turn toward political violence.

However, in Albuquerque it was found that support for the most radical of tactics, terrorism, was more prevalent among those youth who were recent migrants from northern New Mexico, and that long residence in Albuquerque produced support for the more moderate tactics, such as nonviolent protest. Thus, in Albuquerque, city life, through the economy's ability to offer opportunities for mobility, tends to deradicalize the youth.

Finally, the ideology supported by the youth in both cities was found to be associated with whether they supported political violence. The youth who supported capitalism tended strongly to support nonviolent protest, such as boycotts, and moderately to support riots, but they were vehemently opposed to terrorism of any form. However, those youth who supported a separate Chicano country were highly supportive of all forms of political protest, including terrorism, because they believed that a separate Chicano country could not be established unless extreme pressure was exerted, and terrorism was considered the most extreme type of pressure.

Three additional issues deserve some attention. The first has to do with some apparent differences between this study's sample of Chicano youth in Albuquerque and Los Angeles, though not in San Antonio, and a sample of black youth in Los Angeles studied by Sears and McConahay. Probably the greatest difference concerns the ways in which the youth, both Chicano and black, viewed riots. Sears and McConahay reported that the black youth in their study viewed riots as a form of symbolic protest against all of the racism they had endured—in other words, they did not riot for either fun or profit, as Banfield suggested.[41] In this study, those youth who supported riots did so because they wanted to pressure the government and the society to give them some material benefits that they did not now possess. In essence, they saw riots as a political resource to be used in order to secure a political or economic objective. Those who said that they actually would participate in a riot were from lower socioeconomic backgrounds and were more intent upon gaining some economic benefits. They also had less to lose from a white backlash than did their middle-class counterparts, so they were much more willing to participate in this type of activity.

There are two other significant differences between the results of this study and those of the Sears and McConahay study. One has to do with ideology and an individual's attitudes toward protest and political violence. Sears and McConahay did not study their respondents' ideological positions extensively and did not attempt to determine if there was a relationship between ideology and an individual's attitude toward violence, partly because their sample was not conducive to this test. They concluded that no significant relationship existed between black nationalism/separatism and riot participation.[42] The present study, however, found that Chicano nationalist/ separatist ideology was a factor in attitudes toward political violence. Those Chicanos who were separatists were more likely to be positive toward protest and political violence than those who were not. This difference between the findings reported here and those of Sears and McConahay can be explained by two factors. The first has to do with Sears's and McConahay's sample, which was drawn in late 1965 and early 1966, after the riots had occurred. At that time, black nationalism and separatism had not developed as fully as they would in the two years that followed. Thus their findings concerning black nationalism and support for riots might have been more positive if they had undertaken the study at a later time. The second factor has to do with the nature of nationalism in both ethnic communities. Chicano nationalism is stronger than that of blacks because: (1) it is associated with a defined geographic area that was once legally owned by Mexico rather than with a new homeland, as proposed by black nationalists; (2) it has always had a language, Spanish, and customs that are significantly different from mainstream American language and customs and are used as symbols for purposes of identity and mobilization, whereas blacks have had to create a language and customs; and (3) it has been in existence longer.

Sears and McConahay also reported that Mexican Americans, like whites, were fearful for their property while the riots were going on and that they did not think that the riots helped blacks.[43] What one might interpret from these data is that Mexican Americans were opposed to riots. However, the data in this study clearly indicated that Chicanos were not at all opposed to riots. If the Sears and McConahay data are combined with those from the present study, one would conclude more accurately that: (1) the Chicanos in the Sears and McConahay study were opposed to riots because of ethnic differences and antagonisms; and (2) the Chicanos in the present study benefited from the political precedent set by the Watts riot. More specifically, a riot ideology had developed out of the Watts riots, and this ideology had an important political influence on Chicanos. They now could consider riots a legitimate form of protest, as well as an effective political resource in obtaining economic benefits. The Chicanos in the present study exhibited views of riots that were consistent with the arguments of Piven and Cloward in *Regulating the Poor*—that more material resources were directed into the riot communities as a result of the riots.[44] Although political violence in the form of terrorism was not included in the Sears and McConahay questionnaire, it was included in the present study and there were Chicano respondents who were in favor of its use. Here again, the Chicanos in this study, as opposed to the black youth in the Sears and McConahay study, had the benefit of prior acts of terrorism having been committed and reported in the media. This provided them with examples of violence as a legitimate form of political participation, and something to consider within their political spectrum. It will be remembered that many of the youth in this study who supported political terrorism were also separatists, and mentioned the separatists in Quebec as examples of a successful use of these tactics in securing some political and economic concessions.

Finally, Sears and McConahay found little relationship between urbanization and riot participation,[45] whereas this study found that urban life did have an effect on how the young Chicanos in this study thought about political violence, most clearly in the case of the youth from Los Angeles. Those respondents who had the most positive attitudes toward riots and political violence had lived in the city for over ten years. In fact, those who were most willing to use political violence in the form of terrorist bombings were those Chicano youth who were lower-class, had lived in the city with lower-class status for more than ten years, and no longer maintained traditional Chicano culture. They were what Park and Wirth described as "marginal." These youth's positive attitudes toward political violence and toward their own participation in such acts were based on their perceptions of their present conditions. It will be recalled that it was this very group who were the most alienated of all the Chicano youth in this study. It was also this group who consistently maintained radical attitudes toward separatist politics. What this finding suggests is that the urban condition affects both Chicano and blacks in somewhat different ways. Of course, members of all groups, including blacks, whites, Hispanics, and Asians, who are in lower socioeconomic positions and in the process of urbanizing are affected similarly by those urban conditions that accompany the lower-class situation. However, the conditions associated with a lower-class life in conjunction with cultural changes associated with the assimilation process that exists in American cities do work to produce a different experience, and therefore a different response, for Chicanos than for blacks or for members of any other group that is culturally closer to the dominant Anglo-American culture. In sum, the pressures associated with lower-class life are compounded when there are pressures on an individual's cultural orientation, and often this added pressure produces a more extreme political response.

6

Recent Mexican Immigrants
Reinforcing Chicano Ethnicity and Politics?

WHEN PARK, WIRTH, and the Chicago school were involved in analyzing ethnic assimilation in the 1920s and 1930s, immigration to the United States had been severely restricted. The Immigration Act of 1924 had limited immigration to a total of 150,000 per year from all countries while it also established a quota system to help encourage "assimilable" groups.[1] The importance of limited immigration to ethnic assimilation was recognized by Wirth, who stated, in his classic 1928 study of the Jewish ghetto in America:

> While the ghetto has been emptying there have been few new recruits to fill the vacancies. In the past it was the influx of a constant stream of orthodox Jews that was relied upon to hold the community together and to perpetuate the faith. Today, however, this force can no longer be depended upon.[2]

Thus it was under these conditions that Wirth and the Chicago school predicted that the urban environment, with its size, density, and heterogeneity, would be successful in assimilating the many diverse ethnic groups into a common culture—the Anglo American.

This chapter takes up the issue of immigration and its impact on ethnic assimilation by analyzing the effect of Mexican immigration on the Chicano community. More specifically, attention is directed to the newest members of the Chicano community—the Mexican nationals who are in the United States without immigration papers. In recent years estimates of the total number of undocumented Mexican immigrants have been rising steadily. Today these estimates range from two and one-half to seven and one-half million, with more than 600,000 (a conservative estimate) attempting to come to the U.S. each year.[3] The vast majority of these immigrants have been described as coming from extremely poor socioeconomic back-grounds. Many have not had the opportunity to attend school, and are semiliterate and poorly trained in vocational skills. They are also products of a country with a different language and customs. These characteristics have caused social scientists and policy makers to be concerned about the impact of undocumented Mexican nationals on both the Anglo-American and the Chicano communities. Many social scientists and policy analysts have suggested that the continued presence of Mexican nationals has been the dominant force in reinforcing Chicano/Mexican cultural retention and ultimately in retarding Chicano socioeconomic mobility and assimilation.[4]

The presence of Mexican nationals in the United States also raises questions about political socialization. For example, does their presence provide a source of counteridentification (with Mexico) for Chicanos which results in ambivalence toward American politics and subsequent nonparticipation? If these immigrants stay in the country will they, blocked from upward socioeconomic mobility, pose a threat to stability in the urban areas where most now work?

The presence of Mexican nationals has revived the same immigration debates that occurred concerning European ethnic groups in the early part of the twentieth century. These debates, both then and now, can be reduced to two basic positions—restrictionist and nonrestrictionist. There are those who want to restrict the flow of illegal aliens severely because they believe that the Mexican illegals are placing a strain on social services and taking jobs away from disadvantaged Americans, particularly blacks and Chicanos.[5] Those who have argued for a restrictionist policy also have been concerned that the illegal aliens, resenting the exploitation to which they are subject, will become a potential source of political revolt.[6] The second position is held by those who favor either an unrestricted or a moderately restricted policy. They argue that there is insufficient evidence to indicate that the Mexican illegal creates a problem for disadvantaged Americans or for the society as a whole,[7] and some evidence which points to their positive effects.[8]

Of course there are many questions essential to resolving this dispute for which few data are available, and other questions which the data in this study do not address. But the impact of the urban experience on Mexican nationals bears both on the Chicago school hypotheses and on the debate over friction. This chapter assesses the ways in which the undocumented Mexican youth in the present sample have related to Anglo-American and Chicano society. Particular attention is given to socioeconomic backgrounds, goals in life, and attitudes toward politics. It is not the intention of this analysis to provide substantial support for either of the two policy alternatives mentioned. The total number in the sample, as well as the age composition, will not allow for this. However, the analysis will provide some information which is directly relevant to the issues of cultural assimilation and political socialization addressed in this book.

The sample examined in this chapter is composed of seventy-three youth who identified themselves as being in this country illegally. Because all respondents were given the opportunity to identify their own immigration status, some may have lied to protect themselves and their families. For this reason, the teachers of all classes sampled were asked to estimate the number of illegals in their classrooms. It was found that the self-identified sample and the teachers' estimates were almost identical; in fact, the sample had two more members than the teachers' total estimates. This provided evidence that few students had lied about their status.

It is important to point out, however, that this number (seventy-three) is not representative of the total number of illegals attending some of the public schools in the study. Personal observation as well as discussions with teachers and students indicate that the largest number of illegals attending these schools is in the lower high school grades (9–11) rather than in grade 12, from which all of the students interviewed were drawn. There are two reasons for this: (1) many of the illegals are placed at the lower grade levels because of problems involving proficiency in English; and (2) many of those placed at the lower grade levels do not stay in school long enough to reach grade 12. It should be emphasized that these seventy-three Mexican youth are being analyzed for the first time in this work, as they have been excluded from the data analysis in the preceding chapters.

In addition to the data collected from the questionnaire, another valuable source of information was the in-depth interviews. Of the seventy-three Mexican youth who completed the survey, forty-three consented to be interviewed, twenty-seven in Los Angeles and sixteen in San Antonio. Each interview lasted about seventy minutes.

Demographic Characteristics

Most of the studies on illegals indicate that they come into the

Table 6.1
Some Demographic Characteristics of the Illegal Mexican Youth

				San Antonio N=27		Los Angeles N=46	
Sex:							
Male	54	(74%)		22	81%/41%	32	70%/59% *
Female	19	(26%)		5	19%/26%	14	30%/74%
Origin:							
Urban (in Mexico)	40	(55%)		16	59%/40%	24	52%/60%
Rural (in Mexico)	33	(45%)		11	41%/33%	22	48%/67%
Northern Mexico	43	(59%)		23	85%/53%	20	43%/47%
Southern Mexico	30	(41%)		4	15%/13%	26	57%/87%
Length of Urban Residence:							
Two years or less				14	52%/42%	19	44%/58%
Three years to five years				9	33%/36%	16	35%/64%
Six years to ten years				3	11%/27%	8	17%/73%
Over ten years				1	4%/25%	3	7%/75%

*Column Percentages/Row Percentages

U.S. alone.[9] Yet this was not the case with the present sample. In Los Angeles, 9 percent said that they had come alone, 37 percent said that they had come with their father only, and 54 percent said that they had come with their family. The figures for San Antonio are slightly more skewed. No youths said that they had come alone; 26 percent said that they had come with their father, and 75 percent said that they had come with their family.

As might be expected, there are some gender differences in the patterns mentioned above. All of those who had come alone were young males, as were those who had come and now lived exclusively with their fathers. All of the females in the sample had come, and presently lived, with their immediate families.

The rural origins of most illegals is well documented in the literature. More come from towns of fewer than 2,500 than from large cities.[10] However, in this sample there were more who said they were from urban than from rural areas. In Los Angeles, the distribution was 52 percent from urban areas and 48 percent from rural communities. In San Antonio, 59 percent had come from cities and 41 percent from villages (see Table 6.1).

Nearly all of the illegals from the rural areas said that they had come because their villages were in such bad economic condition that migration had become a necessity. Approximately 35 percent said that they had been financed by their villages to come to the United States in order to make money to send back to the villages. These included all those who had come alone and over half of those who had accompanied their fathers only. The other 65 percent said that they had come in order to make money for their own immediate families. This group was composed primarily of those who had arrived with just their fathers. It is particularly interesting that these youth, who were in school, also intended to be helpful to their communities and/or their families. All had jobs after school. These jobs required from six to eight hours a night and six to seven days a week.[11] A wide variety of jobs were held, for example: soda jerk, gas station attendant, waitress, busboy, bakery worker, worker in a dry cleaners, and car wash attendant. When the respondents were asked why they bothered to go to school, three general answers were given: (1) school provided a good cover from the Immigration and Naturalization Service (I.N.S.); (2) they were able to secure a driver's license after their high school driver education class, which added to their file of personal documents; (3) (most often cited) they thought that if they were able to learn a skill and get a high school diploma they would be able to find better jobs when they graduated.

Because those from rural areas were in dire need of quick employment, 65 percent went to Los Angeles, where there were far more opportunities. Of the 35 percent who went to San Antonio, nearly all said that San Antonio was not a good place to work because the wages were too low; and half of these youth went on to say that their fathers were using San Antonio as an initial stopping place and were moving north to Chicago or Detroit in the near future.

The youth who were from urban areas in Mexico also said that their families had come to the United States because of poor economic conditions. But these youth and their fathers had come with the intention of improving the economic condition of the immediate family, which clearly distinguished them from their rural counterparts who, in most cases, had to think of more than their immediate family. Some had made the journey with only their fathers, and 94 percent of this group sent money back to their mothers. In fact, 71 percent said that, as soon as it was possible, they would send for the rest of the family to come to the U.S. Others were already living with their entire families; for these youth there seemed to be less pressure to gain employment. Getting a good education was stressed highly; consequently, they went to public schools with the attitude that they must study hard so that they could secure a good job in the future.[12] Seventy percent of these youth said that they had jobs, but all of these jobs were part-time.

In addition to the rural/urban dichotomy in the origins of illegal immigrants, Bustamante noted in his study of illegal immigration that in the past forty-seven years there had been a general shift in the regional origins of Mexican illegals living in the U.S. Where in the 1920s the bulk of the migration had come from the central plateau region of Mexico, in the 1970s the border states of Mexico were sending increasing numbers, with the state of Chihuahua sending more than any other.[13] In this study the number of youths from the northern part of Mexico, which included all of the border states as well as the states of Durango, Sinaloa and Zacatecas, was slightly higher than the number from the southern region, which included the states of Michoacán, Guanajuato and Jalisco on the central plateau. This increase in immigration from the North is due in part to deteriorating economic conditions there. The north, especially the state of Nuevo León, traditionally has been Mexico's second most industrial area. Recently, the increase in population has produced a larger work force, but industry has not been able to keep pace by employing the vast majority of those eligible.[14] Thus, many of those workers who have experienced chronic unemployment have had to look elsewhere for work, and the United States, partly because of its proximity, has attracted many of them.

In addition to the general shift in the regional origins of illegal immigrants, the interviews revealed that the youth from the North wanted to stay longer in the U.S. than did those from the South. One of the principal reasons for this difference is the northern region's proximity to the United States. Its nearness allows the illegals from this area to visit family and friends easily, reducing feelings of loneliness and alienation.[15] Therefore, the psychological need to return to Mexico is not as strong.

Aspirations, Goals and the Question of Social Imapct on the U.S.

Some researchers have argued that the illegal Mexicans are staying in the U.S. for extended periods of time and taking jobs that Americans otherwise would hold, while not paying taxes.[16] Others have argued that illegals stay in this country for only a short period of time, usually from six to eight months, and that they constitute no economic burden. They take low-paying jobs that Americans could not afford to take or that business could not afford to offer if they had to pay minimum wage. Illegals do pay taxes; they spend their money on U.S. goods, food, clothing, and housing; and they receive few social services.[17]

The data from the interviews clearly indicate two general trends. First, the youth from families with rural origins wanted to stay in the U.S. for shorter periods of time than did those from the urban areas. Secondly, those who came alone or with only their fathers planned to stay an average of six to twenty-four months, depending on the needs of their families and villages. These youth stated that they and their fathers wanted to leave as soon as possible because living in the United States had not been a pleasant experience.[18] The most frequently cited reasons for wanting to go back to Mexico as quickly as possible were: (1) poor treatment at their place of work; (2) living in a big city slum; (3) missing the rest of their families and friends in Mexico; and (4) being tired of the anxiety of worrying whether they would be caught and deported before they had accumulated enough money to help those left in Mexico. However, those youth who were presently living with their families said that their families planned to stay in the U.S. from two to five years. Most of these youth lived in better housing facilities than those who had come alone or with only their fathers—all said that they lived in rented units (some were small houses, but most were apartments) and most said that these units had two bedrooms. They also stated that their fathers believed that the family's most important goal was to accumulate as much money as possible. Absolutely none of the students said that they or their families wanted to live in the U.S. permanently or to become integrated into American society. Probably the most important factor influencing the decision to stay for a number of years was the fact that the whole family was together, which minimized the loneliness and stress occasioned by living in a strange country and having an uncertain legal status.

The illegals who were from urban areas were divided as to how long they wanted to stay in this country. About half said that their parents wanted to move back to Mexico within six to eight years. It was their parents' goal to accumulate as much capital as they could and then go back to Mexico to live "comfortably." Some affirmed that their parents wanted to save their money, take it to Mexico, and establish a small business. The other 50 percent from urban areas stated that their families wanted to stay in the United States indefinitely. It was their desire to take out permanent residency papers, if they could. The long-range goal for 65 percent of those families who wanted to say in America indefinitely was to retire to Mexico with some sort of U.S. pension or with enough money saved to act as a pension.

The question of whether illegal immigrants are a burden on U.S. society has been one of the major concerns of policy makers. As stated above, those who favor a restrictive policy argue that illegals not only take jobs away from Americans, but do not pay taxes. Therefore, they constitute an undue burden on the society. In the present sample, seventy-seven percent of the respondents said that their fathers did have federal and state taxes withheld from their pay checks. In fact, some of the youth actually paid taxes themselves. What is particularly interesting about tax paying among illegals, especially the illegal youth in this study, is that the employer, not the illegal alien, more often than not determined whether the taxes were going to be paid. All of the working youth said that they were very willing to pay taxes because paying taxes was an assurance that they would receive at least minimum wage. However, many of the youth were never in a position to pay taxes because, rather than paying them the minimum wage, some employers chose to pay them in cash. One observation that emerged from the interviews was that no single type of business was more likely to pay "under the table" than any other. Many small and medium-sized businesses that enjoyed good reputations were reported to have paid wages in cash that were below the minimum wage.[19]

A question related to the economic burden issue is whether illegals use the services paid for by the general American public. Part of the argument advanced by those who view illegals as burdens on society is that they use services, but do not pay taxes. As was pointed out above, most of the undocumented workers in this sample paid taxes, and those who did not worked for employers who wanted to pay wages below the minimum. None of the Mexican youth questioned said that they or their families used workmen's compensation when they were injured, welfare of any type, including food stamps, or unemployment. In the area of medical assistance, only 35 percent reported using any of the medical facilities in San Antonio or Los Angeles. Those who did receive medial assistance paid for a portion of the expense. They paid for their medical insurance and for additional services that were not covered by the insurance, such as doctors' fees and portions of any laboratory tests that were performed. For example, those youth who had received outpatient medical care or whose families had received such care reported that they paid for these services when billed. When it was suggested to them by the interviewer that they could have avoided payment, they responded that it was a matter of personal honor to pay.[20]

Some researchers have suggested that a second generation of illegal immigrants will be different from the first in their attitudes and values.[21] Yet what little evidence exists seems to indicate that there are few differences between the illegal immigrants of today and those of past generations.[22] This has been found to be especially true of the illegals' attitudes toward integrating into American society—they come, stay a relatively short time, and then go back to Mexico. In the present study, there were no differences between parents and children who had migrated from rural areas in Mexico with regard to the issue of social integration into American society. Both wanted to spend as little time as possible in the U.S. and to return to their villages. On the other hand, the youth who came from urban areas in Mexico differed from their parents in that they wanted to stay in the United States indefinitely. This included not only the youth whose parents wanted to be long-term residents, but also those whose parents wanted to stay for a relatively short period of time. Eighty-five percent of the youth who lived with their entire families said that they would stay in the U.S. even when their parents went back. It was their goal to work in the United States and make an effort to become a citizen. Of the students who had come from urban areas in Mexico with only their fathers, 80 percent said that they had decided to go back with their fathers, stay in Mexico for a while, and then return to the U.S. to work and live indefinitely. It was clear from the interviews that these youth had become accustomed to the lifestyle in the U.S. and preferred it to that in Mexico. No doubt the availability of jobs was the most important factor in influencing their decisions.

The Relationship Between Chicano and Mexican Youth

One might expect that there would be a close relationship between Chicano and Mexican youth because of their common national origins. Yet such a relationship cannot be immediately inferred. In most of the schools involved in this study, Mexicans and Chicanos formed two distinct social groups. The Chicano students viewed the Mexicans as different from them in terms of language and customs. Clearly, the fact that Spanish was spoken more often by the Mexican youth encouraged this separation. The Chicano youth often felt unsure of their ability to carry on a conversation in Spanish with the Mexican students, fearing that the Spanish they had learned at home was not of the quality spoken in Mexico, or that their speech was not fluent.[23] In addition to these feelings of inadequacy associated with language, 68 percent of the Chicanos said that they did not have a great deal in common with the Mexican students and that they would feel awkward in conversation.

The Mexicans remained somewhat removed from the Chicanos, but this aloofness was associated with general feelings of shyness and rejection. Many felt shy because they did not have a good understanding of English; others became sensitive and shy when they thought that the Chicano students rejected them. The Mexican students' reaction to this perceived rejection was to think of the Chicanos as culturally inferior, in terms of retention of traditional culture. The following response was typical:

Luciano, 18-year-old son of a day worker in Los Angeles:

A lot of Chicanos don't talk to us, but I think that's because they don't speak Spanish good and they are embarrassed. . . . I mean, a lot of them [Chicanos] are *pochos* and they know what we know. [*Pocho* is a word with a somewhat disparaging connotation denoting someone who is assimilated into American society.]

These perceptions on the part of Mexican and Chicano youth usually resulted in their forming friendships within their own groups. This occasionally carried over to extracurricular activities. For example, in two of the high schools in Los Angeles the soccer teams were composed almost exclusively of Mexican students, while the football teams were nearly all Chicano. Of course, some of this dichotomy in athletic participation can be attributed to the fact that each group has a different orientation toward these two sports; that is, in Mexico students are introduced to soccer first, while in the U.S. football is emphasized more. Nevertheless, friendship associations play a very important role in reinforcing the differences that do exist.

The Mexican youth also said that they felt that Chicanos often

Table 6.2
Semantic Differential Mean Scores for Evaluations of
Three Political Parties by Illegal Mexican Youth

	San Antonio	Los Angeles
Democratic Party	1.97 (27)	2.02 (45)
La Raza Unida Party	3.09 (27)	3.21 (46)
Republican Party	6.15 (27)	6.29 (46)

rejected them in the places where they worked. The information from the interviews suggested that when friction did exist between Mexicans and Chicanos in the workplace, it was caused primarily by individuals competing for the better-paying and higher-status jobs.

This conflict in the workplace, which produces antagonistic social relations and disparaging terms such as *pocho*[24] and *mojado* (wetback) has been vividly captured in the film *El Norte*. *El Norte* sensitively depicts the stresses that exist among workers in the highly competitive environment of the secondary labor market, with special reference to the lives of those immigrant workers who come to the United States illegally to build a new future. The main characters in the film are Guatemalan, but the issues are the same as for Mexicans.

Attitudes Toward American Political Parties

The political party receiving the highest evaluation by the Mexican youth was the Democratic Party, followed by the Raza Unida Party and then the Republican Party (see Table 6.2). However, the youth's scores do vary, depending on their area of origin in Mexico. Those who were from rural areas were neutral toward all three parties, and throughout the interviews they repeatedly stated that they did not know much about any of the parties because they did not follow politics. Their attitude conveyed a complete lack of interest in political parties.

On the other hand, the Mexican youth who had migrated from urban areas were very interested in political parties. They were extremely positive toward the Democratic Party, slightly positive toward Raza Unida, and negative toward the Republican Party. Seventy-five percent (thirty) described the Democratic Party as the party that (1) wanted to create more jobs, and (2) supported decent wages for workers. Because they perceived the party in this way, it was their opinion that it would be the party most helpful to them. Their rationale was that the creation of more jobs meant that there would be more jobs available to them as illegals. They also believed that the Democratic Party was responsible for supporting a higher minimum wage, which, they reasoned, was beneficial to them because their wages were determined by the present minimum wage. A number of sources for this information were identified. Approximately 22 percent (nine) said that their opinions about the Democratic Party came from reading the newspapers. Most mentioned newspaper articles in which Democratic presidential candidate Jimmy Carter said that his priority would be more jobs. Another 30 percent (twelve) said that their opinions had come from seeing various Democrats say on television that they were for full employment. About 38 percent (fifteen) said that their views on the Democratic Party came from their teachers' discussion of the elections in 1976. The remaining youth gave various sources, such as family discussions, discussions with friends or coworkers, etc.

The Raza Unida Party was also given a positive evaluation by the Mexican youth from urban areas, but not nearly as strong a one as that given the Democratic Party. The interviews indicated that the scores from the questionnaire were accurate. The prevailing attitudes among these youth was that Raza Unida was good for Chicanos, and they were appreciative of the party's opposition to suggestions that the United States should adopt a policy of mass deportation of Mexican nationals working in the country. They were encouraged by the possibility that the party would be able to help them in the future, yet they thought that the Democratic Party was more important because, at present, it stood a much better chance of winning elections and formulating policy than did Raza Unida.

Luis, 18-year-old son of a construction worker:

I like what the Raza Unida has stood for, but I wouldn't be able to support it because I feel it would be a wasted vote since only the Democrats have a chance to win.

The Republican party was evaluated negatively by these youth, primarily on the basis of two factors. First, they were quite concerned over the Nixon administration's policy toward illegal aliens. Interestingly, 79 percent (thirty-four) of all the respondents, both urban and rural, were aware of recent statements made by then Attorney General Saxbe that called for the deportation of one million Mexican illegals.[25] A small percentage said that they had actually read these statements themselves, but the overwhelming majority said that they had heard them over either Spanish television or radio. The statements by Saxbe left them feeling apprehensive and negative toward the Republican Party. The second factor that influenced their views on the Republican Party was their belief that most businessmen wanted to pay the lowest wages they could. The following comment was typical of those received:

Tito, 17-year-old son of a short-order cook in Los Angeles:

I don't think the Republican party is good because they support the businessmen, and that is not good for me, because businessmen don't want to pay good wages. The Republicans are for business, and all the businessmen I worked for want to pay low wages, so I don't like the Republican Party.

What explains the differences between Mexican youth from rural areas and those from urban centers in terms of their interest in and knowledge of party politics in the U.S.? The evidence here is clear. The fact that nearly all of the youth from urban areas were planning to stay in the U.S., either for an extended period of time or indefinitely, stimulated them to take a greater interest in American politics. In the interviews, 90 percent of this group said that proficiency in English was necessary to function adequately in the U.S., and that they planned to work toward that goal.[26] The students from rural areas had a more limited view of their presence in the United States. Most planned to be here for only a short period of time and then to return to Mexico. Therefore, the vast majority did not have a great interest in U.S. society in general or U.S. politics in particular. Although they could speak English, their skills were more limited. They were in remedial English classes, and their comments indicated that they viewed these classes as a requirement, and not as an experience that might benefit them. What is particularly important about differences in language skills as they relate to interest in American party politics is that those who were more proficient in

English read English-language newspapers and watched television in English, including (and this is critical) the news, which kept them aware of politics in the U.S. Those less proficient naturally gravitated toward the Spanish-language media, with their emphasis on Mexico and Latin America. Thus the youth from rural backgrounds who planned to stay in the U.S. for a short time, and therefore took little interest in learning English at school, were in a much more limited position with regard to receiving information on American politics.

Unions and Unionization

There has long been debate about the role illegal aliens play in labor's attempts to organize. Many labor leaders claim that illegals are an obstacle to organizing because they are fearful that they will lose their jobs and, therefore, are reluctant to become involved in union politics. Another aspect of this argument is that because they themselves are reluctant to become unionized, the types of jobs illegals occupy cannot be organized, thereby preventing the unions from recruiting additional members. In addition, it has been contended that illegals have been involved as strikebreakers in a considerable number of labor disputes in rural areas.[27] This is a curious argument, since, in the past, illegals have joined labor unions and participated actively in union politics.[28] Evidence on illegal immigrants in the European context has shown that illegals are active participants in the unions of the host countries.[29] Furthermore, the trade unions in these European countries view working immigrants, whether legal or illegal, as important resources for their respective organizations, and therefore make concerted efforts at recruiting them.[30] Yet in the United States, organized labor views undocumented workers as threats and makes no attempt to organize them. Why has this occurred? Are illegal aliens from Mexico unusual in that they do not want to be members of unions? Is there something peculiar about organized labor in the United States whereby it is selective with regard to those whom it is willing to organize? Or is there just something unusual about undocumented workers and labor as they interact in the present American context? On the basis of data available here, these questions cannot be answered definitively. However, some evidence of a suggestive nature is available.

In the interviews, the first question asked relating to unions was how many youth had fathers who worked in unions and what types of jobs they held. Twenty-nine percent (twenty) said that their fathers were in unions, 58 percent (forty) said that they were not, and 13 percent (nine) said that they did not know. The types of jobs held by the fathers who belonged to unions varied, but generally they fell into three broad categories: (1) laborers in the construction business; (2) workers in small factory operations such as tool and dye shops or food processing; and (3) maintenance workers in various institutions and businesses.

None of the youth said that they themselves belonged to a union, but 15 percent (eleven) said that they did belong to workers' associations. These associations are types of unions, in that they negotiate contracts and grievances, but they are not recognized formally as unions. Rather, their jurisdiction is limited to the establishment in which their members are based. The types of jobs that had such associations involved custodial work and work in some textile firms.

The percentage of parents participating in unions is rather high, considering the fact that the national average is less than 30 percent. In addition, only 32 percent of the Chicanos in the sample had parents who were in unions. It seems erroneous, therefore, to assume that illegals in general or these illegals in particular do not like unions or jobs that are unionized. Ninety-two percent (sixty-seven) of the youth in this study said that they wanted jobs that were unionized because those were the jobs that paid the most money and gave the best benefits. A small percentage (8 percent, or six) said that they would not like to be in unions, primarily because they thought union jobs, being better jobs, would be more likely to have I.N.S. agents around, thus creating a greater risk of their being apprehended. The only difference found between those who wanted to have union jobs and those who did not was in their present city of residence. All of the Mexican youth who said that they were afraid of unions were from San Antonio. This was due not only to the fear of being apprehended in these types of jobs, but also to the fact that such feelings were reinforced by a general anti-union sentiment in San Antonio.

Most of those who worked and who did not belong to workers' associations were employed in jobs that had not received any attention from unions. Thus a subsequent concern was whether these students would try to find unionized jobs in the future, and, if they were unsuccessful, would they actively try to organize within the jobs that they already had? Ninety-six percent said that they would not be active in organizing either a workers' association or a union within the types of jobs that they now held. The main problem was that these jobs had such a high turnover rate that it would be difficult to maintain a sufficient number of people to found the organization. A second consideration was the fear that if they tried to start a union or an association, their employers might call the I.N.S. or simply fire them. In either instance, they would be left powerless and without recourse. If, on the other hand, someone else did the organizing and was successful, they had every intention of supporting that union. The optimal situation for them was to gain employment in a place where a union already had been established.

In sum, the first consideration of these youth was to protect themselves from being deported. Therefore, being personally involved in union organizing was not seen as a viable alternative to working in jobs that paid poorly and had substandard work conditions.

Exploitation and the Propensity Toward Political Violence

Two positions are predominant in the dispute over the potential of illegal aliens to engage in acts of political violence. Piore, of the Department of Economics, Massachusetts Institute of Technology, and Cornelius, director of the Center for U.S.-Mexican Studies at the University of California, San Diego, have provided excellent examples of each of these two positions.[31] Piore has argued that a second generation of illegal immigrants will become frustrated with their inability to move up to higher-level jobs, and that this will produce enormous social tensions and greater potential for violence. He uses as an example the children of black immigrants in the northern cities of the U.S. who, he suggests, formed the critical mass in the ghetto disturbances of the 1960s. Cornelius has countered this proposition by arguing that (1) illegal immigrants do not stay in the U.S. long enough to develop the same type of second generation (that is, a generation that wants to be integrated into the social structure) that the blacks in the northern U.S. cities did; and (2) given the economic situation in Mexico, these illegal workers do not feel exploited and resentful; therefore, they do not constitute a segment of society that is likely to be involved in violence.[32] Central to his thesis is the argument that the population of Mexican origin[33] has "experienced higher rates of upward occupational mobility in the 1960s," indicating that they are not locked into the very bottom of the labor market, which diminishes the frustrations of living in a "locked-in" situation.[34] Because the present sample is drawn from the sons and daughters of illegals living in the U.S., it provides a good opportunity to analyze these two positions.

At the core of both of these positions are the issues of: (1) a sense of being exploited, (2) feelings of resentment, and (3) attitudes toward the concept of political violence. Each of these will be considered in order. All of the youth in the sample were asked whether they felt they were being exploited. Regardless of any differences in background, all of the youth declared that they were the object of exploitation. Their descriptions of this exploitation involved their places of employment. The vast majority of those who worked received wages below the minimum, and yet they worked with people who were not illegal aliens and who received more than minimum wage. The youth in this situation perceived themselves as being exploited. Those who received more than minimum wage did not feel exploited themselves, but most added that they knew that the majority of illegal Mexicans in this country were exploited. Of course, not all of the youth worked, but even those who did not said that their fathers were being exploited. Two representative comments follow:

Diego, 17-year-old son of a Los Angeles construction worker:

I don't work, so I'm not exploited; but my father does, and he says he makes less than the others even though he does the same job. So he's exploited, and I know other families the same way.

Maurilio, 18-year-old son of a restaurant cook:

I'm not taken advantage of 'cause I don't work, but my father is, 'cause he works for less than they pay others for the same job.

The major point that emerged from the interviews was that all of the youth felt that they were in a vulnerable position, and that Americans took advantage of that situation.

Theoretically, an individual's sense of being exploited could be rationalized and not viewed in negative terms, if he/she were from an extremely poor country such as Mexico. This leads to the question of whether this sense of exploitation was transformed into feelings of frustration and resentment. The data indicate that the answer is affirmative, with the youth citing two objects of their resentment. The first was their employers. Instead of feeling grateful for having jobs in the U.S., as many of their fathers did, the youth were preoccupied with the fact that they were making less money than their fellow workers while doing the same jobs. Although they struggled to keep these feelings in perspective, they still maintained a basic belief that equal work deserved equal pay. One youth was able to articulate this conviction well:

Concilio, 17-year-old son of a furniture factory worker:

I don't think it's right the way they pay us. We do work that most of them [Americans] don't do because it's hard and not high-paying. Then they go and pay us less than somebody who is a citizen for the same work. I mean, the job is already low-paying, so they should give us all the same. I hate those bosses for that 'cause they are not moral [ethical].

Questions of ethics were prevalent among all the Mexican youth. However, among those from urban areas another factor entered into their bitterness toward employers. These youth felt that low-paying jobs were an impediment to their aspirations. As mentioned earlier, many of the youth from urban areas wanted to stay in the United States permanently. For them, always being employed in these low-paying occupations meant that they would be relegated to a life of continuing poverty or even forced to return to Mexico. Such prospects left them both anxious and resentful toward the employers.[35]

Sixty-seven percent (forty-nine) of the Mexican youth in this sample directed their resentment toward the I.N.S.[36] Since most of their hopes for the future were dependent on their remaining in this country, their resentment toward the agency whose duty it was to apprehend and deport them is understandable.

A final question of interest is whether these feelings of resentment produced support for various forms of political violence. As Table 6.3 indicates, there was no support among the Mexican youth in this study for political terrorism, and this was substantiated in the interviews, where only negative comments about such acts were offered. It was the consensus among the respondents that the use of terrorism would result only in negative repercussions for them. The most likely repercussion would be the dispatch of more police to

Table 6.3
Semantic Differential Mean Scores for Evaluations of Three Forms
of Political Violence by Illegal Mexican Youth

	San Antonio	Los Angeles
Terrorist Bombing	6.53 (27)	6.37 (46)
Riots	4.03 (27)	3.94 (43)
Urban Guerrilla Warfare	6.34 (26)	6.29 (45)

patrol Chicano neighborhoods, which would result in a greater risk of deportation. Some of the respondents thought that U.S. officials would blame them for the terrorism and, as a consequence, implement a policy like "Operation Wetback," aimed at massive deportations. Thus the biggest fear concerning terrorism, for these youth, was that it would draw attention to them, something they consistently wanted to avoid.

However, one type of political violence was supported by a segment of the Mexican youth. The Mexican males in the sample were positive toward riots as a form of political expression. These youth gave two general reasons for their support. First, the majority (53, or seventy-three percent) said that riots were a good way for poor people to express their discontent with their living conditions. Second, a minority (thirty, or 41 percent) believed, like many Chicanos in this study, that riots had the potential to create more jobs because governments usually attempted to improve areas affected by riots by creating more jobs for these areas. More jobs meant that they, as illegals, would have a better opportunity to secure higher-paying jobs.

A follow-up question in the interviews asked those respondents who supported riots if they would participate personally in a riot. None said that they would, because they believed that the risks of being arrested were too high. Therefore, their support for riots was only symbolic.

The young women in the sample were almost unanimous in their opposition to all types of violence, including riots. Their rationale mirrored that of those opposing terrorism; that is, that riots would only bring more police into their neighborhoods, which ultimately would cause more harm than good.

Table 6.4
Semantic Differential Mean Scores for the Evaluations of
Five Ideological Concepts by Illegal Mexican Youth

	San Antonio	Los Angeles
Capitalism	3.95 (27)	4.04 (46)
Socialism	4.02 (27)	3.96 (44)
Communism	4.11 (27)	4.08 (45)
Chicano Nationalism	3.97 (27)	3.90 (46)
Workers' Control of Factories	2.88 (26)	2.75 (46)

In sum, there is no evidence to suggest that the illegal migrants in this sample would engage in violent forms of political behavior. The argument expounded by Piore and others that Mexican illegals form an underclass that will become a nucleus for violent social and political behavior is unfounded, at least as it relates to the youth in this study. The evidence here indicates that these youth are too fearful of being deported to become involved in violent social and political behavior. They believe that there is too much to lose economically for them to be actively involved in such behavior. It is this fear of reprisal that distinguishes illegals from the children of black migrants as described by Piore, and this distinction is likely to continue to control the behavior of Mexican nationals as long as they remain in the country illegally.[37]

Political Ideology Among the
Mexican Youth

Among the Mexican youth in this study there was no support for any of the four ideologies presented: capitalism, socialism, communism, and Chicano nationalism. It can be seen in Table 6.4 that all of their scores were near "4," denoting neutrality. The standard deviations in the scores were also small, indicating little variance around these scores. These data suggest that none of the four ideologies had much meaning to these youth. During the interviews, most of the respondents said they did not have a great deal of information about any ideology.[38] In addition to this general lack of information, they also had difficulty relating the information that they did have about ideologies to their personal lives. Seventy-nine percent (fifty-eight) said that they could not see how any of these ideologies related to them and their everyday routines, and because of this, they considered these concepts to have little value.

However, there was one interesting finding concerning a concept that has ideological implications. The concept of "workers' control of factories" was given a strong positive evaluation, and the variance here was quite small. Eighty-nine percent (sixty-five) of the Mexican youth said that they believed that workers should control the factories in which they worked. It was also their belief that most businessmen had failed to be equitable to their employees, in terms of wages, working conditions, benefits, and interpersonal relations and, consequently, that it would be better for workers if they became managers of the places where they worked.

Germán, 17-year-old son of a San Antonio waiter:

We [laborers] would do just as good a job running the businesses as the owners now. We would give higher wages and more benefits. I mean, there would be more justice than there is now.

Concepción, 18-year-old daughter of a Los Angeles clothing worker:

If workers were the owners, managers wouldn't think they were better than us [laborers]. They would have more respect for us. There would be respect for us because we make the product. Also, there would be higher wages, and that would be good for us.

It became clear in the interviews that the reason the concept of "workers' control of factories" was meaningful to the respondents, whereas the other ideological concepts were not, was because they could identify more closely with this concept. Their experiences of working at jobs that were both hard and low-paying had influenced them to view "workers' control of factories" as a salient concept. Somewhat interestingly, although probably predictably, these youth had no idea that this concept was associated with socialism and communism. They merely saw it as being in their interest for workers to have control of the places where they worked.

One would have to conclude that, in spite of the fact that "workers' control" was considered salient, the Mexican youth were not able to expand this concept into a consistent and logical set of ideas that could be thought of as a form of ideology. For the most part, the youth in the sample were nonideological.

Conclusion

This chapter began with the question of whether the increased presence of Mexican nationals constituted a source of reinforcement for Chicano ethnicity. On the basis of the data obtained from the youth in this study, the answer to that question is no, and the reason is that the Mexican national youth who were in the U.S. illegally were isolated from both the Anglo-American and the Chicano communities. This isolation stemmed from their need, sometimes a desperate one, to make enough money to live on and/or to send back to family and friends in Mexico who were dependent on them, combined with their understanding that their illegal status left them in a perpetually tenuous position where contact with all people who were not illegal Mexican immigrants had to be severely limited. In fact, the Chicano and Mexican youth in this study were antagonistic toward each other and had limited social contact. Much of this antagonism emerged from competition for jobs and from cultural orientations that were similar in origin, but different in content. Of course, this type of conflict is not unique to people of Mexican origin, it also occurred among the Italians and the Jews during their immigration periods.[39] Yet the illegal status of the Mexican is unique, and it is likely to cause the antagonisms between the Mexican and Chicano communities to continue. With relatively limited contact with Chicanos, it is difficult for the Mexican nationals to affect the retention of traditional culture among Chicanos. Also, it is apparent from the data that the illegal Mexican youth who wanted to stay in the United States were trying to become more Americanized themselves, so that their total impact on the retention of Chicano culture would be minimized.

The profile of the undocumented Mexican youth in this study is that of the classic immigrants who have come to America to make better lives for themselves and their families. They try to integrate themselves into American society and face the same problems that other ethnic immigrants have faced, but they must face them with the added burden of illegality. In this precarious position, they are vulnerable, as are other members of their families, to being exploited. Exploitation does occur, and a degree of resentment does exist. However, this resentment is always controlled, and could rarely result in violent social or political behavior because of the risks of being deported. Thus the fears of many policy analysts concerning the building of an underclass that will cause social unrest are only partly founded. The conditions under which these illegal immigrants live no doubt will produce an underclass, but the behavior of that underclass nearly always will be held in check because of its legal status.

7

Conclusion

IN RECENT YEARS it has been customary, more often than not, for social scientists to treat Chicano society as a homogeneous unit and compare it as a whole to that of other ethnic groups. One important conclusion that emerges from this study of Chicano youth is that Chicano society is anything but homogeneous. In fact, Chicano society is quite complex, and there is probably nothing that emphasizes the complex nature of it more than (1) the differences that consistently emerged in political attitudes among those Chicanos who came from different social class backgrounds, and (2) the patterned differences in political attitudes that existed between the Chicanos who lived in the three different cities.

First, those differences that occurred between Chicanos of different social class backgrounds will be discussed. The middle-class Chicano wants to become integrated into the American political system. There is a feeling among members of this group that politics can be an effective means of creating an economically secure future. Thus, members of the Chicano middle class attempt to become involved in politics to influence leaders to adopt positions that will help them, but they do not necessarily want Chicanos to take power away from those who now have it. The political goals of middle-class Chicanos are to obtain as many advantages as possible without offending those who now hold power. These attitudes emerge from having been members of an ethnic group with a history of occupying the lower rungs of the socioeconomic ladder and from understanding that they have managed to become middle-class in spite of discriminatory practices by Anglo-Americans. Thus, they have feelings of genuine pride and satisfaction that they now live comfortable lives. However, they also feel that a wrong move on someone's part could leave them vulnerable to regression into a lower-class life. For this reason they are politically cautious and, for the most part, avoid nearly all forms of radical politics. They are prepared to support some pressure being exerted on the existing political order, but their politics remain within the confines of legitimate and acceptable behavior. In addition, they aggressively oppose politics that aim to make fundamental changes in the existing order. They particularly oppose other Chicanos who want to alter the entire system because they believe that these Chicanos jeopardize their own present socioeconomic positions. After all, these persons want to change a system in which they, as members of the middle class, have been relatively successful. Furthermore, they believe that those Chicanos who would challenge the existing economic order would, by such actions, provide the motivation for an Anglo-American backlash that could strip them of their present material positions. Thus, as members of a disadvantaged ethnic minority who have achieved middle-class status, they do not want to have other members of their group create trouble.

Of course, there have been some costs associated with the socioeconomic mobility that concerns middle-class Chicanos. One of these concerns is related to personal identity. As an ethnic minority, Chicanos in general have maintained a strong group identity, despite efforts to assimilate them into the dominant Anglo-American culture. A strong sense of group identity also helps to provide a foundation for a secure personal identity. As socioeconomic mobility has occurred for middle-class Chicanos in post-industrial America, a sense of Chicano group identity has diminished and nothing has emerged to take its place. As a result, some members of the middle class have felt culturally alienated, not knowing whether they should identify with America, Mexico, or a combination of the two. However, even among this segment of the middle class there is a reluctance to become personally involved in those politics that seek to alter the system substantially. If others altered the political system in a direction of which they approved, that would be fine, but they themselves are not willing to become involved because that would be too personally risky. The politics of the middle-class Chicanos, regardless of whether they are alienated from the system or not, are similar to the politics of the middle class of other ethnic groups, such as the blacks and Jews, and are best described as the "politics of moderation."[1]

The lower-class youth in this study had the same goals—a com-

fortable and secure life—as did their middle-class counterparts. However, the vast majority of this group believed that this was possible
only if fundamental changes were to occur in the existing political
order. They did not want merely to influence those in power, as did
their middle-class cohorts; they wanted Chicanos to secure some of
that power and thereby change some of the existing socioeconomic
arrangements. These political attitudes are shaped by the facts that
(1) few of this group are fully integrated into the economic system,
(2) many are not culturally integrated, and (3) most have experienced
social discrimination. In truth, they are separated from the mainstream of America society, and because of this, many of them find
it easy to subscribe to a nationalist, separatist ideology. Finally, because they felt that they had less to lose, the lower-class Chicanos
were willing to take more personal chances than were the middle-
class youth in this study, and this pattern is likely to continue.

In sum, the patterned social class differences in political attitudes
found in this study are the result of a growing Chicano middle class
that has emerged with the increased presence of Chicanos in urban
areas and the increasing numbers of Chicanos continuing their education past high school. These differences in political attitudes between middle- and lower-class Chicanos are likely to continue as
long as Chicanos are able to obtain socioeconomic mobility and be
integrated into the political system. However, the social class differences that do exist within the Chicano population are not, in
terms of the classic Marxist model, likely to develop into class antagonisms because the Chicano lower class does not feel that the
Chicano middle class is their class enemy. The lower-class Chicanos'
conception of politics is mediated by an ethnic understanding of the
world. They see politics as composed of Chicanos, blacks and Anglo-
Americans. Therefore, in their view, the only way that Chicanos
can be effective in politics is for the entire Chicano community to
be mobilized. Consequently, it is imperative that all Chicanos, regardless of their social class standing, work together. Ironically, despite the fact that the middle-class Chicanos do not believe that
total group solidarity is necessary to attain their political goals, or
feel that this would vary according to the political issues and whether
or not it was strategically appropriate, the members of the Chicano
lower class prefer to ignore class differences for fear that they will
lose the middle class as political allies against the Anglo-American
antagonist. In this respect, the Chicano lower class has a political
response similar to that of blacks and dissimilar to that of other

groups, such as Jews, who developed a class-oriented politics even within their own group in many major urban areas. What is unique to Jewish political history is that during the period from 1880 to 1940, Jews suffered persistent and intense discrimination from non-Jews, which resulted in the maintenance of a very strong ethnic identification; however, because Jews had members of their ethnic group on both sides of the class line (owners and producers), they developed a class politics within their group as well.[2] This political-economic experience is significantly different from that of blacks and Chicanos, who never developed a meaningful proprietor class.

Chicano Political Attitudes in Three Cities

As mentioned in the preceding section, middle-class Chicanos tended to be more conservative in their political attitudes than did those from lower- and working-class backgrounds. Social class orientation, and interest, will continue to influence the attitudes of Chicanos. However, the socioeconomic and political environments of the cities in which Chicanos find themselves ultimately will decide the framework within which the formation of political attitudes will occur. What this means is that, although social class background will influence the ways in which Chicanos, or members of any ethnic group, become involved in politics, the kind and degree of involvement will be affected by the socioeconomic and political culture of the cities in which they live. As an example, it can be expected that social class differences in attitudes toward politics will continue in San Antonio, but these attitudes will exist within a politically conservative framework. Given the situation in San Antonio, where the economic system is tightly controlled by Anglo-American businessmen and by the U.S. military establishment, and where the social structure retains tightly stratified, caste-like elements, it is little wonder that Chicanos, who are at the bottom of the social structure, feel constrained in their views concerning political options. In point of fact, the political system here has been controlled tightly by the Democratic Party and by Anglo-American politicians, most of whom have ties to the business community. Thus, the Chicanos in San Antonio accommodate themselves to these political realities, and with the demise of the Raza Unida Party they are likely to do so even more in the foreseeable future. Some who read this book may ask whether the fact that San Antonio has

elected a Chicano mayor and a number of Chicano councilmen sig-
nifies a change in the city's political structure. To some extent,
change has occurred, but in general, the election of Henry Cisneros
has not signified a changing of the political guard in San Antonio
or a transfer of political power.[3] No one knows that better than
Cisneros himself. His political history is one of integrating himself
into the Democratic political organization and moving up the organizational ladder. He was and is accepted by the Anglo-American
elite of the party, and draws a significant amount of his political
clout from their endorsement, even though electoral politics in San
Antonio is non-partisan. Cisneros has continued to work with the
Anglo-American-dominated business community because he real-
izes, as Dennis Kucinich, the ex-mayor of Cleveland, did not, that
if the financial institutions of a city do not want to cooperate, they
can render a mayoral administration powerless.[4] This is especially
true in San Antonio, where a history of racial/ethnic antagonisms
between Chicanos and Anglos, along with the fact that Chicanos
outnumber Anglos, has produced a sensitive Anglo-Texan business
community that is extremely aggressive in punishing those whom
it perceives to be hostile toward it. In general, the Chicano population understands this and has made the accommodations necessary
in order to function. Thus, in terms of electoral politics, one can
expect the Chicanos of San Antonio to follow the lead of the Democratic Party or to vote for a moderate candidate whom the party
endorses. This is the most likely scenario because Chicanos in San
Antonio presently do not see a way to achieve independence from
the Anglo-Texan controlled economy and political structure in San
Antonio. It can also be expected that the Democratic Party will offer
more moderate candidates in order to accommodate "moderately"
what they perceive to be Chicano interests.

Where pressure politics are concerned, the Chicanos of San Antonio are likely to continue to participate in organizations like COPS,
the community-based group that has been involved in moderate
public service issues, and not to become involved with those organizations that would press for fundamental changes in the existing
political and economic power structure.

In sum, the perceptions of the San Antonio Chicanos in this study
are that the options presented to them are tightly controlled and
that they have to be prudent in their political involvement. Hence
San Antonio's socioeconomic and political environment is able to
establish tight parameters for acceptable/unacceptable political be-

havior and thereby establish a functional mechanism for social control.

The Chicanos in Albuquerque operate within a different political milieu than that found in San Antonio. Citizens of Albuquerque, including the Chicano youth in this study, see Albuquerque as a city of opportunity. If one wants to become socioeconomically mobile one can, providing that one works hard enough. If one wants to live anywhere in the city one can, providing that one has enough money; and if one wants to be successful in politics one can, if one takes the correct stand on political issues. In other words, there are few or no barriers caused by the fact of being Chicano. What has developed and has been nurtured by the more influential segments of the society, including influential Chicanos in the middle class, is an ideology which has stressed that Chicanos in New Mexico are different from those in Texas and California, if not racially, then certainly culturally, and that their historical experience is different from that of Chicanos in other states because they have been integrated into the political system. For the most part this ideology has predominated, thereby neutralizing an ethnically-oriented politics while strengthening a class-oriented one. However, although economic assimilation has occurred, it has been much slower for Chicanos in New Mexico than political integration, and the result is that a large lower class still exists, especially when compared with the Anglo lower class. This has caused many Chicanos to maintain an ethnically oriented politics. Thus, from time to time, some issue will fuel the private fires of ethnicity and Albuquerque politics will take on an ethnic character. This occurred when the Alianza Federal de Mercedes and the Raza Unida Party aroused passions associated with ethnicity by politicizing the poor Chicanos' loss of the land given through the Spanish land grant system to wealthy Anglo businessmen and the federal government. Howver, with the demise of the Alianza Federal de Mercedes and Raza Unida, political attitudes in Albuquerque have returned to a social class orientation. Data from both the original and the follow-up study indicate that the youth who once supported Raza Unida, or the Alianza, now support the Democratic Party or no party at all, while many of those who supported the Democrats in the initial 1977 survey have, after experiencing economic mobility, switched to the Republican Party. Interestingly, there is probably no other state with a sizable Chicano population in which as large a proportionate number of Chicanos will support the Republican Party in future elections. This social class pattern is likely to continue, in which the private sentiments associated with an ethnic political consciousness are held in check by the prevailing public ideology that Chicanos in New Mexico are historically unique, have unlimited economic opportunity, and are not, in any significant manner, discriminated against. Consequently, in Albuquerque the power of ideology is able, for the immediate future, to influence political attitudes in a moderate direction.

There was more variation in political attitudes among the Chicano youth of Los Angeles than among the youth of either San Antonio or Albuquerque. No single variable explains the attitudinal orientation of the Chicanos from Los Angeles, since in Los Angeles social class standing alone does not explain the youth's political attitudes. One finds both radical and conservative political attitudes among segments of both the middle and the lower classes. The explanation for this is that Los Angeles' environment is quite different from that of Albuquerque and San Antonio. The city is much larger, both geographically and in terms of population, and more socioeconomically complex than the other two cities. This complexity has given rise to a society with a much more complicated social system, which has stimulated much more range and variety among those factors that influence individual political attitudes. In brief, the socioeconomic environment of Los Angeles has encouraged the development of a wide variety of political attitudes. In looking at the data from this study, it can be seen that more of the youth in Los Angeles feel that there are economic opportunities in their city than do those in San Antonio, for example. There is no feeling of economic intimidation, as there is among the youth in San Antonio. Neither is there a feeling that if individuals hold certain political beliefs they will not get employment. Nor is there any fear that if they subscribe to a particular political belief they will be intimidated by organs of the state, such as the police. There is, instead, the prevailing view that Los Angeles has a tolerant political environment. Los Angeles, with a diversified population in terms of such factors as ethnicity, education, and age, along with a sophisticated media system and a large number of colleges and universities, has stimulated the growth and tolerance of a wide range of political beliefs. The heterogeneity of the population and the complex nature of the social structure have been instrumental in producing an atmosphere that is tolerant toward divergent ideas, primarily as a result of a recognition on the part of most citizens that intolerance would create major cleavages and disruptions in the city's entire system of operation. This tolerant atmosphere has the reciprocal effect of encouraging new ideas to form. Thus, one dynamic of Los Angeles' "mass-like" society is that it is able to control its intrinsic maze of ideas and ideologies because these ideas either counteract one another or fade when confronted by the appeal of newly emerging ones.

The Chicanos of Los Angeles at times evince political attitudes that are quite challenging to the system. In fact, the present study found substantial support among Los Angeles Chicanos, much more than among Chicanos in the other two cities, for nationalist/sepa-ratist politics and violence-oriented protest politics. Given the open sociopolitical milieu of Los Angeles, it is likely that there will always be an abundance of people with ideas and ideologies that they are trying to spread throughout the city's *barrios*. Yet, as with the support for nationalism/separatism and political violence found in this study, the heterogeneity within Chicano society, along with the vastness of the metropolitan area, makes it extremely difficult for political ideas to develop to a level where they are strong enough to be maintained over the time necessary for them to become social movements. In other words, the task of integrating existing ideas into a social movement is too formidable, given the geographically and socially fragmented nature of Los Angeles society.[5] Thus, it is not likely that the same, or similar, political attitudes will be held by the majority of the Chicano population. In addition, because political ideas are subject to rapid change, there will be a tendency for Chicanos, as well as many other groups in Los Angeles, to become frustrated with politics and periodically to become uninvolved. This also will inhibit the emergence of a sustained political movement that defines its agenda as those issues that affect Chicanos directly.[6] Thus, although Los Angeles has had, and is likely always to have, more radical politics among its citizens, the openness and tolerance of the city's "mass-like" society permit the establishment of a form of sociopolitical control which ensures that "moderate" politics constitute the norm. In this regard, all of the three cities share a common element.

Finally, given the theories of the Chicago school, it might be expected that the experience of living in a city would have a uniform effect on the Chicano youth's attitudes toward ethnicity and politics. This study has failed to confirm that hypothesis, and the explanation is that the three cities are quite different from one another. Thus increased length of residence in San Antonio did not reduce attachment to traditional cultural values; instead, longer residence produced political attitudes that were cautious and conservative. In Albuquerque, longer residence produced greater economic mobility and a lessening of ties to traditional culture. In addition, as socio-economic mobility occurred, individuals developed politics based on their social class interests. Finally, in Los Angeles longer residence produced a lessening of ties to traditional culture, regardless of whether or not socioeconomic mobility had occurred. Longer residence also produced more positive attitudes toward radical politics.

Ethnicity, Politics and the City

The findings of this study with regard to Chicanos in the city provide a significant insight into cities in general. If one critical finding has emerged from this study, it is that cities are not similar in the way in which they socialize the individuals who live within their boundaries. This is because cities themselves are quite different, and it is these differences among cities that must be better understood in order to provide a better understanding of the ethnic politics of America, in earlier times as well as today.

San Antonio, Albuquerque, and Los Angeles were chosen for this study because they were large cities, because they were magnet cities for Chicanos in their movement to an urban world, and because as large cities they possessed the characteristics that historically have interested urban sociologists in their study of the city's impact on human behavior—especially how the city has effected ethnic assimilation. The choice of these three cities for this study was an attempt at representing the broad spectrum of Chicano society. On the basis of the three main schools of thought in urban sociology (the Chicago school, the "neighborhood solidarity" school, and the Marxist school) there was reason to hypothesize that separate urban communities would have no differing effects on beliefs and behaviors. Yet the data consistently demonstrated patterned differences in how each city's social and political environment affected the Chicanos who lived there. They emphasized that there were unique socioeconomic and political structures in each of these cities that interacted to influence patterned responses to political involvement. What this suggested was that cities, throughout their histories, develop social orders that are maintained through the establishment of institutions and the concomitant roles that people assume within them. What most societies do is to socialize people into these institutions and social orders. If people are not socialized to think of the existing order as legitimate, then they must be socialized, at a minimum, to accept it. However, those institutions and social orders to which people are in the process of being socialized vary in form and in content, and these variations must be accounted for because they help to explain whether a given individual will think that the existing order is legitimate or merely accept it. Among the Chicanos in this study, three social orders were found to affect political attitudes: one dominated by "caste-like" elements in social relations; a second dominated by social class; and a third dominated by "mass-like" relations. There is no doubt that additional social orders exist and are operating within other cities, and these need to be identified in order to provide a better understanding of the political experiences of various ethnic groups in American cities. This can be done best by identifying those factors that influence the development of the social and political characters of cities, particularly as they affect ethnic groups. The present study has utilized four such factors. First, there is the economic history of the city. This variable includes not only information on how the economic system of a particular city is organized, but information on how it got that way. What particular historical events have occurred to shape its present structure? A city may have come into being for one economic reason, but be organized now for quite a different one. For example, such cities as Chicago and Detroit were organized as trading centers because they were physically located at places that were convenient for transportation. For this same reason, as well as for some other technologically important ones, they developed into production cities. Ultimately, knowing the economic history of a city provides important information about the city's ethnic composition, mainly because it reveals what ethnic groups have come to satisfy the demand for labor at particular points in time.[7] For example, Detroit had a wave of succeeding Eastern European ethnic groups, followed by blacks, Mexicans, Arabs, and Appalachian whites. In Chicago the immigrants were Northern Europeans, Eastern Europeans, Southern Europeans, Jews, Mexicans, blacks, and Appalachian whites—all coming during particular periods of economic activity; and in cities such as New York, Boston, and Los Angeles there were a multitude of ethnic groups who came during overlapping periods of economic activity. Thus the structure of economic life and the concomitant demand for labor at any given time has a significant impact on the ethnic composition of a city.

The degree of local economic diversity also has a profound influence on the character of ethnic relations within a city. Since members of various ethnic groups come to the city to seek employment and to become economically mobile, they are going to be competitive with one another. The diversification of the economy will determine how much opportunity exists for all peoples within the city, which in turn will determine the level of competition and the level of ethnic antagonism.[8] If the economy of a particular city has developed around one particular industry or product, then a more stratified labor market will exist there, with more competition and more ethnic antagonism. In this situation, the antagonism will last over a significant period of time and will assume a particular character. Thus, if the city is a "one-company town," or has many companies, but only one industry, then the options for the individuals who live there will be fewer than they would be for people living in a city with an evenly developed economy, i.e., an even distribution of jobs between services, manufacturing, and government. This was, of course, the case in this study, where San Antonio presented fewer options for its citizens, in terms of both economic mobility and forms of political participation, than existed for the citizens of Los Angeles and, to a lesser extent, Albuquerque. This also would be the case for cities such as Boston, Massachusetts; Birmingham, Alabama; Gary, Indiana; and Pittsburgh, Pennsylvania—all cities organized around one primary industry (for example, steel).[9]

The character of the political system is also an important factor in influencing ethnic relations and politics. Specifically, how "open" is the system in terms of incorporating divergent interests? In many ways, the "openness" of the political system is related directly to the extent of diversification of the economic structure and the number of ethnic groups in that these factors determine the number of interests that must be coordinated, compromised with, governed, and, in general, accommodated. Where there are a significant number of ethnic groups there is a general tendency toward a more open political system. "More open," however, can be understood in two ways. First, there is a tendency for the system to incorporate wider ethnic representation into its various decision-making apparati. This is done because more groups are competing for power within the political market place, and this is a way for systemic control to be administered. Second, as more groups compete, more variety will be evidenced in the strategies used to gain power. There will also be more tolerance of divergent forms of political participation, including violence, because none of the contending groups will feel that any one of them will be able to secure total political power. This is particularly true in cities such as New York, Chicago, and Los Angeles. When a city does not have a diversified economy, and has only a few ethnic groups competing for power, the ideology usually is put forth by the dominant ethnic group that control is necessary in order to maintain the daily work schedule, so that regular economic operations are not disrupted, because the city can ill afford a disruption of production. Of course, there is also the pragmatic understanding that if a competing group seizes power, it will not share that power with the previously dominant group because the political culture does not dictate that it should.

In this situation, the economic and political realities of a particular city dictate strict control over the type of participation that an opposition ethnic group is attempting to undertake. Often, this control is exercised through harsh physical and economic sanctions. For evidence one only has to look to the black political experience in southern cities, or to the Chicano experience in San Antonio. In each of these cases, challenges by the ethnic group not in power usually have been met by rather forceful countermeasures. This does not mean that ethnic groups who are out of political power will be unsuccessful in future attempts to gain such power. As has occurred recently in such cities as Chicago, Gary, Detroit, and Oakland, blacks have been able to secure some political power. However, the transfer of power within government does not carry with it the same kind of political power that is tied to those actors and institutions controlling the economic market places of cities. There are no better examples of this than the cities of Cleveland, Gary, and Detroit, where the mayors from various ethnic groups came into governmental power but failed to deliver benefits to their respective groups because they lacked adequate economic power.[10] Thus, when the role of ethnicity in influencing city politics is analyzed, it is also necessary to assess the impact of the urban political economy.

The fourth variable that influences the formation of political attitudes and behaviors in cities is the legal codes that are in existence. Not much research has been done on this factor, and it was not examined in the present study. It usually is presumed that legal codes affecting social and political attitudes are fairly uniform throughout the nation. However, laws are quite different in different states, and the interpretation of those laws by different elements of the legal system, such as police, lawyers, and courts, varies considerably. This does not go unnoticed by the people who live inparticular cities. Their perceptions of how the legal codes will be enforced, how this will affect their lives, and what chance they have to change current legal thought on the issues that affect them, all contribute to influence their perceptions and attitudes regarding the social and political terrains within which they must operate.

The present inquiry was initiated because of an interest in how living in a city influenced the social and political attitudes of a newly urbanized ethnic group, or what factors explained political learning among Chicano populations now living in urban environments. The study was guided by the dominant sociological theories of urbanization and ethnicity: those of Wirth and Park of the Chicago school, Gans and Suttles of the "neighborhood solidarity" school, and Castells of the marxist school of urban sociology. The data in this study provided supporting evidence for portions of each of the theories mentioned. Probably the theory with the most consistent explanatory power was that of Wirth, Park, and the Chicago school. Yet no one of these theories, including that of the Chicago school, went far enough in explaining why there were differences between cities controlling for the same ethnic group—Chicanos. The "social order" conceptual framework used in this study goes farther in explaining a city's impact on a given ethnic group's political attitudes. Doubtless there is a need to specify more precisely the factors used as variables in this study, but this will remain for future work. What the present study has shown is that the Chicanos not only are bound for cities, but, like other urban groups, are politically and economically bound by them as well.

Appendix
Notes on the Sample and Data Gathering Procedures

THE INTENT of this study was to determine what effects urban life has on an ethnic group. Special attention was given to how urban life affected attitudes about politics, about one's own ethnic culture, and the relationship between them. It was determined that the study could be most valuable if it focused on a particular age group, and those chosen were young Chicanos between the ages of seventeen and nineteen. There were a number of reasons for choosing such a group. First, I was interested in generational change and the impact of the urban environment on change. Since I was looking to see if a new generation was emerging with a new set of attitudes, I could not select a group that was younger than seventeen because these individuals would be more likely to reflect their parents than they would a new generation. In addition, the selection of an older group would be inappropriate because it would not reflect a new generation. Second, members of this age group were about to become, or had just become, voters and so their attitudes toward what they perceived to be their political world was important. Finally, because one of the objectives of the study was that it be longitudinal, beginning with this age group provided opportunities to study it periodically throughout the generation's lifetime.

The sample for this study combined both stratification and clustering methods. As has been previously mentioned, the target population of the sample was Chicano youth seventeen to nineteen years of age living in Los Angeles, San Antonio, and Albuquerque. There were a number of considerations in selecting the sample. It was decided, first, that it would be more economical to select the sample from among seventeen to nineteen year-olds attending school rather than to try to secure a random sample of seventeen to nineteen year-olds from the entire city population. To be most efficient and to maximize the representativeness of the sample, a number of geographic areas were identified that had significant numbers of Chicanos living in them. Each of these areas represented a different socioeconomic neighborhood. There were areas where nearly all of the residents were poor or working class, while there were other areas where the inhabitants were nearly all middle class. In addition, within these areas there were neighborhoods that had various degrees of population density, as well as variations in the degree of ethnic heterogeneity.

From the broad-based geographic areas, three areas corresponding to school subdistricts were chosen; and from these areas, three schools were chosen. One school contained a student body from predominantly lower-class families, another represented middle-class families, and a third was composed of roughly fifty percent middle- and lower-class. This last school was in an area that was going through residential change. In all three areas the broad spectrum of socioeconomic strata within the Chicano community was well represented. In addition, the sampling areas chosen included the broad spectrum of physical conditions associated with urbanism.

All nine high schools selected (three in each city) were public schools. This raises two questions concerning possible biases in the sample. The first has to do with omitting students who attended Catholic high schools. Having checked the enrollments of Chicanos in Catholic high schools for the period I was studying, I found that enrollments were small. Thus if there is bias here, it is relatively insignificant. The second question has to do with student dropout rates and whether the fact that Chicanos historically have had high dropout rates biased the sample. Here again I thoroughly checked the attendance records of each school and interviewed the appropriate school officials. I found that the dropout rate for the past four-year period (for these areas) was quite low. In fact, the dropout rate had been less than 8 percent of the enrolled freshmen in each of the schools sampled. Therefore, I do not believe the dropout rate was high enough to become a significant factor in biasing the sample of high school seniors.

Once the school was selected, contact was made with the various school authorities and little difficulty arose in gaining the cooperation of the various school officials. The next step in securing the sample was to identify those courses that every student was required to take. There were two such courses and, if the student was not enrolled in one, he/she was enrolled in the other. In this way, I was able to identify the entire population of high school seniors at the school. From the entire senior population the sample was drawn first by a random start and then by selecting every third person. Each student was then approached in class and asked to participate in the research project. The entire extent of the project was explained. Only six students in all three cities refused to participate. Because there was a self-administered component to the questionnaire, class attendance was taken the day the first part of the questionnaire was administered. I had decided not to administer the questionnaire if there was more than a 5 percent absentee rate among the students, but that never turned out to be the case. Each student completed the questionnaire and returned it with his or her address listed on the cover. Students were told that within the week they would be contacted by an interviewer who would ask them a series of questions that would constitute the second half of the project. Within the week, a team of interviewers contacted the students outside of the school. Each of the interviewers was fully trained in face-to-face interviewing techniques prior to the study, but there were two training sessions for this project as well. Before the interview began, a question was asked as to whether the student had talked to other students about the first part of the questionnaire. If students indicated that they had talked about specific questions and had done so for more than a short time (a few minutes), their questionnaires were marked to indicate a possible bias. Only 8 students from San Antonio, 10 students from Albuquerque, and 16 from Los Angeles indicated they had talked about the questionnaire extensively. Interestingly enough, their questionnaires were checked with those who had not discussed the questionnaire and no significant differences were found between the two groups.

When the interviewer had finished going through the questionnaire, he/she asked whether the respondent would be willing to answer another questionnaire some time in the future. All the students said they would participate at a future time. The total in the sample was 1,040 youths.

With the questionnaire portion of the study completed, the data were taken back to M.I.T. and coded, and a computer file was created. After some preliminary analyses had been made, I returned to each of the three cities to conduct in-depth interviews with a selected group of students. Two hundred students were selected from all three cities (67 from L.A., 67 from San Antonio, and 66 from Albuquerque). Only 16 of the students contacted said they could not participate. If a student could not participate, another was chosen until the desired number (200) was achieved. Each of the in-depth interviews lasted about 90 minutes and was recorded on a tape recorder. The interviews were then transcribed in a form that was used to validate what the survey data indicated or clarified some of the ambiguities that existed in the survey data.

The last phase of the research project was to return to each of the three cities five years after the original survey was completed and reinterview 300 of the students who had participated in the first survey. In the follow-up study, 500 names were randomly selected, and the process of locating them began. If a person could not be found, then another person was drawn from the random 500 until the desired 300 was achieved. Thus, the first of a scheduled three follow-up studies was completed. Data from this questionnaire were coded and a new computer file created for longitudinal study.

Finally, a brief note on the questionnaire itself and the data. Before the questionnaire was printed in final form it was given as a pretest in each of the three cities to 75 Chicanos (38 young men, 37 young women) who were of the same age group. This was done to determine the overall effectiveness of the questionnaire in ascertaining the information desired. Where problems existed in question wording and/or ordering, they were corrected for the final form. Because of space problems, the questionnaire used in this study could not be reproduced in the appendix. For those interested in obtaining the various questionnaires, they are included in the data sets and are available from the Survey Research Center at the University of California, Berkeley, or from the author in care of the Department of Sociology, University of California, Berkeley, California 94720.

Notes

Chapter 1

1. The early studies of ethnicity are too numerous to record. Some, although not all, of the standard works would include: John Higham, *Strangers in the Land* (New Brunswick, N.J.: Rutgers University Press, 1955); Oscar Handlin, *The Uprooted* (Boston: Little, Brown, 1951); Handlin, *Children of the Uprooted* (New York: Grosset & Dunlop, 1968); Handlin, *Boston's Immigrants: A Study in Acculturation* (Cambridge: Harvard University Press, 1941; rev. ed., New York: Atheneum, 1971); Julius Drachsler, *Democracy and Assimilation: The Blending of Immigrant Heritages in America* (New York: MacMillan Co., 1920).

2. Of those studies that have been done, a few are: L. Paul Metzger, "American Sociology and Black Assimilation: Conflicting Perspectives," *American Journal of Sociology* 76 (January 1971): 627–647; sections of Leo Grebler, Joan Moore, and Ralph Guzman, *The Mexican American People: The Nation's Second Largest Minority* (New York: Free Press, 1970); Edward Murguia, *Assimilation, Colonialism and the Mexican American People*, Mexican American Monograph Series 1 (Austin: University of Texas Press, 1975). American Indians, as an ethnic group, faced a unique set of issues related to their historical and legal position in America. Studies that discuss assimilation or acculturation of American Indians do so in the context of the government projects which relocated them to cities. See J. O. Waddel and O. M. Watson, *The American Indian in Urban Society* (Boston: Little, Brown, 1971); Joan Ablon, "Relocated American Indians in the San Francisco Bay Area: Social Interaction and Indian Identity," *Human Organization* 23 (1964):362–371; J. H. Stauss and Bruce A. Chadwick, "Urban Indian Adjustment," *American Indian Culture and Research Journal* 2(3) (1979):23–38. Alan L. Sorkin, *The*

Urban American Indian (Lexington, Mass.: Lexington Books, 1978).

3. There are many names used to designate American citizens of Mexican origin. This study uses "Chicano" and, occasionally, "Hispano." The use of the term Hispano is limited to the people who live in New Mexico because they have a unique relationship with Mexico. For the most part, these people were ruled by Spain for some 300 years, and were under Mexican rule for only 28 years before the United States took over. Therefore, they consider themselves Hispanos and not Chicanos. In general, the term "Anglo" or "Anglo-American" is used to designate the aggregate group of white Americans; however, where necessary, the specific ethnic identification is used.

4. Milton Gordon was one of the first to conceptualize that assimilation involves many areas of social life. See his *Assimilation in American Life: The Role of Race, Religion and National Origins.* (New York: Oxford University Press, 1964).

5. See Dwaine Marvick, "The Political Socialization of the American Negro," *The Annals 361* (September 1965):112–127; Sidney Verba, Bashir Ashmed, and Anil Bhatt, *Caste, Race and Politics* (Beverly Hills, Cal.: Sage Publications, 1971); David O. Sears and John B. McConahay, "Racial Socialization, Comparison Levels, and the Watts Riot," *Journal of Social Issues 26* (1970): 121–140; James W. LaMare, "Language Environment and Political Socialization of Mexican-American Children," in Richard Niemi and Associates, eds., *The Politics of Future Citizens* (San Francisco: Jossey-Bass, 1974), pp. 63–82; F. Chris Garcia, *Political Socialization of Chicano Children: A Comparative Study with Anglos in California* (New York: Praeger, 1973); Dean Jaros, Herbert Hirsch, and Frederick Fleron, "The Malevolent Leader: Political Socialization in an American Sub-Culture," *American Political Science Review 62* (1968):169–184; Sarah F. Liefschutz and Richard G. Niemi, "Political Attitudes Among Black Children." in Richard Niemi and Associates, eds., *The Politics of Future Citizens*, pp. 83–102.

6. For a discussion of the issues related to the rapid growth of the Chicano and Hispanic population, see Leobardo F. Estrada, F. Chris Garcia, Reynaldo Flores Macias, and Lionel Maldonado, "Chicanos in the United States: A History of Exploitation and Resistance," *Daedalus 110*(2) (Spring 1981): 103–133.

7. See Marc R. Levy and Michael S. Kramer, *The Ethnic Factor: How America's Minorities Decide Elections* (New York: Simon and Schuster, 1972).

8. Rodolfo Acuña, *Occupied America: A History of Chicanos* (New York: Harper and Row, 1981), p. 320; David Montejano, "A Journey Through Mexican Texas, 1900–1930: The Making of a Segregated Society" (Ph.D. dissertation, Yale University, 1982), p. 305–308.

9. See Mario Barrera, *Race and Class in the Southwest* (South Bend, Ind.: University of Notre Dame Press, 1979); Andrés Jímenez, "Political Domination in the Labor Market: Racial Division in the Arizona Copper Industry" (Berkeley: University of California, Institute for the Study of Social Change, Working Paper No. 103, 1977).

10. Carey McWilliams, *North From Mexico* (New York: Greenwood Press, 1948), is considered the classic portrayal of the constant flow of Mexican immigrants in both directions.

11. See M. Kent Jennings and Richard G. Niemi, *The Political Character of Adolescence: The Influence of Families and Schools* (Princeton, N.J.: Princeton University Press, 1974); Sandra Kenyon, "The Development of Political Cynicism Among Negro and White Adolescents," paper presented at the annual meeting of the American Political Science Association, New York, September 1969.

12. See Sidney Verba and Norman H. Nie, *Participation in America: Political Democracy and Social Equality* (New York: Harper and Row, 1972), Chapter 10.

13. See Sidney Verba, et al., *Caste, Race and Politics;* David Sears and John B. McConahay, *The Politics of Violence;* Richard D. Shingles, "Black Consciousness and Political Participation: The Missing Link," *American Political Science Review* 75(1) (March 1980): 76–91.

14. See F. Chris Garcia, *The Political Socialization of Chicano Children;* James LaMare, "Language Environment and Political Socialization of Mexican-American Children;" and George Antunes and Charles M. Gaitz, "Ethnicity and Participation: A Study of Mexican-Americans, Blacks and Whites," *American Journal of Sociology* 80: 1192–1211.

15. For a good treatment of the ethnic experience see Thomas J. Archdeacon, *Becoming American: An Ethnic History* (New York: The Free Press, 1983).

16. See David Montejano, "A Journey Through Mexican Texas, 1900–1930," Chapter 8.

17. See the 1980 *United States Census,* vol. 1, General Population Characteristics for Texas, (PC80-1-B45); . . . for California (PC80-1-B6); and . . . for New Mexico (PC80-1-B33).

18. See David O. Sears, "Political Socialization," in Fred I. Greenstein and Nelson Polsby, eds., *The Handbook of Political Science,* Vol. 2: *Micropolitical Theory* (Reading, Mass.: Addison-Wesley, 1975).

19. For general reference to the Chicago school see Robert E. L. Faris, *Chicago Sociology: 1920–1932* (Chicago: University of Chicago Press, 1970). Specifically, see Robert Park, Ernest Burgess, and R. D. McKenzie, *The City* (Chicago: University of Chicago Press, 1925); Louis Wirth, *On Cities and Social Life,* ed. Albert J. Reiss (Chicago: University of Chicago Press, 1964).

20. See Robert Park, "Racial Assimilation of Secondary Groups," *American Journal of Sociology 19* (March 1914):606–623; Park, *Race and Culture* (Glencoe, Ill.: Free Press, 1950).

21. See Louis Wirth, *The Ghetto* (Chicago: University of Chicago Press, 1928); Wirth, "Urbanism as a Way of Life," *American Journal of Sociology 44* (July 1938):3–24; Wirth, "The Problem of Minority Groups," in Ralph Linton, ed., *The Science of Man in the World Crisis* (New York: Columbia University Press, 1945).

22. Michael P. Smith, *The City and Social Theory* (New York: St. Martin's Press, 1979), p. 172.

23. See Herbert Gans, *Urban Villagers: Group and Class in the Life of Italian-Americans* (New York: The Free Press, 1962); Jane Jacobs, *The Death and Life of Great American Cities* (New York: Vintage, 1961); Gerald Suttles, *The Social Order of the Slum: Ethnicity and Territory in the Inner City* (Chicago: University of Chicago Press, 1968); Herbert Gans, "Urbanism and Suburbanism as Ways of Life," in A. M. Rose, ed., *Human Behavior and Social Processes* (Boston: Houghton and Mifflin, 1962), pp. 625–648.

24. One important exception is the theory advanced by Claude Fischer, "Toward a Subcultural Theory of Urbanism," *American Journal of Sociology 80* (May):1319–1341. Fischer integrated many of the ideas of both of these schools into his theory.

25. See Manuel Castells, *The Urban Question: A Marxist Approach* (Cambridge: Massachusetts Institute of Technology Press, 1977); Castells, *City, Class and Power* (New York: St. Martin's Press, 1978); Michael Harloe, ed., *Captive Cities: Studies in the Political Economy of Cities and Regions* (New York: John Wiley and Sons, 1977); C. G. Pickvance, ed., *Urban Sociology: Critical Essays* (London: Methuen, 1976).

26. See Castells, *The Urban Question*, chapter 5; C. G. Pickvance, *Urban Sociology*.

27. Michael P. Smith, *The City and Social Theory*, p. 171.

28. See Ira Katznelson, *City Trenches: Urban Politics and the Patterning of Class in the United States* (New York: Pantheon, 1982).

29. Ibid., p. 214.

30. For a general discussion of the mathematical principles of path analysis, see Otis Dudley Duncan, "Path Analysis: Sociological Examples," *American Journal of Sociology 72* (July 1966):1–16; David R. Heise, *Causal Analysis* (New York: John Wiley and Sons, 1975), pp. 111–147; Sewell Wright, "Path Coefficients and Path Regressions: Alternative or Complementary Concepts?," *Biometrics 16* (June 1960):189–202.

The general equation used by Asher to explain path analysis is:

$$r_{ij} = \Sigma \ p_{ik} r_{jk}$$

"where k is an index referencing those variables having a direct impact on x_1 and the subscript i references the dependent variable in the pair." See Herbert Asher, *Causal Modeling*, Sage Paper on Quantitative Applications in Social Sciences (Beverly Hills, Cal.: Sage Publications, 1976), pp. 32–35.

31. Both of these variables were constructed in the following manner: first the students were asked to name the streets on which they lived and give the house numbers rounded off to the hundred. Thus, if a student lived at 213 Spruce Street, he/she would put "200 block Spruce Street." After the student's block was recorded, it was matched with the information provided by the three city planning departments on population density and ethnic composition of the neighborhoods. Because of the tendency of planning departments to not focus on ethnicity and the degree of difficulty in accurately assessing its composition in neighborhoods, the statistics provided by the city planning department were checked, and where discrepancies were found, they were corrected.

32. Socioeconomic status was determined by an index developed by Otis Dudley Duncan, "A Socioeconomic Index for All Occupations," in Albert Reiss, Jr., ed., *Occupations and Social Status* (New York: Free Press, 1960), pp. 109–33; and elaborated on by David L. Featherman and Robert M. Hauser, "On the Measurement of Occupations in Social Survey," *Sociological Methods and Research 2* (November 1973):239–251.

33. It was necessary to construct an index because it would not have been accurate to analyze the effects of any one variable alone. These four variables were chosen to be indexed because they were theoretically important for analyzing traditional Chicano culture. Factor analysis also was used in order to determine if they clustered together empirically, and it was found that they did. By using Osgood's formula (the "D" Statistic) for factor analysis, which is:

$$D_{kj}\sqrt{\Sigma \ dij^2}$$

where D is the linear distance between any two concepts i and j, and d is the algebraic difference between the coordinates of i and j on the same factor, the following results were obtained:

Spanish	2.67
Compadrazgo	2.70
Curanderismo	2.75
Catholic Church	2.77

See Charles Osgood, George J. Suci, and Percy H. Tannenbaum, *The Measurement of Meaning*, (Urbana, Ill.: U. of Illinois Press, 1957), pp. 332–335. If principal factor analysis is utilized, the following loadings are obtained:

Spanish   .834
Compadrazgo   .791
Curanderismo   .776
Catholic Church   .768

Consult Norman H. Nie et al, *Statistical Package for the Social Sciences*, 2nd ed. (Chicago: McGraw-Hill, 1975), pp. 468–513 for a discussion of factor analysis, particularly the varimax orthogonal rotation method.

34. The social relations in San Antonio result from Anglo/Mexican interaction that developed during one particular historical period in Texas and have managed, at least in terms of certain elements, to persist into the present. For a discussion of the historical emergence of these social relations see David Montejano, "Frustrated Apartheid: Race, Repression, and Capitalist Agriculture in South Texas, 1920–1930," in Walter Goldfrank, ed., *The World-System of Capitalism: Past and Present* (Beverly Hills, Cal.: Sage Publications, 1979), pp. 131–168; Montejano, "Is Texas Bigger Than the World-System?," *Review 4* (Winter 1981):597–628.

Many of the characteristics associated with the social relations of this earlier period have persisted and are similar to those described by John Dollard, *Caste and Class in a Southern Town* (Garden City, N.Y.: Doubleday & Co., Inc., 1949). Also see John Hart Lane, Jr., *Voluntary Organizations Among Mexican Americans in San Antonio, Texas* (New York: Arno Press, 1976), pp. 28–29; Ozzie G. Simmons, "Anglo-Americans and Mexican-Americans in South Texas: A Study in Dominant Subordinate Group Relations," (Ph.D. dissertation, Harvard University, 1952); and Leo Grebler, John Moore, and Ralph Guzman, *The Mexican American People*, pp. 322–325.

35. Most of the Chicanos who work hold the lowest-paying jobs in the service sector, which is oriented primarily toward the military bases. Others work for the government (on the military bases) and are supervised by Anglos. See George L. Wilber and Robert T. Hagan, *Metropolitan and Regional Inequalities Among Minorities in the Labor Market* (Lexington, Ky.: Social Welfare Research Institute, University of Kentucky, 1975), Tables 2-A.

36. Los Angeles, of course, has innumerable ethnic groups from all of the world's continents. Albuquerque has four main groups, Anglos, Chicanos, blacks and Indians; but with increasing migration from the East, many more Caucasian subgroups are joining the ranks of the Anglo population. Recently some Asians, mostly Vietnamese and Cambodians, have come to Albuquerque.

37. *United States Census*, 1980, General Population Characteristics: Texas, California, New Mexico

38. For the origins of this conflict see David Montejano, "A Jour-

ney Through Mexican Texas, 1900–1930," Mario Barrera, *Race and Class in the Southwest;* Rodolfo Acuña, *Occupied America.*

39. James Kurth and Steven Rosen, eds., *Testing the Theory of the Military Industrial Complex* (Lexington, Mass.: Lexington Books, 1972). John Mollenkoff, *The Contested City* (Princeton, N.J.: Princeton University Press, 1983), p. 240.

40. Robert Garland Landolt, *The Mexican-American Workers of San Antonio, Texas* (New York: Arno Press, 1976).

41. Politics in San Antonio were tightly controlled by Anglos through the strength of the Democratic political machine. See Rodolfo Acuña, *Occupied America,* p. 320; O. Douglas Weeks, "The Texas-Mexican and the Politics of South Texas," *American Political Science Review 24* (August 1930):608–615.

42. See Arnold Fleischmann, "Sunbelt Boosterism: The Politics of Postwar Growth and Annexation in San Antonio," in David C. Perry and Alfred J. Watkins, eds., *The Rise of the Sunbelt Cities* (Beverly Hills, Cal.: Sage Publications, 1977), p. 158; John Mollenkopf, *The Contested City,* p. 248.

43. For Mexican/police relations see Julian Samora, Joe Bernal, and Albert Peña, *Gunpowder Justice; A Reassessment of the Texas Rangers* (South Bend, Ind.: University of Notre Dame Press, 1979); Rodolfo Acuña, *Occupied America,* pp. 414–415.

44. John Mollenkopf, *The Contested City,* p. 214.

45. Much of the economic activity was focused around Sandia Laboratories, Kirtland Air Force Base, and the Los Alamos testing site for atomic weapons.

46. *United States Bureau of the Census, 1980,* General Population Characteristics: California, New Mexico, Texas.

47. Nancie L. Gonzales, *The Spanish Americans of New Mexico: A Heritage of Pride* (Albuquerque: University of New Mexico Press, 1969); Carey McWilliams, *North From Mexico;* and F. Chris Garcia, "Manitos and Chicanos in New Mexico Politics," *Aztlan: Chicano Journal of the Social Sciences and Arts 4* (2):177–188.

48. See Raymond J. Brady and Larry D. Adcock, "Economic and Demographic Forecasts and Projections: Bernalillo County and City of Albuquerque, 1975–1980–1985," (Albuquerque: Albuquerque Department of Urban Planning, 1976), "Socio-Economic Mini-Profile for the Greater Albuquerque Area," Special Report No. 61-65 (Albuquerque: Middle Rio Grande Council of Governments of New Mexico, 1975), Table 2.

49. See Paul L. Hain and José Z. Garcia, "Voting, Elections and Parties," in F. Chris Garcia and Paul L. Hain, eds., *New Mexico Government* (Albuquerque: University of New Mexico Press, 1981).

50. Interestingly, for involvement in the opening ceremonies of the 1984 Summer Olympic Games that were held in Los Angeles,

the city was able to find among its citizens representatives of every country participating.

51. See Rodolfo Acuña, *Occupied America*, pp. 292–342.

52. See John Mollenkopf, *The Contested City*, pp. 213–253.

53. For a description of the Los Angeles Police Department's operating code, see James Q. Wilson, *Varieties of Police Behavior* (Cambridge: Harvard University Press, 1968), pp. 172–199. The Los Angeles Police usually operate under what Wilson calls "the legalistic style."

54. For a discussion of the Chicanos' early relationship to the media in general, see Francisco J. Lewels, *The Uses of the Media by the Chicano Movement* (New York: Praeger, 1974).

55. See Robert E. Park, "Human Migration and the Marginal Man," *American Journal of Sociology* 33 (May 1928):881–893.

56. See William Kornhauser, *The Politics of Mass Society* (New York: The Free Press, 1959), pp. 74–101.

Notes for Chapter 2

1. See Joel D. Aberback and Jack L. Walker, "Political Trust and Racial Ideology," *The American Political Science Review* 64(4) (December 1970):1199–1219; Dean Jaros, Herbert Hirsch, and Frederic J. Fleron, Jr., "The Malevolent Leader: Political Socialization in an American Sub-Culture"; Stanley Greenberg, *Politics and Poverty: Modernization and Response in Five Poor Neighborhoods* (New York: John J. Wiley, 1974).

2. See Louis Wirth, "Urbanism as a Way of Life." Most importantly, see Robert Park, especially *Race and Culture*, "Racial Assimilation of Secondary Groups; "Human Migration and the Marginal Man."

3. See Herbert Gans, *Urban Villagers*; Gerald Suttles, *The Social Order of the Slum*. Interstingly, Gans, in a more recent article, seems to have moved closer to an assimilationist position. See his "Symbolic Ethnicity: The Future of Ethnic Groups and Cultures in America," *Ethnic Racial Studies* 2 (January 1979):1–18.

4. A large number of cultural variables were included in the questionnaire. Generally speaking, these included cultural artifacts and concepts associated with folk medicine, various foods, clothing styles, reading materials, media presentations and preferences, and Chicano/Mexican music.

5. For literature reviews, see R. N. Morris, *Urban Sociology* (New York: Praeger, 1968); Richard Sennett, *Families Against the City* (Cambridge, Mass.: Harvard University Press, 1970); Michael P. Smith, *The City and Social Theory*, pp. 229–230.

6. See Louis Wirth, "Urbanism as a Way of Life"; Robert Park, "Human Migration and the Marginal Man." Also see Louis Wirth, *The Ghetto* (Chicago: University of Chicago Press, 1928); and his "Localism, Regionalism, and Centralization," *American Journal of Sociology* 44 (May 1939):494–507.

7. See William Madsen, *Mexican Americans of South Texas* (New York: Holt-Rinehart and Winston, 1964); and Arthur Rubel, *Across the Tracks: Mexican/Americans in a Texas City* (Austin: University of Texas Press, 1966). Both of these works have been heavily criticized. For a reconceptualized view of the Chicano family, see Alfredo Mirandé and Evangelina Enriquez, *La Chicana: The Mexican-American Woman* (Chicago: University of Chicago Press, 1979), Chapter 4.

8. See Celia Heller, *Mexican American Youth: Forgotten Youth at the Crossroads* (New York: Random House, 1966); Lyle Shannon and Magdalene Shannon, *Minority Migrants in the Urban Community: Mexican-American and Negro Adjustment to Industrial Society* (Beverly Hills, Cal.: Sage Publications, 1973).

9. Maxine Baca Zinn, "Chicano Family Research: Conceptual Distortions and Alternative Directions," *Journal of Ethnic Studies* 7:(3) (Fall, 1979):59–71.

10. In addition to residence in communities that were primarily rural and within the United States, whether respondents come from Mexico was also considered. Those from Mexico displayed the same attitudes toward extramarital sex as did those from the rural Southwest. Semantic differential scores were: U.S., D = 2.56 and Mexico, D = 2.49, indicating the same positive meaning for both groups.

11. The questions read: "How many children would you like to have in your family?" and "What would you say were your two most important considerations in deciding how many children you would have?"

12. From the question, the mean was actually 2.92 children desired.

13. From the question, the mean for Los Angeles as 1.62 and for Albuquerque 1.89 children desired.

14. For Puerto Rican adaptation, see Helen Safa, "Puerto Rican Adaptation to the Urban Milieux," in Peter Orleans and William Ellis, eds., *Race, Change and Urban Society* (Beverly Hills: Sage, 1971); for Italians see Humberto Nelli, *Italians in Chicago, 1880–1930: A Study in Ethnic Mobility* (New York: Oxford, 1970); for Poles see Neil Sandberg, *Ethnic Identity and Assimilation, The Polish American Community: A Case Study of Metropolitan Los Angeles* (New York: Praeger, 1974); Stephan Thernstrom, *The Other Bostonians: Poverty and Progress in the American Metropolis 1880–1970* (Cambridge: Harvard University Press, 1973); for southern Slavs

see Josef Barton, *Peasants and Strangers: Italians, Rumanians and Slovaks in an American City, 1890–1950* (Cambridge: Harvard University Press, 1975).

15. See Manuel Carlos, "Traditional and Modern Forms of Compadrazgo among Mexicans and Mexican Americans: A Survey of Continuities and Changes," paper presented at the meeting of the Fortieth International Congress of Americanists, Rome, September 3–10, 1972.

16. The debate continues among sociologists as to whether primary group relations continue within the city or simply erode away after the first generation or with length of residence in the city. For arguments for assimilation, see Louis Wirth, "Social Interaction: The Problem of the Individual and the Group," *American Journal of Sociology 44* (May 1939):493–509; Robert Park, "Racial Assimilation in Secondary Groups," *American Journal of Sociology, 19* (March 1914):606–623. For the "neighborhood solidarity" theory see Herbert Gans, *Urban Villagers;* Gerald Suttles, *The Social Order of the Slum.*

17. Redlining exists in the majority of America's cities, and this has had an enormous impact on racial/ethnic housing patterns. Racial discrimination also affects racial/ethnic housing patterns, particularly discrimination on the part of the lending agency. Although this is very difficult to document, one conclusive study exists. It empirically demonstrates racial discrimination by the banks of New York State in lending to nonwhites. See Robert Schafer, *Mortgage Lending Decisions: Criteria and Constraints* (Cambridge, Mass.: Joint Center for Urban Studies of the Massachusetts Institute of Technology and Harvard University, 1978).

18. This is similar to the situation described by Richard Sennett, in *The Uses of Disorder: Personal Identity and City Life* (New York: Vintage, 1970), in which ethnic groups learned about one another because they had to in order to function.

19. This also was found to be true of migrants to other cities throughout the world. See Wayne Cornelius, *Politics and the Migrant Poor in Mexico City* (Palo Alto, Cal.: Stanford University Press, 1975); Janet Abu-Lughod, "Migrant Adjustment to City Life: The Egyptian Case," *American Journal of Sociology, 67* (July 1961):22–32.

20. The importance of parents in maintaining the *compadrazgo* system can not be overemphasized since it is the parents who make the original contact and who are usually friends with the *comadre/compadre.*

21. Their attitudes were similar to those expressed by Richard Rodriguez, *Hunger of Memory: The Education of Richard Rodriguez* (New York: Bantam Books, 1982).

22. For corroboration of the fact that urban living reduces the

importance and use of extended kinship, independent of other factors, see Claude Fischer, *To Dwell Among Friends: Personal Networks in Town and City* (Chicago: University of Chicago Press, 1982), pp. 80–88.

23. See Robert E Park, "Human Migration and the Marginal Man."

24. See Joshua Fishman, Vladimir C. Nahirny, John E. Hofman, Robert G. Hayden, *Language Loyalty in the United States* (The Hague: Mouton, 1966):363.

25. Fluency was measured by each of the persons who administered the questionnaire, all of whom were completely fluent in speaking, reading, and writing Spanish themselves. Each of the respondents was asked a series of questions that would lead to a conversation in Spanish. The questions were such that the respondents were required to utilize those verbal language skills that they possessed in order to express themselves.

26. In the eastern and midwestern cities there were, and still are, a multitude of people from various ethnic origins. This has occurred because the industrialization of America began in those cities, and there was a demand for cheap labor from all available sources. The result of the immigration process was the settlement in these cities of many people who spoke different languages. All of these people needed to function in their new environment, so they communicated in English, partly because English was the language of the work place, partly because English was a neutral language for most of these groups, so that any antagonism between different groups could be circumvented by the universal use of English.

27. For evidence supporting the argument that in places where there are two primary linguistic groups such as San Antonio, there will be strong resistance on the part of both toward mother-tongue shift, see Stanley Lieberson and Timothy J. Curry, "Language Shift in the United States: Some Demographic Clues," *International Migration Review 5* (Summer):125–137.

28. The Spanish language is reinforced because it can be used at work. Also, the fact that San Antonio is so ethnically segregated reinforces language maintenance independently of social class, social mobility. See Stanley Lieberson, *Language and Ethnic Relations in Canada* (New York: Wiley 1970); Stanley Lieberson, Guy Dalton, and Mary Ellen Johnston, "The Course of Mother-Tongue Diversity in Nations," *American Journal of Sociology 81* (July 1975):34–61, for corroborating evidence of the effect of ethnic segregation on language shift, or the lack thereof.

29. The correlation (zero-order) of proficiency in Spanish and amount of Spanish spoken in the home is .72 (<.001).

30. This notion of moving out of the cultural milieu of the *barrio*

is similar to the experience of other ethnic groups. Louis Wirth describes this process for Jews in *The Ghetto*, pp. 241–261.

31. See Stanley Lieberson, "Bilingualism in Montreal: A Demographic Analysis," *American Journal of Sociology 71* (July 1965):10–25.

32. Ninety-three percent (290) of the youth from Albuquerque said that they believed that English was the only language that would be used in daily economic activity, and that if you did not know English you did not stand a good chance of becoming economically mobile.

33. See Richard Sennett, *The Uses of Disorder.* Sennett argues that contact with a variety of ethnic groups forces all ethnic groups to accommodate one another.

34. Stanley Lieberson and Timothy J. Curry, "Language Shift in the United States," p. 131.

35. Many of these stories were in the form of *corridos,* or folk ballads, which often describe political events. Many of these events involve the conflict between Anglos and Chicanos. One example is the *corrido* of Gregorio Cortez, which deals with ethnic conflict, and especially Chicano resistance. For an in-depth analysis of the *corrido* in general and this *corrido* in particular see Americo Paredes, *With a Pistol in His Hand—A Border Ballad and Its Hero* (Austin: University of Texas Press, 1971). Many other stories of Chicano resistance to perceived Anglo intrusions are simply passed on verbally. Such stories, as told in South Texas, have involved the Plan of San Diego, a separatist conspiracy, and the story of Juan Cortina; in New Mexico, "Las Gorras Blancas," "La Mano Negra," and the story of Elfego Baca, among numerous others; in California, the histories of Joaquin Murieta and Tiburcio Vasquez. See Pedro Castillo and Alberto Camarillo, *Furia y Muerte: Los Bandidos Chicanos,* Monograph No. 4, Aztlan Publications (Los Angeles: University of California, Chicano Studies Center, 1973).

36. See Stanley Lieberson and Timothy J. Curry, "Language Shift in the United States: Some Demographic Clues."

37. See Stanley Lieberson, Guy Dalton, and Mary Ellen Johnston, "The Course of Mother-Tongue Diversity in Nations," pp. 55–57.

38. See Harold Isaacs, *Idols of the Tribe: Group Identity and Political Change* (New York: Harper and Row, 1975).

39. Wirth and Park would have argued that urban life would diminish an individual's association with traditional institutions such as religion. See Wirth, "Urbanism as a Way of Life"; Park, "The City: Suggestions for the Investigation of Human Behavior in the Urban Environment," in Robert E. Park, Ernest W. Burgess, and Roderick D. McKenzie, *The City* (Chicago: University of Chicago Press, 1925),

pp. 1–46. Also consult Gerhard Lenski, *The Religious Factor* (New York: Anchor Books, 1963).

40. There are innumerable examples of ethnic groups sponsoring their cultural events under the auspices of a particular religious institution. The Jews have their religious institution, the Gypsies theirs, the Latvians theirs (Lutheran), the Russians theirs (Russian Orthodox), the Greeks theirs (Greek Orthodox), the Armenians theirs (Armenian Orthodox), and the Serbians theirs (Eastern Orthodox). There are various ethnic groups who are Roman Catholic and who have developed their own cultural orientations with regard to clergy and/or cultural events. For example one can find German priests serving German parishes, Polish priests serving Polish parishes, etc., and each promoting ethnic cultural events.

41. Women attended church an average (as recorded from the interviews) of 4.71 times a month, while men estimated that they attended church an average of 4.03 times a month. For each individual, this could represent as high a rate of attendance as once a day for thirty to thirty-one days or even several times a day for thirty to thirty-one days. What these mean scores represent are once a week for men (usually on Sunday), and roughly the same for women, or perhaps once more during the month for women.

42. In point of fact, neither density nor heterogeneity had any effect whatsoever. However, "length of time in the city" did have a slight effect. Those youth who had lived in the city for more than seven years tended to go to church an average of 3.88 times a month, as compared to 4.89 times for those who had been in the city less than seven years.

43. Among the youth of San Antonio there existed a double standard with regard to what was good for men and what was good for women. What is interesting about this is that both the women and the men in this sample thought that women should be virgins before they were married, whereas it was not important that men should be. In other words, both the men and the women in the San Antonio sample upheld this double standard.

44. The only form of birth control that was considered appropriate by these youth was the "rhythm method," and this was considered appropriate only for those who were married.

45. No effect was found for the other urban variables such as "population density' or "ethnic heterogeneity."

46. This figure is taken from those youth who reported that their families had arrived in the city at one level of socioeconomic status and had moved up to a higher status. The total number of respondents who had experienced this mobility is 184.

47. No effect was found for "ethnic heterogeneity" of the neighborhood or for "population density."

48. The questions read: "Do you consider premarital sex to be immoral?'; "Do you think you would ever be involed in premarital sex?"; and "If you do think you will be involved in premarital sex under what circumstances would that occur?" The rationale given most by the youth for becoming involved in premarital sex was whether they were in love with the person with whom they were involved. There was no substantial difference between men and women on the question of premarital sex, as one might have expected. Seventy-one percent of the men said that they had no problem with premarital sex if they loved the other person, and 69 percent of the young women said the same thing.

49. The questions read: "Do you approve of the use of contraceptives?"; "If you do approve of their use, would you use them yourself?"; and "If you do think you would use contraceptives what would you consider using (you may choose more than one)?" On the issue of contraceptives there was virtually no difference between the responses of men and women.

50. The questions read: "Do you consider abortion to be immoral?"; "Would you ever consider an abortion for yourself or the person you are with?"; "Under what circumstances would you consider the use of an abortion?" The conditions specified "under certain circumstances" were: 1) loss of the father (death), 2) complications with the pregnancy, 3) rape.

51. The sources of information mentioned were: school, pamphlets passed out to the public by various women's groups, information received from doctors or the health center with which the respondents were associated.

52. See Frances Swadesh, *Los Primeros Pobladores: Spanish Americans on the Ute Frontier,* sections on baptism and the Penitente Brotherhoods.

53. The "right circumstances" for Los Angeles were the same as for Albuquerque: that those involved loved one another.

54. See Humberto Nelli, *Italians in Chicago 1880–1930,* pp. 181–200.

55. The question read: "How would you categorize your city in terms of its tolerance of ideas and behavior that are different from what everyone else thinks? Would you say it is a tolerant place to live? Explain."

56. Albuquerque and Los Angeles would tend to support Wirth's and Park's assertions that traditional values would diminish with city life. The findings in these two cities are also consistent with what Fischer found when studying the effects of city life on religiosity. See Claude Fischer, "The Effects of Urban Life on Traditional Values," *Social Forces* 53 (March 1975):422–427; Fischer, *To Dwell Among Friends,* p. 208–215.

Chapter 3

1. See Richard M. Merelman, "The Development of Political Ideology: A Framework for the Analysis of Political Socialization," *American Political Science Review* 63 (September 1969):750–767; Joseph Adelson and Robert O'Neil, "The Growth of Political Ideas in Adolescence: The Sense of Community," *Journal of Personality and Social Psychology* 6 (September 1966):295–306; Joseph Adelson, Bernard Green, and Robert O'Neil, "Growth of the Idea of Law in Adolescence," *Development Psychology* 1 (July 1969):327–332.

2. See Louis Wirth, "Ideological Aspects of Social Disorganization," *American Sociological Review* 5 (August 1940):472–482.

3. See Herbert Gans, *The Urban Villagers,* pp. 163–180; and Gerald Suttles, *The Social Order of the Slum,* pp. 99–101.

4. Fascism was also included in the questionnaire, but none of the respondents identified with it or knew about it.

5. See John L. Sullivan, George E. Marcus, and Daniel Richard Minns, "The Development of Political Ideology: Some Empirical Findings," *Youth and Society* 7 (December 1975):148–170.

6. The idea of an independent country is not a new one to Chicanos. Since Texas independence in 1836 and the Mexican War of 1848, when the United States annexed what is now the southwestern part of the country (California, Arizona, New Mexico, Colorado, and Nevada) the question of whether allegiance should be given to the United States has never been completely resolved. At various times in the past, political movements have emerged with the expressed desire of creating a separate Chicano country. Probably the most important reason why Chicano nationalism has not died out is that ethnic conflict between Anglos and Chicanos has persisted. This has tended to reinforce ethnic group identification more than would have been the case otherwise. Furthermore, these antagonisms have reinforced the themes of countless stories of the failure of Chicano to attain their own statehood. These stories have been kept alive through conventional story telling, folk ballads (*corridos*), and, more recently, Chicano studies programs in high schools and colleges. Thus, in spite of the fact that the Civil War seems to have ended the possibility of legal or military secession, separatism, or nationalism, still is viewed as a legitimate ideology within the Chicano community and tends to elicit emotional responses from both supporters and opponents. See Martín Sánchez Jankowski, "The Social and Political Origins of The Chicano Separatist Movement," (M.A. thesis, Dalhousie University, Halifax, Nova Scotia, 1972).

7. None of the teachers indicated any familiarity in the interviews with the philosophical foundations of socialism or communism.

8. Even the radio and television stations which are Chicano-run

are relatively conservative in their presentation of the news. This is due principally to the tenuous position of these stations with regard to their financial situation vis-à-vis the Anglo financial community. See Francisco J. Lewels, Jr., *The Uses of the Media by the Chicano Movement.*

9. For the most part, the remaining Chicanos said they did not know what communism was, but they were against it because they heard that it was a terrible system. This is similar to the point that Edelman makes, that Americans have been so socialized through language that the mere mention of communism evokes a negative response. See Murray Edelman, *The Symbolic Uses of Politics* (Urbana, Ill., Illini Books, 1964), pp. 116–117.

10. Four socialist parties were named by these students, but no single party received more mention than the others. These parties were: The Socialist Workers Party, The Spartacus League, the Socialist Labor Party, and the A.T.M. (August Twenty-fourth Movement, a Chicano nationalist-socialist group).

11. Some of the respondents said they thought that a separate Chicano country would be multilingual, with Spanish and the various Native American languages being the primary languages. English was mentioned, but most thought that it should be taught as a foreign language, in the way that French and German are now taught.

12. "Aztlán" is the name given by the Aztecs to identify the place to which they had originally come from before their migration to the Mexico City area. This place is thought to have been the Southwestern part of the United States. See Miguel Leon-Portilla, *Aztec Thought and Culture* (Norman, OK: University of Oklahoma Press, 1963).

13. See Leonard Doob, *Patriotism and Nationalism: Their Psychological Foundations* (New Haven: Yale University Press, 1964), p. 228; Harold R. Isaacs, "Basic Group Identity: The Idols of the Tribe," in Nathan Glazer and Daniel P. Moynihan (eds.), *Ethnicity: Theory and Experience* (Cambridge: Harvard University Press, 1975), pp. 29–54; Karl Deutsch, *Nationalism and Social Communications: An Inquiry into the Foundations of Nationality*, 2nd ed. (Cambridge, Mass.: M.I.T. Press, 1966), pp. 29–72.

14. Leonard Doob, *Patriotism and Nationalism*, p. 231.

15. There are, of course, many examples, a few of which are the Bretons in France, the Kurds in Iraq, the Basques and Catalonians in Spain, the Tyroleans in Italy, and the Jurasians in Switzerland.

16. See Harold Isaacs, "Basic Group Identity: The Idols of the Tribe," pp. 29–52.

17. Richard Merelman, "The Development of Ideology," p. 751.

18. See Philip E. Converse, "The Nature of Belief Systems in Mass

Publics," in David E. Apter, ed., *Ideology and Discontent* (Glencoe,' Ill.: The Free Press, 1964), pp. 238–245.

19. Merelman has found that certain psychological factors, including child rearing practices, influence cognitive styles, policy thinking, and ideological development. However, the present study found that the adolescents' contacts with the social conditions around them were the most influential. This, of course, does not deny that psychological factors may have an impact. See Richard Merelman, "The Development of Ideology," and his *Political Reasoning in Adolescence: Some Bridging Themes* (Beverly Hills, Cal.: Sage Paper on American Politics, 1976).

20. A good review of this literature can be found in Wayne A. Cornelius, Jr., "Urbanization as an Agent in Latin American Political Instability: The Case of Mexico," *American Political Science Review* 63 (September 1969):833–857. Also see Samuel P. Huntington, *Political Order in Changing Societies* (New Haven: Yale University Press, 1968), pp. 278–283.

21. See Milton Gordon, "Theory of Racial and Ethnic Group Relations," in Nathan Glazer and Daniel P. Moynihan, eds., *Ethnicity: Theory and Experience*, pp. 84–110, and especially pp. 99–107.

22. For a summary of much of the literature on blacks, see Stanley B. Greenberg, *Politics and Poverty: Modernization in Five Poor Neighborhoods* (New York: John Wiley and Sons, 1974), pp. 249–251; see also Joel D. Aberback and Jack L. Walker, "Political Trust and Racial Ideology," *American Political Science Review* 64 (December 1970): 1199–1219.

23. These high density areas are marked by housing projects and the blocks immediately adjacent to the project on all sides.

24. Putnam's study of the local community also found that extended friendship groups were the most important in influencing political attitudes. See Robert Putnam, "Political Attitudes and the Local Community," *American Political Science Review* 60 (September 1966):647–652.

25. This is a standard complaint among blacks who live in poor, overcrowded areas as well. See Stanley B. Greenberg, *Politics and Poverty*, p. 249; Angus Campbell and Howard Schuman, "Racial Attitudes in Fifteen American Cities," *The National Advisory Commission of Civil Disorders, Supplemental Studies* (Washington, D.C.: U.S. Government Printing Office, July 1968).

26. James Q. Wilson, *Varieties of Police Behavior: The Management of Law and Order in Eight Communities* (Cambridge: Harvard University Press, 1968), p. 172; see also pp. 172–199.

27. Cornelius also found this in his study of Mexico City. See Wayne A. Cornelius, *Politics and the Migrant Poor in Mexico City*, pp. 63–67.

28. A number of studies have noted the relationship between ethnic antagonisms, group discrimination, and the rise of ethnic nationalism. See Karl Deutsch, *Nationalism and Social Communication: An Inquiry into the Foundations of Nationality,* pp. 129–130; William Kornhauser, "Rebellion and Political Development," in Harry Eckstein, ed., *Internal War* (New York: The Free Press: 1964), p. 153.

29. New Mexico State Planning Office, *Emundo Report* (Santa Fe: 1961); Clark Knowlton, "Land Grant Problems Among the State's Spanish Americans," (Albuquerque: Bureau of Business Research, 1967).

30. Both the federal and state governments have accumulated most of the land relinquished by Chicano ranchers. Not only does the federal government have control over nine million acres (six times the size of the famous King ranch of Texas), but these nine million acres comprise most of the best grazing land in the state. It is not surprising that antagonisms between Chicanos and the National Forest Service, the agency charged with the administration of this area, are at times quite intense. See H. Paul Friesma, "The Forest Service in Crisis in Northern New Mexico," paper presented at the annual meeting of the Midwest Political Science Association, Chicago, 1971.

31. For a discussion of the Alianza movement, see Peter Nabokov, *Tijerina and the Courthouse Raid* (Albuquerque: University of New Mexico Press, 1969); Richard Gardner, *Grito! Reies Tijerina and the New Mexico Land Grant War of 1967* (Indianapolis: Bobbs-Merrill, 1970).

32. Chicanos and blacks have not had a history of mutual understanding, trust, and empathy. In fact, many Chicanos have, at different times and locations adopted racist attitudes toward blacks. A number of explanations can be offered for this occurrence. First, as predominantly lower-class groups, Chicanos and blacks compete for the same types of jobs, and this has produced antagonisms. Second, Chicanos have tried to reduce the psychological anguish caused by Anglo racism by becoming racists themselves. They have found it necessary to consider another group of people as being below them in psychological, social, and economic development, thereby reinforcing albeit fallaciously, their own sense of worth. Third, social encounters with blacks who are somewhat more extroverted and aggressive have produced feelings of resistance toward what are perceived to be black attempts to manipulate Chicano. For a study which found Chicanos to be antagonistic or racist toward blacks, see Leo Grebler, et al., *The Mexican-American People,* p. 392.

33. See Stanley Greenberg, *Poverty and Politics,* pp. 146–150, 153–156. Greenberg found ethnic neighborhoods to be an important factor in facilitating group consciousness. More generally, see Karl

Deutsch, *Nationalism and Social Communication*, p. 119; Leonard Doob, *Patriotism and Nationalism*, pp. 251–252.

34. Although this pattern was more prevalent in Los Angeles, it existed among the adolescents of Albuquerque as well.

35. See the classic work by E. Franklin Frazier, *Black Bourgeoisie* (New York: MacMillan/Collier Books, 1957), pp. 77–79.

36. It was expected that the greatest concern for jobs would be found among the males in this study. However, no differences were found between the sexes. The young women were as concerned as the young men about where they were going to work upon graduation from high school. They also displayed the same frustrations with the existing system as did the young males in this study.

37. For a similar reaction among middle-class black Americans against the nationalist movement of Marcus Garvey as well as the Black Muslim movement, see Frazier, *Black Bourgeoisie*, pp. 103–167; E. U. Essien-Udom, *Black Nationalism: A Search for Identity in America* (New York: Dell Publishing Co., 1964), pp. 328–333.

38. A very similar reaction occurred among lower-class blacks, and many joined the Black Muslim movement as well as such groups as the Republic of New Africa (a black nationalist group from Detroit). See Essien-Udom, pp. 328–333, 354–358. For a discussion of the Republic of New Africa, see Raymond Hall, *Black Separatism in the United States* (Hanover, N.H.: The University Press of New England, 1978), pp. 129–138.

39. Although this has occurred in a number of countries, one of the best examples is found in South Africa. See Edwin S. Munger, *Afrikaner and African Nationalism: South African Parallels and Parameters* (London: Oxford University Press, 1967), pp. 24–43.

40. See Theodore Roszak, *The Making of a Counter Culture: Reflections on the Technocratic Society and Its Youthful Opposition* (Garden City, N.Y.: Anchor Books, 1968); Kenneth Kenniston, *The Uncommitted, Alienated Youth in American Society* (New York: Delta Books, 1965).

41. This can be seen quite clearly in the case of Quebec, Canada, where the retention of traditional culture, especially the French language, has become the most salient political issue. See Lorenzo Morris, "The Politics of Education and Language in Quebec: A Comparative Perspective," *Canadian and International Education 5* (December 1976):1–36.

42. A large number of these youth (64%) were from broken homes, where the mothers had the responsibility of raising the children, and 85% of these families were on public assistance. Perhaps the fact that the family life of these youth was so tenuous contributed to their identification with an ideology which offered an identity com-

pletely different from that which they were presently experiencing and disliking so much.

43. These youth envisioned a system similar to that described in much of the sociological literature on pluralism. See Arend Lijphart, *Democracy in Plural Societies: A Comparative Exploration* (New Haven: Yale University Press, 1972).

44. The alienation of the youth who no longer adhered to traditional culture is close to that described by Kenneth Kenniston in *Young Radicals: Notes on Committed Youth* (New York: Harcourt, Brace and World, 1968).

45. The youth experiencing the greatest social dislocation were those who were lower-class and who had lost their association with traditional Chicano culture. They comprised that segment of ethnic society that has been described as "marginal" by Robert Park. See his "Human Migration and Marginal Man."

Chapter 4

1. The early studies were Fred I. Greenstein, *Children and Politics* (New Haven: Yale University Press, 1965); Robert Hess and Judith Torney, *The Development of Political Attitudes in Children* (Garden City, N.Y.: Anchor Books, 1968); David Easton and Jack Dennis, *Children in the Political System* (New York: McGraw-Hill, 1969).

2. There have been some studies on adolescents, the more recent of which have been summarized in David O. Sears, "Political Socialization in Fred I. Greenstein and Nelson Polsby (eds.), *Handbook of Political Science*, Vol. 2; Micro-Political Theory (Reading, Mass.: Addison-Wesley, 1975).

3. See especially M. Kent Jennings and Richard G. Niemi, *The Political Character of Adolescence*.

4. See Walter Dean Burnham, "Party Systems and the Political Process," in William Nisbet Chambers and Walter Dean Burnham, eds., *The American Party System: Stages of Political Development* (New York: Oxford University Press, 1967).

5. Much has been written on the relationship of the political machine to ethnic groups. Much of the early writing emphasized that ethnic groups were willing simply to sell their role or to give it away; and that this occurred because these groups were ignorant of civil responsibility. See James Q. Wilson and Edward Banfield, *City Politics* (Cambridge: Harvard University Press, 1963), Chapters 3 and 16; Wilson and Banfield, "Political Ethos Revisited," *American Political Science* 64(4) (Dec. 1971):1048–1062. See also Daniel P. Moynihan, "The Irish," in Nathan Glazer and Daniel P. Moynihan,

eds., *Beyond the Melting Pot* (Cambridge: M.I.T. Press, 1963), pp. 221–229; Elmer Cornwell, "Bosses, Machines, and Ethnic Group," *The Annals of the American Academy of Political and Social Sciences 353* (May 1964):27–39.

6. See O. D. Weeks, "The Texas-Mexican and the Politics of South Texas"; Clifton McClosky, *The Government and Politics of Texas* (Boston: Little, Brown & Co., 1969), pp. 101–102; E. R. Fincher, *Spanish Americans as a Political Factor in New Mexico, 1912–1950* (New York: Arno Press, 1974), pp. 49, 53, 68, 69, 77.

7. See Angus Campbell, Philip E. Converse, Warren E. Miller, Donald E. Stokes, *The American Voter: An Abridgement* (New York: John Wiley & Sons, 1964); Angus Campbell, Gerald Gurin, and Warren Miller, *The Voter Decides* (Evanston, Ill.: Row, Peterson, 1954).

8. See Ralph Guzman, "Political Socialization of the Mexican American People" (Ph.D. dissertation, University of California, Los Angeles, 1970); Leo Grebler et. al., *The Mexican American People,* pp. 557–572, a work hypothesizing that Chicanos would have a low sense of political efficacy. Also see F. Chris Garcia, *Political Socialization of Chicano Children,* pp. 124–127.

9. See Robert D. Hess, "Political Socialization in the Schools," *Harvard Educational Review 38* (Summer 1968):528–536; George B. Levinson, "The Schools' Contribution to Learning of Participatory Responsibility" in Byron G. Massialas, ed., *Political Youth, Traditional Schools: National and International Perspectives* (Englewood cliffs, N.J.: Prentice-Hall Inc., 1972), pp. 129–30.

10. Sidney Verba and Norman Nie, *Participation in America: Political Democracy and Social Equality* (New York: Harper & Row, 1972).

11. See Samuel Popkin, John W. Gorman, Charles Phillips, Jerry A. Smith; "Comment: What Have You Done for Me Lately? Toward an Investment Theory of Voting," *American Political Science Review 60* (September 1976):779–805.

12. M. Kent Jennings and Richard G. Niemi, *The Political Character of Adolescence,* p. 42.

13. Voting studies have shown blacks overwhelmingly to vote Democratic. See Sidney Verba and Norman Nie, *The Changing American Voter* (Cambridge: Harvard University Press, 1980), pp. 226–229. This was also true of black voters in the 1984 presidential election where they voted overwhelmingly for Walter Mondale, the Democratic candidate. See Raymond E. Wolfinger, "Dealignment, Realignment, and Mandates in the 1984 Election," paper prepared for Public Policy Week of the American Enterprise Institute, Washington, D.C., Dec. 3, 1984, pp. 14–17.

14. See John Schockley, *Chicano Revolt in a Texas Town* (South Bend, Ind.: University of Notre Dame Press, 1974).

15. See Armando Navarro, "The Evolution of Chicano Politics," *Aztlan: International Journal of Chicano Studies and Research* 5 (Spring and Fall 1974):76–78.

16. See Martha Derthick, *New Towns in Town: Why a Federal Program Failed* (Washington, D.C.: The Urban Institute, 1972), pp. 41–46, for a description of how Congressman Henry B. Gonzalez (Democrat, San Antonio) stopped the Model Cities Program in San Antonio because it was perceived as a threat to the military bases.

17. Much of the bitterness and disappointment came from the fact that it was frustrating to live in densely populated areas that were overwhelmingly Chicano. The youth complained about the inadequacy of their physical environments. Youth from public housing complexes indicated that they were frustrated over their own or their parents' attempts to correct the situation by contacting the Public Housing Authority or the city representative for their district. The most frequent grievance of those youth who lived in densely populated and ethnic areas focused on the inadequate collection of garbage, unclean streets, and insufficient police protection. The Democratic Party was perceived by all of these youth, whether accurately or not, to be in a position to effect change if it wanted to. Their negative feelings toward the Democratic Party were directed at what they perceived as the party's unresponsiveness to their needs.

18. See John Saywell, *The Rise of the Parti Quebecois: 1967–1976* (Toronto: University of Toronto Press, 1977).

19. French culture and its maintenance is one of the primary issues that has brought the *Parti Quebecois* to provincial power in Quebec. The party has always stressed two issues: one, that the French-speaking population has not received its share of economic benefits from the English-speaking minority; and two, that the French culture and language are slowly dying because of Quebec's association with the rest of English-speaking Canada. For a general background on the Quebec situation, see Marcel Rioux, *Quebec in Question* (Toronto: James and Samuel, 1971); see John Porter, "Ethnic Pluralism in Canada," in Nathan Glazer and Daniel P. Moynihan, eds., *Ethnicity: Theory and Experience*, pp. 267–300. For a discussion of the *Parti Quebecois*, see John Saywell, *The Rise of the Parti Quebecois: 1967–1976.*

20. The "militant ethnic core" of the ethnic population which Wolfinger discusses is relevant here. Members of the "militant core" stay in the old ethnic neighborhoods regardless of whether they have experienced economic mobility. See Raymond Wolfinger, "The Development and Persistence of Ethnic Voting," *American Political Science Review* 54 (December 1965):896–909.

21. See Phillip E. Converse, "The Nature of Belief Systems in Mass Publics" in David E. Aptek (ed.), *Ideology and Discontent*

(Glencoe: Free Press, 1964); Donald Stokes and Warren E. Miller, "Party Government and the Saliency of Congress," in Angus Campbell, Philip E. Converse, Warren E. Miller, and Donald E. Stokes, *Elections and the Political Order* (New York: John Wiley and Sons, 1966), p. 199; David RePass, "Issue Salience and Party Choice," *American Political Science Review* 65 (June 1971):389–400.

22. See Arthur E. Miller, Warren E. Miller, Alden S. Raine, and Thad A. Brown, "A Majority Party in Disarray," *American Political Science Review* 70 (2) (Sept. 1976):753; also see the adjoining comments.

Chapter 5

1. The best example of this effort to look at the black urban experience was the Kerner report, formally known as *The National Advisory Commission on Civil Disorders* (New York: Bantam, 1968).

2. See Louis Wirth, "Culture Conflict and Misconduct," *Social Forces 9* (June 1931):485–491; Robert E. Park, "Collective Behavior," in Ralph H. Turner, ed., *Robert E. Park: On Social Control and Collective Behavior* (Chicago: University of Chicago Press, 1967), pp. 225–239.

3. Consult *The National Advisory Commission on Civil Disorders.*

4. Hannah Arendt, *On Violence* (New York: Harcourt, Brace and World, 1969), p. 63.

5. David O. Sears and John B. McConahay, *The Politics of Violence: The New Urban Blacks and the Watts Riot* (Boston: Houghton-Mifflin Co., 1973).

6. Peter A. Lupsha and Catherine MacKinnon, "Domestic Political Violence, 1965–1971: A Radical Perspective," in Herbert Hirsch and David C. Perry, eds., *Violence as Politics: A Series of Original Essays* (New York: Harper and Row, 1973), pp. 5–40.

7. Michael Lipsky, *Protest in City Politics: Rent Strikes, Housing and the Power of the Poor* (Chicago: Rand McNally & Co., 1970), p. 2.

8. Hannah Arendt, *On Violence*, p. 46.

9. Peter Lupsha and Catherine MacKinnon, "Domestic Political Violence, 1965–1971," p. 11.

10. Peter Eisinger, "The Conditions of Protest Behavior in American Cities," *American Political Science Review* 67 (March 1973), 14.

11. Ibid., p. 15.

12. For the importance of fear in protests see H. L. Nieburg, *Po-*

litical Violence: The Behavioral Process (New York: St. Martin's Press, 1969), p. 129; and Peter Eisinger, "The Conditions of Protest Behavior in American Cities," p. 13, note 17.

13. This is Eisinger's main argument. See "The Conditions of Protest Behavior in American Cities."

14. Eisinger found in his study of blacks that there was more support for protest among the middle class. See Peter Eisinger, "Racial Differences in Protest Participation," *American Political Science Review 68* (June 1974):592–606.

15. Peter Eisinger, "The Conditions of Protest Behavior in American Cities," p. 13.

16. What is particularly interesting about this attitude is that Stokely Carmichael made the same point before breaking away from the Student Non-Violent Coordinating Committee (SNCC).

17. See Stan Steiner, *La Raza: The Mexican Americans* (New York: Harper & Row Publishers, 1970), pp. 324–388, for a discussion of the cultural renaissance and the *Teatro Campesino.*

18. See Peter Eisinger, "Racial Differences in Protest Participation," p. 602. Eisinger found this to be second to housing issues in causing blacks to protest.

19. See Edgar Z. Friedenberg, "The High School as A Focus of 'Student Unrest,' " *The Annals of the American Academy of Political and Social Science 395* (May 1971):118.

20. See U.S. Commission on Civil Rights, *Mexican-American Educational Series, Study Report I: Ethnic Isolation of Mexican Americans in the Public Schools of the Southwest* (Washington, D.C.: U.S. Government Printing Office, 1971).

21. See Carlos Muñoz, "The Politics of Educational Change in East Los Angeles," in Alfredo Castañeda, Mario Barrera, Carlos Cortes, Manuel Ramírez, eds., *Mexican-Americans and Educational Change* (New York: Arno Press, 1973).

22. See Lewis Anthony Dexter, *The Tyranny of Schooling: An Enquiry Into the Concept of 'Stupidity'* (New York: Basic Books, 1964), pp. 18–71, for a discussion of how schools perpetuate the fear of being labelled stupid.

23. See Lester M. Salamon and Stephen Van Evera, "Fear, Apathy, and Discrimination: A Test of Three Explanations of Political Participation," *American Political Science Review 67* (December 1973):1288–1306 for an analysis of the effects of fear on black participation in the south.

24. Sears and McConahay reported the same complaints in their study of the Watts riot. See David O. Sears and John B. McConahay, *The Politics of Violence*, pp. 55–58.

25. See David O. Sears and John B. McConahay, *The Politics of Violence*, pp. 170–196; and T. M. Tomlinson, "Riot Ideology Among

Urban Negroes," in Louis H. Masotti and Don R. Bowen, eds., *Riots and Rebellion: Civil Violence in the Urban Community* (Beverly Hills, Cal.: Sage Publications, 1968), pp. 417–427.

26. Eisinger has stressed this point in his studies of protest. See both of the studies cited above.

27. See Robert Fogelson, *Violence as Protest* (Garden City, N.Y.: Doubleday and Company, Inc., 1971)

28. See Edward Banfield, *The Unheavenly City Revisited* (Boston: Little Brown Co.), pp. 211–233.

29. David O. Sears and John B. McConahay, *The Politics of Violence*, Chapter 2, p. 124.

30. See Jay Shulman, "Ghetto Area Residence, Political Alienation and Riot Orientation," in Louis H. Masotti and Don R. Bowen, eds., *Riots and Rebellion*, pp. 261–284. Also see Bernard N. Grofman and Edward N. Muller, "The Strange Case of Relative Gratification and Potential for Political Violence: The V-Curve Hypothesis," *American Political Science Review* 67 (June 1973):536, which argues that the potential for violence goes up as expectations rise.

31. See Don R. Bowen, Elinor Bowen, Sheldon Gawiser, and Louis H. Masotti, "Deprivation, Mobility and Orientation Toward Protest of the Urban Poor," in Louis H. Masotti and Don R. Bowen, eds., *Riots and Rebellion: Civil Violence in the Urban Community*, pp. 187–200.

32. This sense of personal honor is discussed in Armando Morales, *Ando Sangrando: A Study of Mexican American-Police Conflict* (La Puente, Cal.: Perspective Publications, 1972).

33. Social factors also include those that are political.

34. The concepts of "urban guerrilla warfare" and "terrorist bombing" have a high correlation $(r = .84)$, and information from the interviews clearly indicated that they were measuring the same thing. Therefore, it was decided that "terrorist bombing" would be the only concept presented.

35. As can be seen on the path diagrams, all the coefficients are small. This occurred because one segment of the sample was consistently in favor of terrorism and possessed a number of attributes measured by all the variables. Thus, when the equation partials out the effects of influencing variables, all the coefficients are reduced in significance. It is better, therefore, to look at the model as a whole.

36. For a discussion of the relationship between population density and violence see Susan Welch and Alan Booth, "Crowding and Civil Disorder: An Examination of Comparative National and City Data" *Comparative Political Studies* 8 (April 1975):58–74.

37. Some middle-class youth were positive toward terrorism also, but all these students were from high density neighborhoods. These youth were not frustrated with their own living conditions; rather,

they were frustrated with the living conditions of their lower-class neighbors and negative toward the Anglo society and government. This group is captured in the coefficient P_{62} in Figure 5.7, which is .293.

38. A small minority of the youth in Los Angeles (2%) who supported terrorism did so because they saw it as Chicanos asserting themselves against the Anglo oppressors. Its meaning to them was purely symbolic—they were striking back at Anglo society for what they believed to be its unfair treatment of Chicanos. This view of violence is similar to that presented by Frantz Fanon, *Wretched of the Earth* (New York: Grove Press, 1966), where violence is seen as a type of liberating act.

39. Hannah Arendt makes a similar point concerning the glorification of violence in *On Violence*, p. 83.

40. See Douglas Hibbs, Jr., *Mass Political Violence: A Cross-National Causal Analysis* (New York: John J. Wiley & Sons, 1973), pp. 138–146.

41. See David O. Sears and John B. McConahay, *The Politics of Violence*, pp. 158–164.

42. Ibid., pp. 107–108.

43. Ibid., pp. 164–166.

44. Frances Fox Piven and Richard Cloward, *Regulating the Poor* (New York: Randon House, 1971), Chapters 8, 9, and 10.

45. David O. Sears and John B. McConahay, *The Politics of Violence*, p. 174.

Chapter 6

1. See Thomas J. Archdeacon, *Becoming American: An Ethnic History*, Chapter 6.

2. Louis Wirth, *The Ghetto*, p. 279.

3. These figures are from various sources, but primarily from the Immigration and Naturalization Service. See Wayne A. Cornelius, "Mexican Migration to the United States: Causes, Consequences, and U.S. Responses," Monographs on Migration and Development, No. C/78-9 (Cambridge, Mass.: Center for International Studies, M.I.T., 1978), pp. 3–13.

4. For good examples see Neal Juston, "Mexican-American Achievement Hindered by Cultural Conflict," *Sociology and Research 56* (July): 471–479; Celia Heller, *Mexican-American Youth*.

5. Former Secretary of Labor Ray Marshall was an adherent of this position; see his "Economic Factors Influencing the International Migration of Workers," in Stanley R. Ross, ed., *Views Across*

the Border: The United States and Mexico, pp. 163–182; Vernon M. Briggs, Jr., Walter Fogel, and Fred H. Schmidt, *The Chicano Worker* (Austin: University of Texas Press, 1977), pp. 103–104; and Vernon M. Briggs, Jr., *Chicanos and Rural Poverty* (Baltimore, Md.: Johns Hopkins University Press, 1973).

6. See Michael Piore, "The 'Illegal Aliens' Debate Misses the Boat," *Working Papers For a New Society* (March/April, 1978):61.

7. See Wayne A. Cornelius, "Briefing Paper on Illegal Mexican Migration to the United States," paper prepared for the National Security Council, February 7, 1977.

8. See Wayne A. Cornelius, "Mexican Migration to the United States: Causes, Consequences, and U.S. Responses."

9. See Jorge Bustamante, "Undocumented Immigration from Mexico: Research Report," *International Migration Review 2* (Summer 1977):149–177; Wayne A. Cornelius, "Mexican Migration to the United States: Causes, Consequences, and U.S. Response," p. 19.

10. Jorge Bustamante, "Undocumented Immigration from Mexico."

11. See Wayne A. Cornelius, "Mexican Migration to the United States: The View from Rural Sending Communities," Monographs on Migration and Development, No. C/76-12 (Cambridge, Mass.: Center for International Studies, 1976), pp. 31–41. This study found remittances from illegals to their families and rural communities to be of substantial importance.

12. See Margarita B. Melville, "Mexican Women Adapt to Migration," *International Migration Review 12* (Summer 1978):225–235. In this research it was reported that the women who had accompanied their families to the United States illegally thought that education for their children was extremely important. Because the students who thought education was important were also with their entire families, the fact that they had less pressure on them to find a job complements the findings of Melville's study.

13. Jorge Bustamante, "Commodity-Migrants: Structural Analysis of Mexican Immigration to the United States," in Stanley R. Ross, ed., *Views Across the Border,* pp. 198–201.

14. See Victor Urquidi and Sofia Mendez Villarreal, "Economic Importance of Mexico's Northern Border Region," pp. 141–162; F. Ray Mrashall, "Economic Factors Influencing the International Migration of Workers," pp. 163–182; both in Stanley R. Ross, ed., *Views Across the Border.*

15. Cornelius in his study of illegals, has made a similar point about the importance of being close to Mexico. See Wayne A. Cornelius, "Mexican Migration to the United States: Causes, Consequences, and U.S. Responses," p. 25.

16. Although the question of tax evasion is not discussed explic-

itly, it seems to be assumed by those who argue that illegal aliens take jobs away from disadvantaged Americans. Basically, the rationale is that Mexicans take jobs away because they will work for less than the minimum wage. Thus it seems to be assumed that because they do receive below the minimum they will not pay taxes, since the studies are concerned that the illegal alien uses the social services of this country without paying for them.

17. Wayne A. Cornelius, "Mexican Migration to the United States: Causes, Consequences, and U.S. Responses," p. 89. Cornelius presents a number of other studies with some of the same findings.

18. See Robert L. Derbyshire, "Adaptation of Adolescent Mexican-Americans to United States Society," *American Behavioral Scientist* 13 (September/October 1969):88–103. This study reported that Mexican adolescents had a difficult time adjusting to U.S. society in Los Angeles.

19. Blaming the victim is something that has been especially common with regard to Mexican illegals. Two studies that discuss the dynamics of this situation are Jorge A. Bustamante, "The 'Wetback' as Deviant: An Application of Labelling Theory," *American Journal of Sociology* 77 (January 1972):106–178; Mauricio Mazon, "Illegal Alien Surrogates: A Psycho-historical Interpretation of Group Stereotyping in Time of Economic Stress," *Aztlan: International Journal of Chicano Studies Research* 6 (Summer 1975):305–324.

20. Personal honor has been an important element of Mexican and Chicano culture. Celia Heller noted this in *Mexican American Youth: Forgotten Youth at the Crossroads.*

21. This is implicit in Piore, "The 'Illegal Aliens' Debate Misses the Boat"; and F. Ray Marshall, "Economic Factors Influencing the International Migration of Workers," p. 171.

22. See Jorge Bustamante, "Commodity-Migrants: Structural Analysis of Mexican Immigration to the United States"; Wayne A. Cornelius, "Mexican Migration to the United States: Causes, Consequences, and U.S. Responses."

23. This same problem is present in Quebec, where tension exists between French Canadians and French nationals over the "proper usage" of the French language. The French nationals are often heard saying that the French Canadians do not speak "proper French." Frantz Fanon discusses this in *Black Faces, White Masks* (New York: Grove Press, 1968) concerning the person from Martinique's preoccupation with speaking French like they do in France.

24. See Jose Antonio Villarreal's novel *Pocho* (New York: Anchor Books, 1970) for a sensitive treatment of this concept.

25. Former Attorney General William Saxbe's statement was reported in the *Los Angeles Times*, October 31, 1974.

26. The language teachers in the schools all reported that there

were pronounced differences between the Mexican sudents in their attitudes toward learning English. Those who did not speak well also did not put a great deal of effort into learning and were usually much more transient, i.e., they would be at the school for only a limited time.

27. Cesar Chavez of the United Farm Workers Union has complained on a number of occasions about the farm owner's use of Mexican nationals as strikebreakers. See the September 23, 1974 edition of the *Washington Post* for an example of this criticism. Since 1977, however, he has been supportive of the illegal Mexican worker and has encouraged the government to formulate a less restrictive immigration policy. See also Ricardo Romo, "Responses to Mexican Immigration, 1910–1930," *Aztlan: International Journal of Chicano Studies Research* 6 (Summer 1975):174–194.

28. See Ricardo Romo, "Responses to Mexican Immigration, 1910–1930," p. 186; Andrés Jímenez, "Political Domination of the Labor Market: Racial Division in the Arizona Copper Industry," Working Paper Series #103 (Berkeley: Institute for the Study of Social Change), pp.25–28.

29. See Martin Slater, "Migration and the Workers' Conflicts in Western Europe" (Ph.D. dissertation, Massachusetts Institute of Technology, 1976), Chapter 6.

30. Ibid., pp. 220–221, 236–240.

31. See Michael Piore, "The 'Illegal Aliens' Debate Misses the Boat," pp. 61–63; Piore, *Birds of Passage and Promised Lands* (Cambridge, Mass.: Cambridge University Press, 1979); see also Wayne Cornelius, "Mexican Migration to the United States: Causes, Consequences, and U.S. Responses," p. 91.

32. Cornelius has suggested this. Ibid., p. 65.

33. Presumably Cornelius's use of this term in this context refers to Chicanos (Mexican Americans) as well as to Mexican nationals.

34. Wayne Cornelius, "Mexican Migration to the United States: Causes, Consequences, and U.S. Responses," p. 91.

35. The low-paying employer is defined here as one who pays wages well below the going rate for any given type of work. Usually this means around the minimum wage.

36. This percentage also represents some overlap because many of the youth mentioned both the I.N.S. and the employers.

37. *The National Advisory Commission on Civil Disorders* found that recent migrants to the riot cities were not participants in the riots.

38. Eighty-three percent of those who had any knowledge of the ideologies said that the source for their information was their high school social studies teacher.

39. See Irving Howe, *World of Our Fathers: The Journey of the*

East European Jews to America and the Life They Found and Made (New York: Simon and Schuster, 1976), chapters 2–4; Humberto S. Nelli, *Italians in Chicago,* p. 154.

Chapter 7

1. For a discussion of the conservative tendencies of the black middle class, see E. Franklin Frazier, *Black Bourgeoisie;* Ira Katznelson, *Black Men, White Cities: Race Politics and Migration in the United States, 1900–30, and Britain, 1948–68* (Chicago: University of Chicago Press, 1976); William Julius Wilson, *The Declining Significance of Race: Blacks and Changing American Institutions* (Chicago: University of Chicago Press, 1978), pp. 134–143. For Jews see Irving Howe, *World of Our Fathers,* p. 384.

2. See Irving Howe, Ibid., chapter 9.

3. See David Montejano, "The Demise of 'Jim Crow' for Texas Mexicans, 1940–1970," *Aztlan: International Journal of Chicano Studies Research,* forthcoming, 1985.

4. For the case of Dennis Kucinich in Cleveland see Dan Marshall, ed., "The Battle for Cleveland: Public Interest Challenges Corporate Power," Conference on Alternative State and Local Policies, Washington, D.C., 1979. Also see the interview Dennis Kucinich gave in *Playboy,* June, 1979, pp. 81–118. The power of the business community in neutralizing the political policies of urban black mayors has been documented in William E. Nelson, Jr. and Philip J. Meranto, *Electing Black Mayors: Political Action in Black Community* (Columbus, Ohio: Ohio State University Press, 1977); Edward Greer, *Big Steel: Black Politics and Corporate Power in Gary, Indiana* (New York: Monthly Review Press, 1979).

5. For a discussion of the fragmented nature of Los Angeles society and its effects on political attitudes and participation, see J. David Greenstone, *Labor in American Politics* (Chicago: University of Chicago Press, 1969), pp. 141–175; J. David Greenstone and Paul E. Petersen, *Race and Authority in Urban Politics: Community Participation and the War on Poverty* (Chicago: University of Chicago Press, 1962), pp. 96–125.

6. Los Angeles' political and economic environment is unlikely to produce those criteria that Castells has identified as necessary for a "successful" social movement. See Manuel Castells, *The City and the Grassroots: A Cross-Cultural Theory of Urban Social Movements* (Berkeley: University of California Press, 1983).

7. See William Kornblum, *Blue Collar Community* (Chicago: University of Chicago Press, 1974), pp. 9–35. For ethnic succession in

the early years of Detroit see Olivier Zunz, *The Changing Face of Inequality: Urbanization, Industrial Development, and Immigrants in Detroit, 1880–1920* (Chicago: University of Chicago Press, 1982).

8. See Edna Bonacich, "A Theory of Ethnic Antagonism: The Split Labor Market," *American Sociological Review 37* (1972):547–559.

9. For a prime example see Edward Greer, *Big Steel.*

10. See William E. Nelson, Jr. and Philip J. Meranto, *Electing Black Mayors.* For a study that did find that political inclusion of Hispanics and blacks had a positive effect on policies impacting on minorities, see Rufus B. Browning, Dale Rogers Marshall, and David H. Tabb, *Protest is Not Enough: The Struggle of Blacks and Hispanics for Equality in Urban Politics* (Berkeley: University of California Press, 1984). However, most of the cities in this study, all of which were in northern California, were ones with relatively diversified economies, which provided policy makers with more flexibility.

Bibliography

Aberback, Joel D., and Walker, Jack L. "Political Trust and Racial Ideology." *American Political Science Review 64* (December 1970):1199–1219.

Ablon, Joan. "Relocated American Indians in the San Francisco Bay Area: Social Interaction and Indian Identity." *Human Organization 23* (1964):362–71.

Abu-Lughod, Janet. "Migrant Adjustment to City Life: The Egyptian Case." *American Journal of Sociology 67* (July 1961):22–32.

Acuña, Rodolfo. *Occupied America: A History of Chicanos.* New York: Harper and Row, 1981.

Adelson, Joseph, and O'Neil, Robert. "The Growth of Political Ideas in Adolescence: The Sense of Community." *Journal of Personality and Social Psychology 7* (September 1966):295–306.

Adelson, Joseph, Green, Bernard, and O'Neil, Robert. "Growth of the Idea of Law in Adolescence." *Development Psychology 1* (July 1969):327–332.

Antunes, George, and Gaitz, Charles M. "Ethnicity and Participation: A Study of Mexican-Americans, Blacks and Whites." *American Journal of Sociology 80* (March 1975):1192–1211.

Archdeacon, Thomas J. *Becoming American: An Ethnic History.* New York: The Free Press, 1983.

Arendt, Hannah. *On Violence.* New York: Harcourt, Brace and World, 1969.

Asher, Herbert. *Causal Modeling.* Beverly Hills, Cal.: Sage Publications, 1976.

Banfield, Edward C. *The Unheavenly City Revisited.* Boston: Little, Brown Co., 1970.

Barrera, Mario. *Race and Class in the Southwest: A Theory of Inequality.* Notre Dame, Ind.: University of Notre Dame Press, 1979.

Barton, Josef. *Peasants and Strangers: Italians, Rumanians and Slo-*

vaks in an American City, 1890–1950. Cambridge: Harvard University Press, 1975.

Bonacich, Edna. "A Theory of Ethnic Antagonism: The Split Labor Market." *American Sociological Review* 37 (1972):547–559.

Bowen, Don R., Bowen, Elinor, Gawiser, Sheldon, and Massoti, Louis. "Deprivation, Mobility and Orientation Toward Protest of the Urban Poor." In Louis H. Massoti and Don R. Bowen, eds., *Riots and Rebellion: Civil Violence in the Urban Community.* Beverly Hills: Sage Publications, 1968.

Brady, Raymond J., and Adcock, Larry D. "Economic and Demographic Forecasts and Projections: Bernalillo County and City of Albuquerque, 1975–1980–1985." Albuquerque Department of Urban Planning, "Socio-Economic Mini-Profile for the Greater Albuquerque Area," Special Reort No. 61-5, Table 2, Albuquerque: Middle Rio Grande Council of Governments of New Mexico, 1975.

Briggs, Vernon M., Jr. *Chicanos and Rural Poverty.* Baltimore: Johns Hopkins University Press, 1973.

Briggs, Vernon M., Jr., Fogel, Walter, and Schmidt, Fred. *The Chicano Worker.* Austin: University of Texas, 1977.

Browning, Rufus T., Marshall, Dale R., and Tabb, David H. *Protest is Not Enough: The Struggle of Blacks and Hispanics for Equality in Urban Politics.* Berkeley: University of California Press, 1984.

Burnham, Walter Dean. "Party Systems and the Political Process." In William N. Chambers and Walter D. Burnham, eds., *The American Party System: Stages of Political Development.* New York: Oxford University Press, 1967.

Bustamante, Jorge A. "The 'Wetback' as Deviant: An Application of Labelling Theory." *American Journal of Sociology* 77 (January 1972):706–718.

———. "Commodity-Migrants: Structural Analysis of Mexican Immigration to the United States." In Stanley R. Ross, ed., *Views Across the Border.* Albuquerque: University of New Mexico Press, 1978.

Campbell, Angus, Gurin, Gerald, and Miller, Warren. *The Voter Decides.* Evanston, Ill.: Row, Peterson, 1954.

Campbell, Angus, Converse, Philip E., Miller, Warren E., and Stokes, Donald E. *The American Voter: An Abridgement.* New York: John Wiley & Sons, Inc., 1964.

Campbell, Angus, and Schuman, Howard. "Racial Attitudes in Fifteen American Cities." *The National Advisory Commission of Civil Disorders, Supplemental Studies.* Washington, D.C.: U.S. Government Printing Office, July 1968.

Carlos, Manuel. "Traditional and Modern Forms of Compadrazgo

Among Mexicans and Mexican Americans: A Survey of Continuities and Changes." Paper presented at the meeting of the Fortieth International Congress of Americanists, Rome, September 3–10, 1972.

Castells, Manuel. *The Urban Question: A Marxist Approach.* Cambridge: Massachusetts Institute of Technology Press, 1977.

———. *City, Class and Power.* New York: St. Martin's Press, 1978.

———. *The City and the Grassroots: A Crosscultural Theory of Urban Social Movements.* Berkeley: University of California Press, 1983.

Castillo, Pedro, and Camarillo, Alberto. *Furia y Muerte: Los Bandidos Chicanos.* Monograph No. 4, Aztlan Publications. Los Angeles: Chicano Studies Center, University of California, 1973.

Converse, Philip E. "The Nature of Belief Systems in Mass Publics." In David E. Apter, ed., *Ideology and Discontent.* Glencoe, Ill.: The Free Press, 1964.

Cornelius, Wayne A. "Urbanization as an Agent in Latin American Political Instability: The Case of Mexico." *American Political Science Review 63* (September 1969):833–857.

———. *Politics and the Migrant Poor in Mexico City.* Stanford: Stanford University Press, 1975.

———. "Mexican Migration to the United States: The View From Rural Sending Communities." Monograph on Migration and Development. Cambridge, Mass.: Center for International Studies, 1976.

———. "Briefing Paper on Illegal Mexican Migration to the United States." Paper prepared for the National Security Council, February, 1977.

———. "Mexican Migration to the United States: Causes, Consequences, and U.S. Responses." Monographs on Migration and Development, No. C/78-9. Cambridge, Mass.: Center for International Studies, M.I.T., 1978.

Cornwell, Elmer. "Bosses, Machines and Ethnic Groups." *The Annals of the American Academy of Political and Social Sciences 353* (May 1964):27–39.

Derbyshire, Robert L. "Adaptation of Adolescent Mexican-Americans to United States Society." *American Behavioral Scientist 13* (September/October 1969):88–103.

Derthick, Martha. *New Towns in Town: Why a Federal Program Failed.* Washington, D.C.: The Urban Institute, 1972.

Deutsch, Karl. *Nationalism and Social Communication: An Inquiry into the Foundation of Nationality,* 2nd ed. Cambridge, Mass.: M.I.T. Press, 1966.

Dexter, Lewis A. *The Tyranny of Schooling: An Enquiry Into the Concept of Stupidity.* New York: Basic Books, 1964.

Dollard, John. *Caste and Class in a Southern Town.* Garden City, N.Y.: Doubleday & Co., Inc., 1949.

Doob, Leonard. *Patriotism and Nationalism: Their Psychological Foundations.* New Haven: Yale University Press, 1964.

Drachsler, Julius. *Democracy and Assimilation: The Blending of Immigrant Heritages in America.* New York: MacMillan Co., 1920.

Duncan, Otis D. "A Socioeconomic Index for all Occupations." In Robert J. Reiss, ed., *Occupations and Social Status.* New York: Free Press, 1961.

——. "Path Analysis: Sociological Examples." *American Journal of Sociology 72* (July 1966):1–16.

Easton, David, and Dennis, Jack. *Children in the Political System. New York: McGraw-Hill, 1969.*

Edelman, Murray, The Symbolic Uses of Politics. Urbana, Ill.: University of Illinois Press, 1964.

Eisinger, Peter. "The Conditions of Protest Behavior in American Cities."*American Political Science Review 67* (March 1973):11–28.

——. "Racial Differences in Protest Participation." *American Political Science Review 68* (June 1974):592–606.

Erikson, Erik, *Childhood and Society.* New York: W. W. Norton & Co., Inc., 1963.

——. *Identity: Youth and Crisis.* New York: W. W. Norton & Co., Inc., 1968.

Essien-Udom, E. U. *Black Nationalism: A Search for Identity in America.* New York: Dell Publishing Co., 1964.

Estrada, Leobardo F., Garcia, F. Chris, Macías, Reynaldo F., and Maldonado, Lionel. "Chicanos in the United States: A History of Exploitation and Resistance." *Daedalus 110* (Spring 1981):103–133.

Fanon, Frantz. *Wretched of the Earth.* New York: Grove Press, 1966.

——. *Black Faces, White Masks.* New York: Grove Press, 1968.

Faris, Robert E. L. *Chicago Sociology: 1920–1932.* Chicago: University of Chicago Press, 1970.

Featherman, David L., and Hauser, Robert M. "On the Measurement of Occupations in Social Survey." *Sociological Methods and Research 2* (November 1973):239–251.

Fincher, E. R. *Spanish Americans as a Political Factor in New Mexico, 1912–1950.* New York: Arno Press, 1974.

Fischer, Claude S. "The Effects of Urban Life on Traditional Values." *Social Forces 53* (March 1975):420–432.

——. "Toward a Subcultural Theory of Urbanism."*American Journal of Sociology 80* (May 1975):1319–1341.

———. *To Dwell Among Friends: Personal Network in Town and City.* Chicago: University of Chicago Press, 1982.

Fishman, Joshua, Nahirny, Vladamir C., Hofman, John E., Hayden, Robert G. *Language Loyalty in the United States.* The Hague: Mouton, 1966.

Fogelson, Robert. *Violence as Protest.* Garden City, N.Y.: Doubleday and Company, Inc., 1971.

Frazier, E. Franklin. *Black Bourgeoisie.* New York: MacMillan, 1957.

Friedenberg, Edgar Z. "The High School as a Focus of 'Student Unrest.' " *The Annals of the American Academy of Political and Social Sciences 395* (May 1971):117–126.

Friesma, Paul. "The Forest Service in Crisis in Northern New Mexico." Paper presented at the annual meeting of the Midwest Political Science Association, Chicago, 1971.

Gans, Herbert. 'Urbanism and Suburbanism as Ways of Life: A Reevaluation of Definitions." In Arnold Rose, ed., *Human Behavior and Social Processes.* Boston: Houghton-Mifflin Co., 1962.

———. *The Urban Villagers: Group and Class in the Life of Italian-Americans.* New York: The Free Press, 1964.

———. "Symbolic Ethnicity: The Future of Ethnic Groups and Cultures in America." *Ethnic and Racial Studies 2* (January 1979):1–20.

García, F. Chris. *Political Socialization of Chicano Children: A Comparative Study with Anglos in California.* New York: Praeger Publishers, 1973.

García, F. Chris. "Manitos and Chicanos in New Mexico Politics." *Aztlan: Chicano Journal of the Social Sciences and Arts 4* (Spring and Fall, 1974):177–188.

Gardner, Richard. *Grito! Reies Tijerina and the New Mexico Land Grant War of 1967.* Indianapolis: Bobbs-Merrill, 1970.

Glazer, Nathan, and Moynihan, Daniel P. *Beyond the Melting Pot.* Cambridge, Mass.: M.I.T. Press, 1970.

Gonzalez, Nancie. *The Spanish Americans in New Mexico: A Heritage of Pride.* Albuquerque: University of New Mexico Press, 1969.

Gordon, Milton. *Assimilation in American Life: The Role of Race, Religion and National Origins.* New York: Oxford University Press, 1964.

———. "Theory of Racial and Ethnic Group Relations." In Nathan Glazer and Daniel P. Moynihan, eds., *Ethnicity: Theory and Experience.* Cambridge, Mass.: Harvard University Press, 1975.

Grebler, Leo, Moore, Joan, and Guzman, Ralph. *The Mexican-American People: The Nation's Second Largest Minority.* New York: Free Press, 1970.

Greenberg, Stanley, *Politics and Poverty: Modernization and Re-*

sponse in Five Poor Neighborhoods. New York: John J. Wiley, 1974.

Greenstein, Fred. *Children and Politics.* New Haven: Yale University Press, 1965.

Greenstone, J. David. *Labor in American Politics.* Chicago: University of Chicago Press, 1969.

Greenstone, J. David, and Petersen, Paul E. *Race and Authority in Urban Politics: Community Participation in the War on Poverty.* Chicago: University of Chicago Press, 1973.

Greer, Edward. *Big Steel: Black Politics and Corporate Power in Gary, Indiana.* New York: Monthly Review Press, 1979.

Grofman, Bernard N., and Muller, Edward N. "The Strange Case of Relative Gratification on Potential for Political Violence: The V-Curve Hypothesis." *American Political Science Review* 67 (June 1973):514–539.

Guzman, Ralph. "Political Socialization of the Mexican American People." Ph.D. Dissertation, University of California, Los Angeles, 1970.

Hall, Raymond. *Black Separatism in the United States.* Hanover, N.H.: The University Press of New England, 1978.

Handlin, Oscar. *The Uprooted.* Boston: Little, Brown, 1951.

Handlin, Oscar. *Children of the Uprooted.* New York: Grosset & Dunlop, 1960.

Handlin, Oscar. *Boston's Immigrants.* New York: Atheneum, 1968.

Harloe, Michael, ed. *Captive Cities: Studies in the Political Economy of Cities and Regions.* New York: John Wiley & Sons, 1977.

Heise, David R. *Causal Analysis.* New York: John Wiley & Sons, 1975.

Heller, Celia. *Mexican American Youth: Forgotten Youth at the Crossroads.* New York: Random House, 1966.

Hess, Richard, and Torney, Judith. *The Development of Political Attitudes in Children.* Garden City, N.Y.: Anchor Books, 1968.

Hess, Robert D. "Political Socialization in the Schools." *Harvard Educational Review* 38 (Summer 1968):528–536.

Hibbs, Douglas. *Mass Political Violence: A Cross-National Causal Analysis.* New York: John Wiley & Sons, 1973.

Higham, John. *Strangers in the Land.* New Brunswick, N.J.: Rutgers University Press, 1955.

Howe, Irving. *World of Our Fathers: The Journey of the East European Jews to America and the Life They Found and Made.* New York: Simon and Schuster, 1976.

Huntington, Samuel P. *Political Order in Changing Societies.* New Haven: Yale University Press, 1968.

Isaacs, Harold. *Idols of the Tribe: Group Identity and Political Change.* New York: Harper & Row, 1975.

————. "Basic Group Identity: The Idols of the Tribe." In Nathan Glazer and Daniel P. Moynihan, eds., *Ethnicity: Theory and Experience*. Cambridge: Harvard University Press, 1975.

Jacobs, Jane. *The Death and Life of Great American Cities*. New York: Vintage, 1961.

Jankowski, Martin L. "The Social and Political Origins of the Chicano Separatist Movement." M.A. thesis, Dalhousie University, Halifax, Nova Scotia, 1972.

Jaros, Dean, Hirsch, Herbert, and Fleron, Frederick. "The Malevolent Leader: Political Socialization in an American Sub-Culture." *American Political Science Review* 62 (June 1968):564–575.

Jennings, M. Kent, and Niemi, Richard G. *The Political Character of Adolescence: The Influence of Families and Schools*. Princeton, N.J.: Princeton University Press, 1975.

Jímenez, Andrés. "Political Domination in the Labor Market: Racial Division in the Arizona Copper Industry." Working Paper Series, no. 103. Berkeley: Institute for the Study of Social Change, University of California, 1977.

Katznelson, Ira. *Black Men, White Cities: Race, Politics and Migration in the U.S. 1900–30, and Britain, 1948–68*. Chicago: University of Chicago Press, 1976.

Katznelson, Ira. *City Trenches: Urban Politics and the Patterning of Class in the United States*. New York: Pantheon, 1982.

Kenniston, Kenneth. *The Uncommitted: Alienated Youth in American Society*. New York: Delta Books, 1965.

Kenniston, Kenneth. *Young Radicals: Notes on Committed Youth*. New York: Harcourt, Brace and World, 1968.

Kenyon, Sandra. "The Development of Political Cynicism Among Negro and White Adolescents." Paper presented at the annual meeting of the American Political Science Association, New York, 1969.

Knowlton, Clark. "Land Grant Problems Among the State's Spanish Americans." Albuquerque, Bureau of Business Research, 1967.

Kornblum, William. *Blue Collared Community*. Chicago: University of Chicago Press, 1974.

Kornhauser, William. *The Politics of Mass Society*. New York: The Free Press, 1959.

————. "Rebellion and Political Development." In Harry Eckstein, ed., *Internal War*. New York: The Free Press, 1964.

Kurth, James, and Rosen, Steven J., eds. *Testing the Theory of the Military Industrial Complex*. Lexington, Mass.: Lexington Books, 1972.

La Mare, James W. "Language Environment and Political Socialization of Mexican-American Children." In Richard Niemi and

Associates, eds., *The Politics of Future Citizens*. San Francisco: Jossey-Bass, 1974.

Landolt, Robert Garland. *The Mexican-American Workers of San Antonio, Texas*. New York: Arno Press, 1976.

Lane, John Hart, Jr. *Voluntary Organizations Among Mexican Americans in San Antonio, Texas*. New York: Arno Press, 1976.

Lenski, Gerhard. *The Religious Factor*. New York: Anchor Books, 1963.

Leon-Portilla, Miguel. *Aztec Thought and Culture*. Norman, OK.: University of Oklahoma Press, 1963.

Levesnon, George B. "The Schools' Contributions to Learning of Participatory Responsibility." In Byron G. Massialas, ed., *Political Youth, Traditional Schools: National and International Perspectives*. Englewood Cliffs, N.J.: Prentice-Hall, 1972.

Levy, Mark R., and Kramer, Michael S. *The Ethnic Factor: How America's Minorities Decide Elections*. New York: Simon and Schuster, 1973.

Lewels, Francisco J., Jr. *The Uses of the Media by the Chicano Movement: A Study of Minority Access*. New York: Praeger Publishers, 1974.

Lieberson, Stanley. "Bilingualism in Montreal: A Demographic Analysis." *American Journal of Sociology 71* (July 1965):10–25.

―――. *Language and Ethnic Relations in Canada*. New York: Wiley, 1970.

Lieberson, Stanley, Dalton, Guy, and Johnston, Mary Ellen. "The Course of Mother-Tongue Diversity in Nations." *American Journal of Sociology 81* (July 1975):34–61.

Lieberson, Stanley, and Curry, Timothy J. "Language Shift in the United States: Some Demographic Clues." *Internatinal Migration Review 5* (Summer):125–137.

Liefschutz, Sarah F., and Niemi, Richard G. "Political Attitudes Among Black Children." In Richard Niemi and Associates, eds., *The Politics of Future Citizens*. San Francisco: Jossey-Bass, 1974.

Lijphart, Arend. *Democracy in Plural Societies: A Comparative Exploration*. New Haven: Yale University Press, 1972.

Lipsky, Michael. *Protest in City Politics: Rent Strikes, Housing and the Power of the Poor*. Chicago: Rand McNally & Co., 1970.

Lupsha, Peter A., and MacKinnon, Catherine. "Domestic Political Violence 1965–1971: A Radical Perspective." In Garry Gappert and Harold M. Rose, eds., *The Rise of the Sun Belt Cities*. Urban Affairs Annual Review, Vol. 9. Beverly Hills, Cal.: Sage Publications, 1975.

Madsen, William. *Mexican-Americans of South Texas*. New York: Holt, Rinehart, and Winston, 1964.

Marshall, Daniel. "The Battle of Cleveland: Public Interest Challenges Corporate Power." Conference on Alternative State and Local Policies, Washington, D.C., 1979.

Marshall, Ray. "Economic Factors Influencing the International Migration of Workers." In Stanley R. Ross, ed., *Views Across the Border: The United States and Mexico.* Albuquerque: University of New Mexico Press, 1978.

Marvick, Dwaine. "The Political Socialization of the American Negro." *The Annals 361* (September 1965):112–127.

Mazon, Mauricio. "Illegal Alien Surrogates: A Psychohistorical Interpretation of Group Stereotyping in Time of Economic Stress." *Aztlan: International Journal of Chicano Studies Research 6* (Summer 1975):305–324.

McClosky, Clifton. *The Government and Politics of Texas.* Boston: Little, Brown & Co., 1969.

McWilliams, Carey. *North From Mexico.* New York: Greenwood Press, 1968.

Melville, Margarita B. "Mexican Women Adapt to Migration." *International Migration Review 12* (Summer 1978):225–235.

Merelman, Richard M. "The Devleopment of Political Ideology: A Framework for the Analysis of Political Socialization." *American Political Science Review 63* (September 1969):750–767.

———. *Political Reasoning in Adolescence: Some Bridging Themes.* Beverly Hills, Cal.: Sage Publications, 1976.

Metzger, L. Paul. "American Sociology and Black Assimilation: Conflicting Perspectives." *American Journal of Sociology 76* (January 1971):627–647.

Miller, Arthur H., Miller, Warren E., Raine, Alden S., and Brown, Thad A. "A Majority Party in Disarray: Policy Polarization in the 1972 Election." *American Political Science Review 70(3)* (September 1976):753–778.

Mirandé, Alfredo, and Enriquez, Evangelina. *La Chicana: The Mexican-American Woman.* Chicago: University of Chicago Press, 1979.

Mollenkopf, John. *The Contested City.* Princeton, N.J.: Princeton University Press, 1983.

Montejano, David. "Frustrated Apartheid: Race, Repression, and Capitalist Agriculture in South Texas, 1920–1930." In Walter Goldfrank, ed., *The World-System of Capitalism: Past and Present.* Beverly Hills, Cal.: Sage Publications, 1979.

———. "Is Texas Bigger Than the World-System?" *Review 4* (Winter 1981):597–628.

———. "A Journey Through Mexican Texas, 1900–1930: The Making of a Segregated Society." Ph.D. dissertation, Yale University, 1982.

———. "The Demise of 'Jim Crow' for Texas Americans, 1940–1970."

Aztlan: International Journal of Chicano Studies, forthcoming, 1985.

Morales, Armando. *Ando Sangrando: A Study of Mexican American-Police Conflict.* La Puente, Cal.: Perspective Publications, 1972.

Morris, Lorenzo. "The Politics of Education and Language in Quebec: A Comparative Perspective." *Canadian and International Education 51* (December 1976):1–36.

Morris, R. N. *Urban Sociology.* New York: Praeger, 1968.

Munger, Edwin S. *Afrikaner and African Nationalism: South African Parallels and Parameters.* London: Oxford University Press, 1967.

Muñoz, Carlos. "The Politics of Educational Change in East Los Angeles." In Alfredo Castañeda, ed., *Mexican-Americans and Educational Change.* New York: Arno Press, 1973.

Murguia, Edward. *Assimilation, Colonialism and the Mexican American People,* Mexican American Monograph Series 1. Austin: University of Texas Press, 1975.

Nabobov, Peter. *Tijerina and the Courthouse Raid.* Albuquerque: University of New Mexico Press, 1969.

The National Advisory Commission on Civil Disorders. New York: Bantam. 1968.

Navarro, Armando. "The Evolution of Chicano Politics." *Aztlan: International Journal of Chicano Studies and Resarch 5* (Spring and Fall 1975):57–84.

Nelli, Humbert S. *Italians in Chicago 1880–1930: A Study in Ethnic Mobility.* New York: Oxford University Press, 1970.

Nelson, William E., Jr., and Meranto, Philip J. *Electing Black Mayors: Political Action in the Black Community.* Columbus: Ohio State University Press, 1977.

New Mexico State Planning Office. *Emundo Report.* Santa Fe: 1961.

Nie, Norman H. Hull, C. Hadlai, Jenkins, Jean G., SteinBrenner, Karin, and Bent, Dale H. *Statistical Package for the Social Sciences,* 2nd ed. New York: McGraw-Hill, 1975.

Nieburg, H. L. *Political Violence: The Behavioral Process.* New York: St. Martin's Press, 1969.

Orleans, Peter, and Ellis, William, eds. *Race, Change and Urban Society.* Beverly Hills, Cal.: Sage Publications, 1971.

Osgood, Charles, Suci, George J., and Tannenbaum, Percy H. *The Measurement of Meaning.* Urbana, Ill.: University of Illinois Press, 1957.

Paredes, Americo. *With a Pistol in His Hand.* Austin: University of Texas Press, 1971.

Park, Robert E. "Racial Assimilation of Secondary Groups." *American Journal of Sociology 19* (March 1914):606–623.

Park, Robert E., Burgess, Ernest W., and McKenzie, R. D. *The City.* Chicago: University of Chicago Press, 1925.

Park, Robert E. "Human Migration and the Marginal Man." *American Journal of Sociology 33* (May 1928):881–893.

———. *Race and Culture.* Glencoe, Ill.: Free Press, 1950.

———. "Collective Behavior." In Ralph H. Turner, ed., *Robert E. Park: On Social Control and Collective Behavior.* Chicago: University of Chicago Press, 1967.

Pickvance, C. G., ed. *Urban Sociology: Critical Essays.* London: Methuen, 1976.

Piore, Michael. *Birds of Passage and Promised Lands.* Cambridge, Mass.: Cambridge University Press, 1979.

———. "The 'Illegal Aliens' Debate Misses the Boat." *Working Papers for a New Society,* March/April 1978.

Popkin, Samuel, Gorman, John W., Phillips, Charles, and Smith, Jerry A. "Comment: What Have You Done for Me Lately? Toward an Investment Theory of Voting." *American Political Science Review 70* (September 1976):779–805.

Porter, John. "Ethnic Pluralism in Canada." In Nathan Glazer and Daniel P. Moynihan, eds., *Ethnicity: Theory and Experience.* Cambridge: Harvard University Press, 1975.

Putnam, Robert. "Political Attitudes and the Local Community." *American Political Science Review 60* (September 1966):640–654.

RePass, David. "Issue Salience and Party Choice." *American Political Science Review 65* (June 1971):389–400.

Rioux, Marcel. *Quebec in Question.* Toronto: James and Samuel, 1971.

Rodriguez, Richard. *Hunger of Memory: The Education of Richard Rodriguez.* New York: Bantam Books, 1982.

Romo, Ricardo. "Responses to Mexican Immigration, 1910–1930." *Aztlan: International Journal of Chicano Studies Research 6* (Summer 1975):174–194.

Ross, Stanley, R., ed. *Views Across the Border.* Albuquerque: University of New Mexico Press, 1978.

Roszak, Theodore. *The Making of a Counter Culture: Reflections on the Technocratic Society and Its Youthful Opposition.* Garden City, N.Y.: Anchor Books, 1968.

Rubel, Arthur. *Across the Tracks: Mexican-Americans in a Texas city.* Austin: University of Texas Press, 1966.

Safa, Helen. "Puerto Rican Adaptation to the Urban Milieux." In Peter Orleans and William Ellis, eds., *Race, Change, and Urban Society.* Beverly Hills, Cal.: Sage Publications, 1971.

Salamon, Lester M., and Van Evera, Stephen. "Fear, Apathy, and Discrimination: A Test of Three Explanations of Political Participation." *American Political Science Review 67* (December 1973):1288–1306.

Samora, Julian, Bernal, Joe, and Peña, Albert. *Gunpowder Justice: A Reassessment of the Texas Rangers.* South Bend, Ind.: University of Notre Dame Press, 1979.

Sandberg, Neil. *Ethnic Identity and Assimilation: The Polish American Community: A Case Study of Metropolitan Los Angeles.* New York: Praeger Publishers, 1974.

Saywell, John. *The Rise of the Parti Quebecois,1967–1976.* Toronto: University of Toronto Press, 1977.

Schafer, Robert. *Mortgage Lending Decisions: Criteria and Constraints.* Cambridge, Mass.: Joint Center for Urban Studies of M.I.T. and Harvard University, 1979.

Sears, David O., and McConahay, John B. "Racial Socialization, Comparison Levels, and the Watts Riot." *Journal of Social Issues 26* (1970):121–140.

Sears, David O., and McConahay, John B. *The Politics of Violence: The New Urban Blacks and the Watts Riot.* Boston: Houghton-Mifflin Co., 1973.

Sears, David O. "Political Socialization." In Fred I. Greenstein and Nelson W. Polsby, eds., *Handbook of Political Science, Vol 2: Micropolitical Theory.* Reading, Mass.: Addison-Wesley, 1975.

Sennett, Richard. *The Uses of Disorder: Personal Identity and City Life.* New York: Vintage, 1970.

Sennett, Richard. *Families Against the City.* Cambridge: Harvard University Press, 1970.

Shannon, Lyle, and Shannon, Magdalene. *Minority Migrants in the Urban Community: Mexican-American and Negro Adjustment to Industrial Society.* Beverly Hills, Cal.: Sage Publications, 1973.

Shockley, John. *Chicano Revolt in a Texas Town.* South Bend, Ind.: University of Notre Dame Press, 1974.

Shulman, Jay. "Ghetto Area Residence, Political Alienation and Riot Orientation." In Louis H. Masotti and Don R. Bowen, eds., *Riots and Rebellion: Civil Violence in the Urban Community.* Beverly Hills, Cal.: Sage Publications, 1968.

Simmons, Ozzie G. "Anglo-Americans and Mexican-Americans in South Texas: A Study in Dominant-Subordinate Group Relations." Ph.D. dissertation, Harvard University, 1952.

Shingles, Richard D. "Black Consciousness and Political Participation: The Missing Link." *American Political Science Review* 75(1) (March 1980):76–91.

Slater, Martin. "Migration and the Workers' Conflicts in Western Europe." Ph.D. dissertation, Massachusetts Institute of Technology, 1976.

Smith, Michael P. *The City and Social Theory.* New York: St. Martin's Press, 1979.

Sorkin, Alan L. *The Urban American Indian.* Lexington, Mass.: Lexington Books, 1978.

Stauss, J. H., and Chadwick, Bruce, A. "Urban Indian Adjustment." *American Indian Culture and Research Journal* 2(3) (1979):23–38.

Steiner, Stan. *La Raza: The Mexican Americans.* New York: Harper & Row Publishers, 1970.

Stokes, Donald E., and Miller, Warren E. "Party Government and the Saliency of Congress." In Angus Campbell, Philip Converse, Warren E. Miller, and Donald E. Stokes, eds., *Elections and the Political Order.* New York: John Wiley & Sons, Inc., 1966.

Sullivan, John L., Marcus, George E., and Minns, Daniel Richard. "The Development of Political Ideology: Some Empirical Findings." *Youth and Society* 7 (December 1975):148–170.

Suttles, Gerald. *The Social Order of the Slum: Ethnicity and Territoriality in the Inner City.* Chicago: University of Chicago Press, 1968.

Swadesh, Frances. *Los Primeros Pobladores: Spanish-Americans on the Ute Frontier.* South Bend, Ind.: University of Notre Dame Press, 1974.

Thernstrom, Stephan. *The Other Bostonians: Poverty and Progress in the American Metropolis, 1880–1970.* Cambridge: Harvard University Press, 1973.

Tomlinson, T. M. "Riot Ideology Among Urban Negroes." In Louis H. Masotti and Don R. Bowen, eds., *Riots and Rebellion: Civil Violence in the Urban Community.* Beverly Hills, Cal.: Sage Publications, 1968.

United States Commission on Civil Rights. *Mexican-American Educational Series, Study Report I: Ethnic Isolation of Mexican Americans in the Public Schools of the Southwest.* Washington, D.C.: U.S. Government Printing Office, April 1971.

United States Bureau of the Census, vol. 1, General Population Characteristics for Texas (PC80-1-B45), California (PC80-1-B6); New Mexico (PC80-1-B33). 1980.

Urquidi, Victor, and Villarreal, Sofia Mendez. "Economic Importance of Mexico's Northern Border Region." In Stanley R. Ross, ed., *Views Across the Border.* Albuquerque: University of New Mexico Press, 1978.

Verba, Sidney, Ashmed, Bashir, and Bhatt, Anil. *Caste, Race and Politics.* Beverly Hills, Cal.: Sage Publications, 1971.

Verba, Sidney, and Nie, Norman. *Participation in America: Political Democracy and Social Equality.* New York: Harper & Row, 1972.

Verba, Sidney, Nie, Norman, and Petrocik, John. *The Changing American Voter.* Cambridge, Mass.: Harvard University Press, 1976.

Villarreal, Jose Antonio. *Pocho.* New York: Anchor Books, 1970.

Waddell, J. O., and Watson, O. M. *The American Indian in Urban Society.* Boston: Little, Brown, 1971.

Weeks, O. D. "The Texas-Mexican and the Politics of South Texas." *American Political Science Review 24* (August 1930):608–615.

Welch, Susan, and Booth, Alan. "Crowding and Civil Disorder: An Examination of Comparative National and City Data." *Comparative Political Studies 8* (April 1975):58–74.

Wilber, George L., and Hagen, Robert J. *Metropolitan and Regional Inequities Among Minorities in the Labor Market.* Lexington, Ky.: Social Welfare Research Institute, University of Kentucky, 1975.

Wilson, James Q. *The Amateur Democrat.* Chicago: University of Chicago Press, 1962.

Wilson, James Q., and Banfield, Edward, *City Politics.* Cambridge, Mass.: Harvard University Press, 1963.

Wilson, James Q. *Varieties of Police Behavior: The Management of Law and Order in Eight Communities.* Cambridge, Mass.: Harvard University Press, 1968.

Wilson, James Q., and Banfield, Edward. "Political Ethos Revisited." *American Political Science Review 65*(4) (December 1971):1048–1062.

Wilson, William Julius. *The Declining Significance of Race: Blacks and Changing American Institutions.* Chicago: University of Chicago Press, 1978.

Wirth, Louis. *The Ghetto.* Chicago: University of Chicago Press, 1928.

———. "Culture Conflict and Misconduct." *Social Forces 9* (June 1931):484–492.

———. "Urbanism as a Way of Life." *American Journal of Sociology 44* (July 1938):3–24.

———. "Localism, Regionalism, and Centralization." *American Journal of Sociology 42* (May 1937):493–509.

———. "Social Interaction: The Problem of the Individual and the Group." *American Journal of Sociology 44* (May 1939):965–979.

———. "Ideological Aspects of Social Disorganization." *American Sociological Review 5* (August 1940):472–482.

———. "The Problem of Minority Groups." In Ralph Linton, ed., *The Search of Man in the World Crisis.* New York: Columbia University Press, 1945.

———. *On Cities and Social Life,* edited by Albert J. Reiss. Chicago: University of Chicago Press, 1964.

Wolfinger, Raymond E. "The Development and Persistence of Ethnic Voting." *American Political Science Review 54* (December 1965):896–909.

Wolfinger, Raymond E. "Dealignment, Realignment, and Mandates in the 1984 Election." Paper prepared for Public Policy Week of the American Enterprise Institute, Washington, D.C., December 3, 1984.

Wright, Sewell. "Path Coefficients and Path Regressions: Alternative or Complementary Concepts?" *Biometrics* 16 (June 1960):189–202.

Zinn, Maxine Baca. "Chicago Family Research: Conceptual Distortions and Alternative Directions." *Journal of Ethnic Studies* 7(3) (Fall 1979):59–71.

Zunz, Olivier. *The Changing Face of Inequality: Urbanization, Industrial Development, and Immigrants in Detroit, 1880–1920.* (Chicago: University of Chicago Press, 1982).

Index